Peach Girl

Also Available from TOKYOPOP®:

MARMALADE BOY 1-3 (of 8)
A tangled teen romance for the new millennium.

REAL BOUT HIGH SCHOOL 1-3 (of 4+)
At Daimon High, teachers don't break up fights…they grade them.

MARS 1-3 (of 15)
Biker Rei and artist Kira are as different as night and day, but fate binds them in this angst-filled romance.

GTO 1-5 (of 23+)
Biker gang member Onizuka is going back to school…as a teacher!

CHOBITS 1-2 (of 5+)
In the future, boys will be boys and girls will be…robots? The newest hit series from CLAMP!

PARADISE KISS 1-2 (of 3+)
High fashion and deep passion collide in this hot new shojo series!

KODOCHA: Sana's Stage 1-3 (of 10)
There's a rumble in the jungle gym when child star Sana Kurata and bully Akito Hayama collide.

ANGELIC LAYER 1-2 (of 5)
In the future, the most popular game is Angelic Layer, where hand-raised robots battle for supremacy.

LOVE HINA 1-5 (of 14)
Can Keitaro handle living in a dorm with five cute girls…and still make it through school?

Peach Girl

by Miwa Ueda

6

TOKYOPOP®

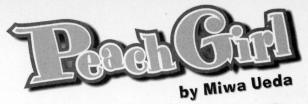

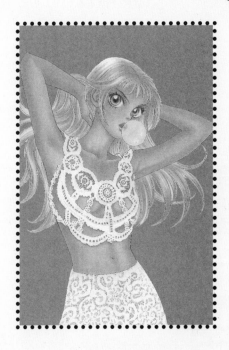

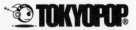

TOKYOPOP® Presents
Peach Girl 6 by Miwa Ueda
TOKYOPOP is a registered trademark
of Mixx Entertainment, Inc.
ISBN: 1-931514-16-X
First Printing September 2002

10   9   8   7   6   5   4   3   2   1

Translator - Dan Papia.
Retouch and Lettering - Paul Tanck.
English Adaptation - Jodi Bryson.
Graphic Designer - Anna Kernbaum.
Senior Editor - Julie Taylor.
Production Managers - Jennifer Wagner and Mario M. Rodriguez.
Art Director - Matt Alford.
VP of Production - Ron Klamert. Publisher - Stuart Levy.

Email: editor@TOKYOPOP.com
Come visit us at www.TOKYOPOP.com

TOKYOPOP®
Los Angeles - Tokyo

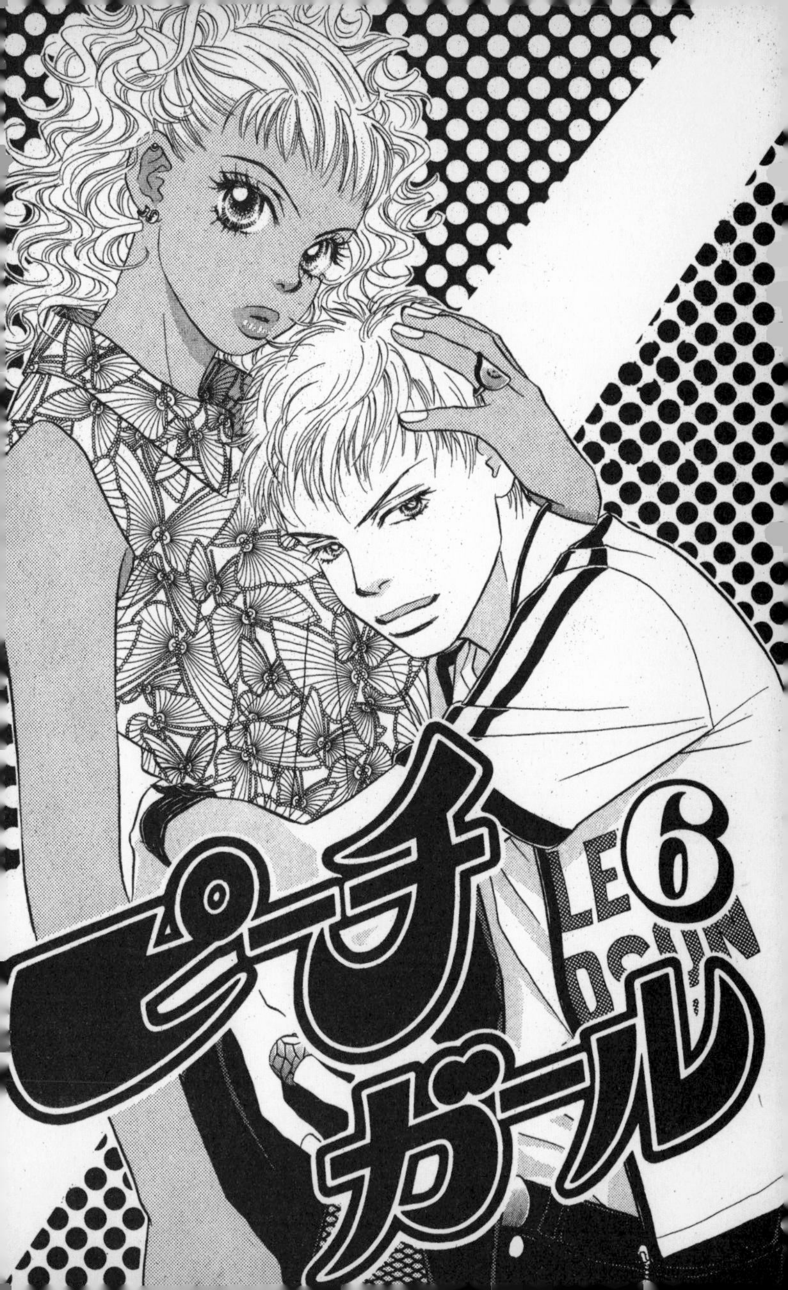
ピーチガール
6

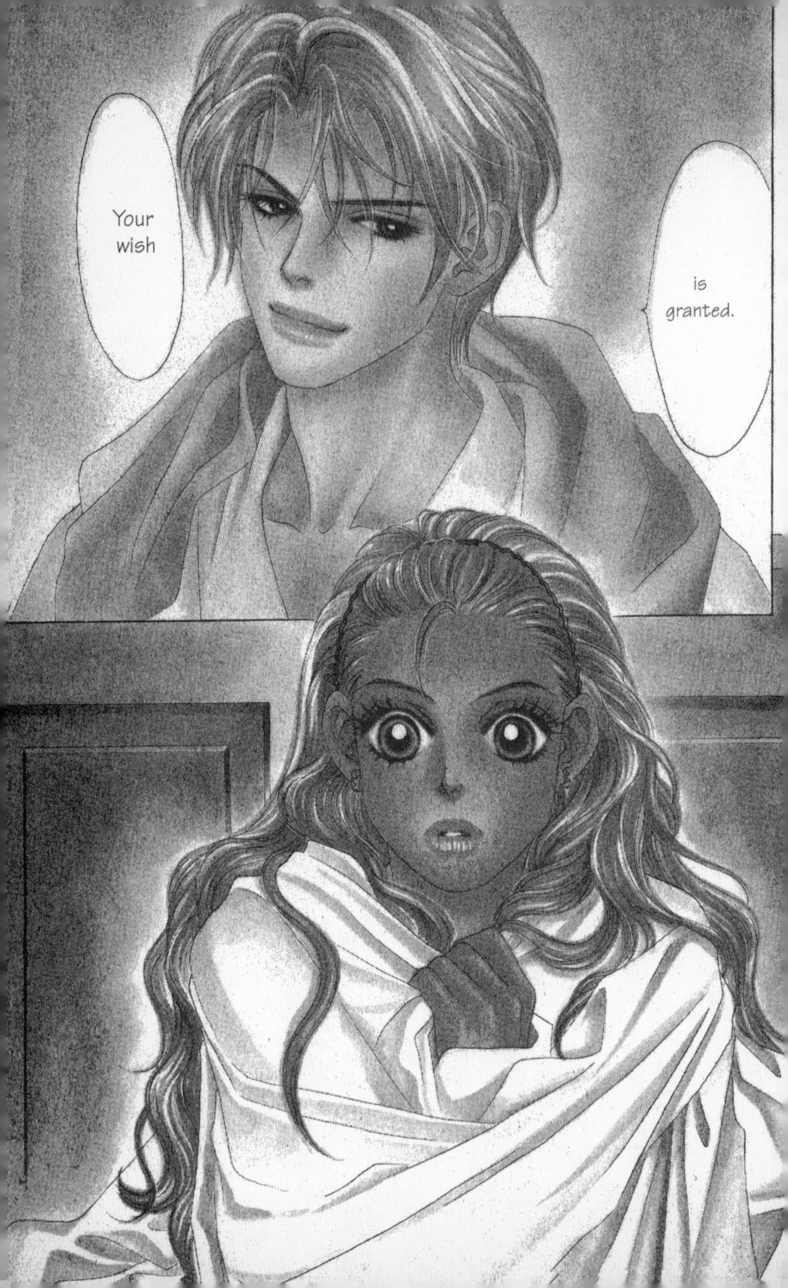
Your wish
is granted.

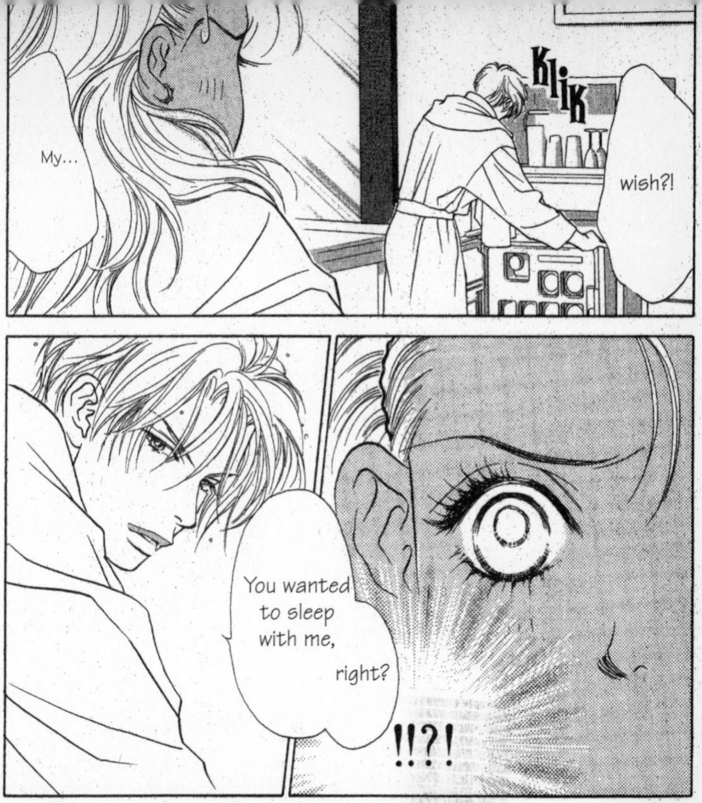
My...
KLIK
wish?!
You wanted to sleep with me, right?
!!?!

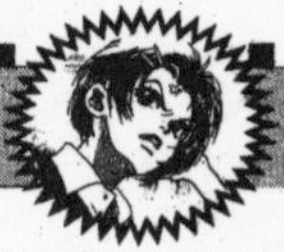

MOMO vs SAE: Death match, part 1

When Toji, the guy Momo has adored since junior high, admitted his love for her, everything seemed perfect. But Sae, who covets *everything* Momo has, spread a rumor that Momo was dating Kiley, and tried to wreck things with Toji. Kiley intervened to clear up the misunderstanding, and the couple happily resumed dating. Sae started dating the supermodel called Goro, and her confidence was restored. However, Sae dumped him then got back with him so she could use him to resume her plot to steal Toji. During Momo's birthday party at Toji's house, Sae drugged Momo and sent her off to a hotel with Goro. As the story begins, it appears Momo has had her virginity *stolen*!

Everything you need to know.

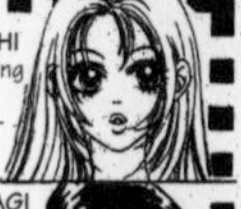

MOMO ADACHI
Currently dating Toji. Has she lost her virginity to GORO?

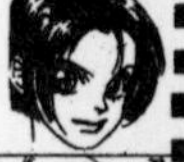

SAE KASHIWAGI
Momo's relentlessly jealous enemy. Loser in Round 1. Vows to steal Toji anyway.

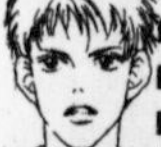

TOJI TOJIGAMORI
Momo's boyfriend He once kissed Sae, but he's in love with Momo now.

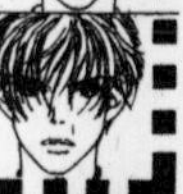

GORO
The male supermodel who declared his love to Sae. Did he really deflower Momo?

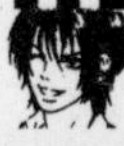

KILEY OKAYASU
He knows Momo better than anyone. When it's time to take Sae down, Kiley's the man!

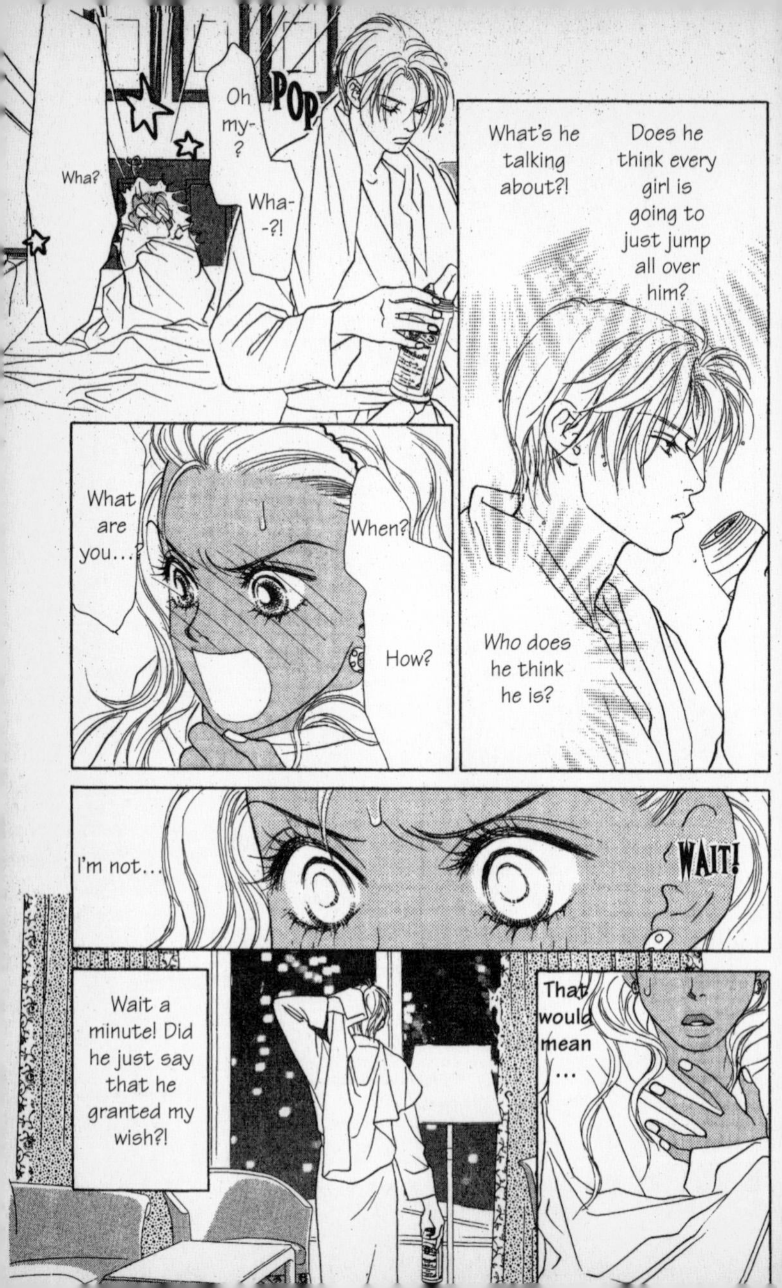
Wha?
Oh my-?
POP
Wha- -?!
What's he talking about?!
Does he think every girl is going to just jump all over him?
Who does he think he is?
What are you...?
When?
How?
I'm not...
WAIT!
Wait a minute! Did he just say that he granted my wish?!
That would mean ...

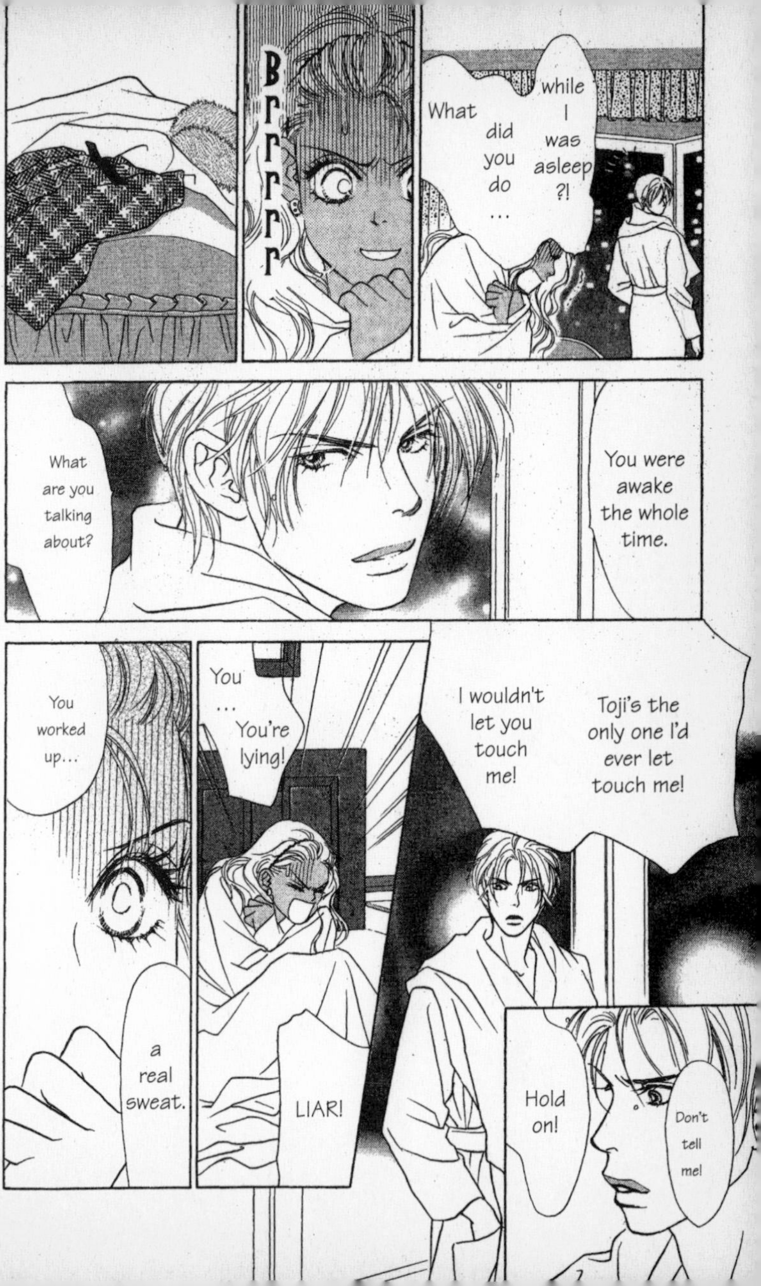
Brrrrr
What did you do...
while I was asleep?!
What are you talking about?
You were awake the whole time.
You worked up...
a real sweat.
You... You're lying!
LIAR!
I wouldn't let you touch me!
Toji's the only one I'd ever let touch me!
Hold on!
Don't tell me!

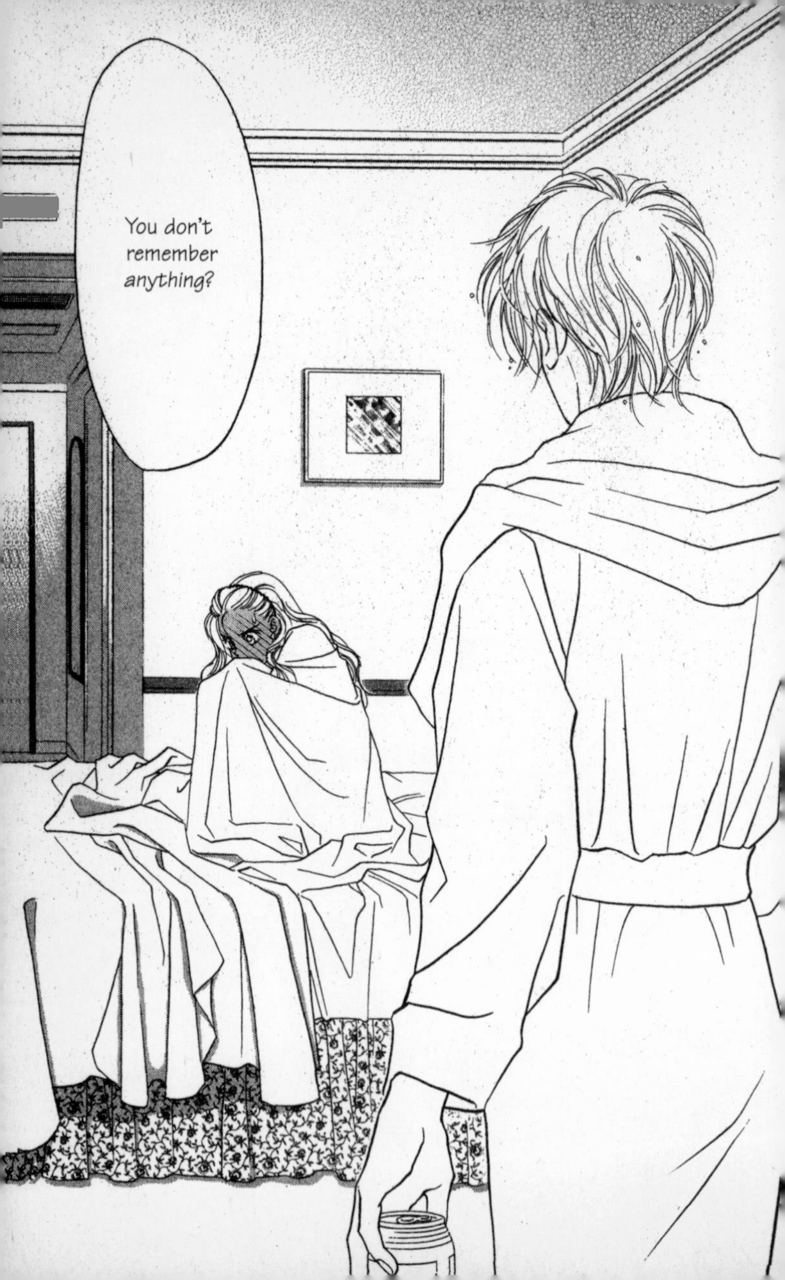
You don't remember anything?

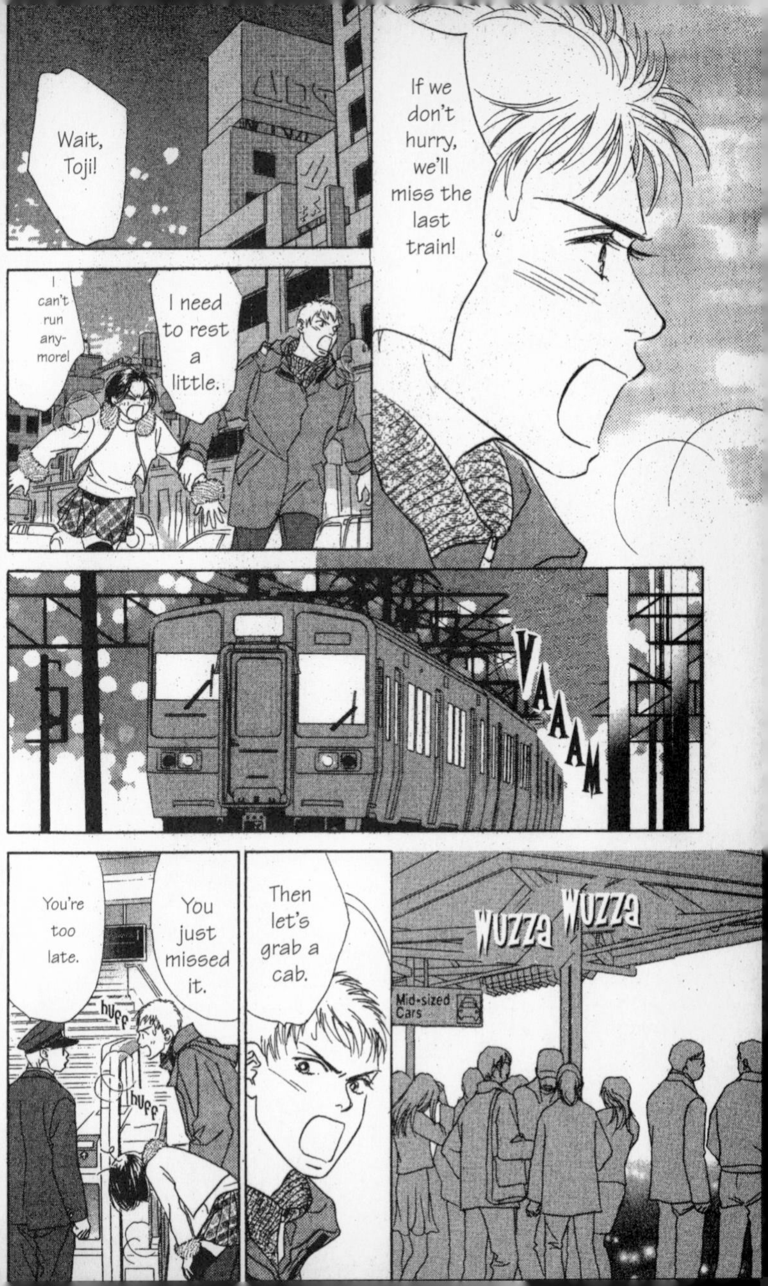
Wait, Toji!
I can't run anymore!
I need to rest a little.
If we don't hurry, we'll miss the last train!
VAAAAM
You're too late.
You just missed it.
huff
huff
Then let's grab a cab.
Wuzza Wuzza
Mid-sized Cars

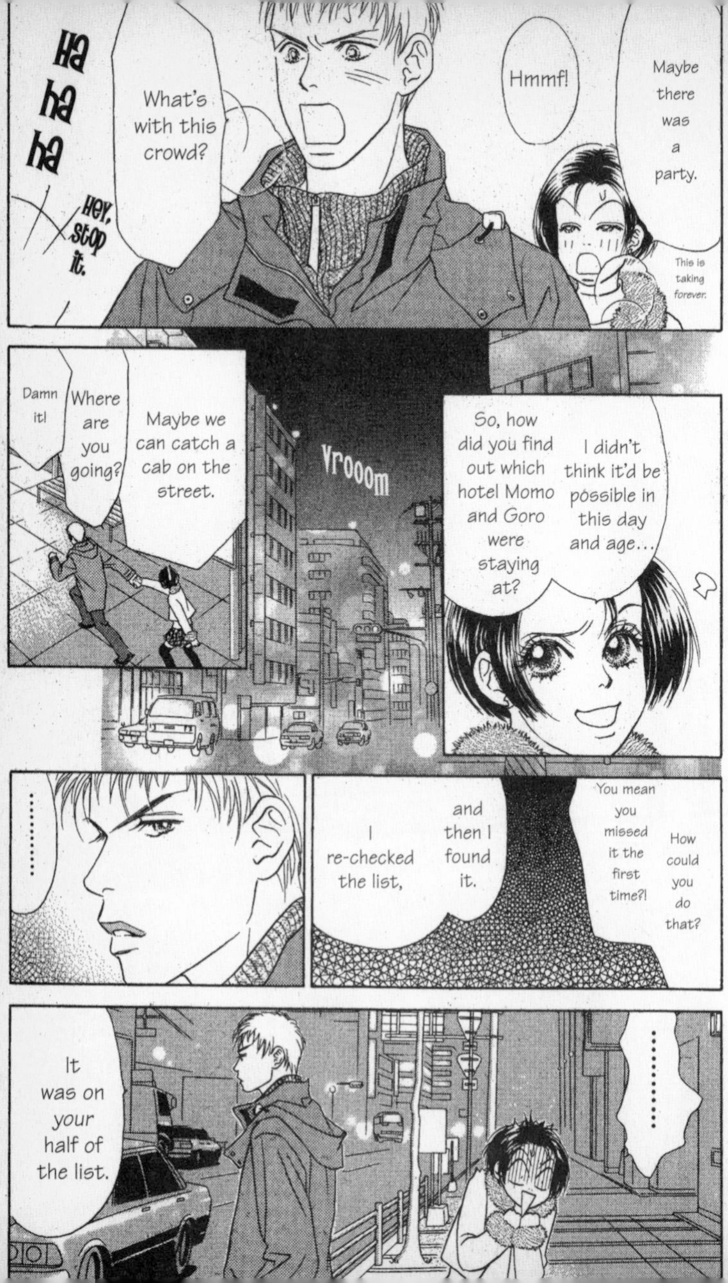

Ha ha ha
Hey, stop it.
What's with this crowd?
Hmmf!
Maybe there was a party.
This is taking forever.
Damn it!
Where are you going?
Maybe we can catch a cab on the street.
Vrooom
So, how did you find out which hotel Momo and Goro were staying at?
I didn't think it'd be possible in this day and age...
....
I re-checked the list,
and then I found it.
You mean you missed it the first time?!
How could you do that?
It was on your half of the list.
....

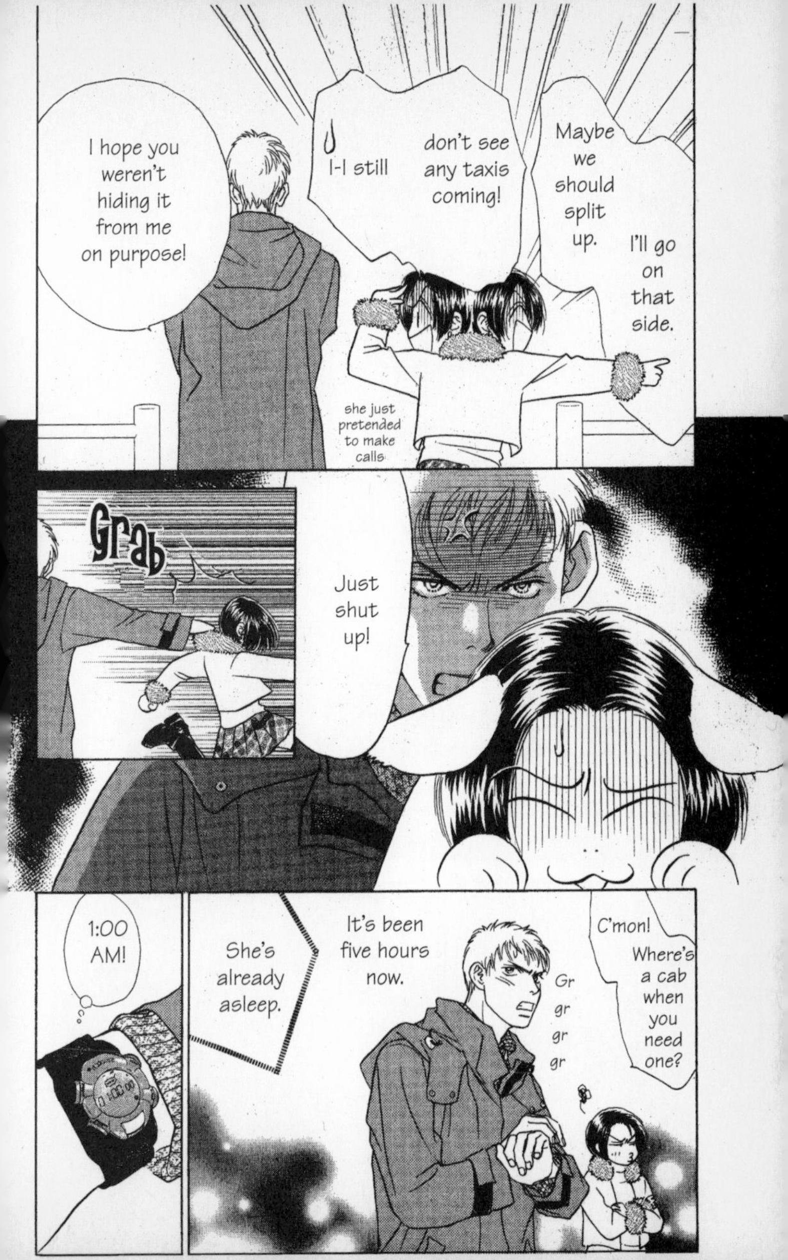
I hope you weren't hiding it from me on purpose!
I-I still
don't see any taxis coming!
Maybe we should split up.
I'll go on that side.
she just pretended to make calls
Grab
Just shut up!
1:00 AM!
She's already asleep.
It's been five hours now.
Gr gr gr gr
C'mon! Where's a cab when you need one?

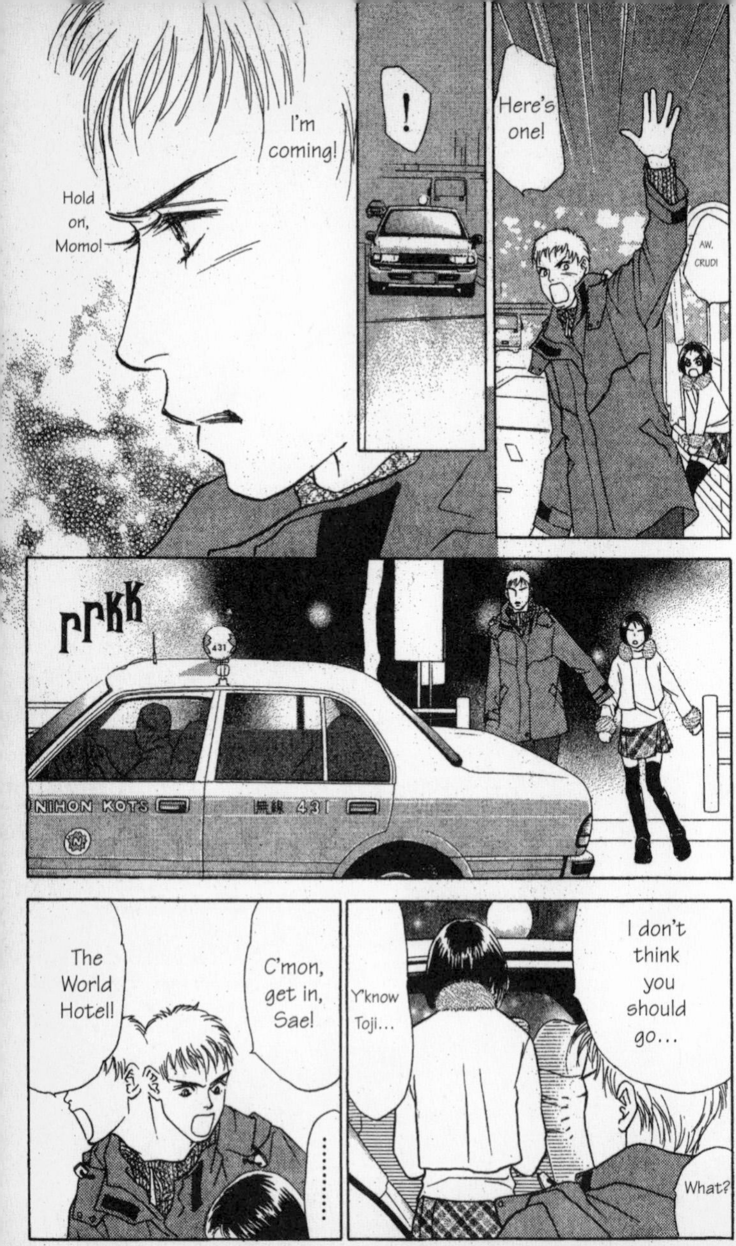

Hold on, Momo!
I'm coming!
!
Here's one!
AW, CRUD!
431
NIHON KOTS
無線 431
The World Hotel!
C'mon, get in, Sae!
....
Y'know Toji...
I don't think you should go...
What?

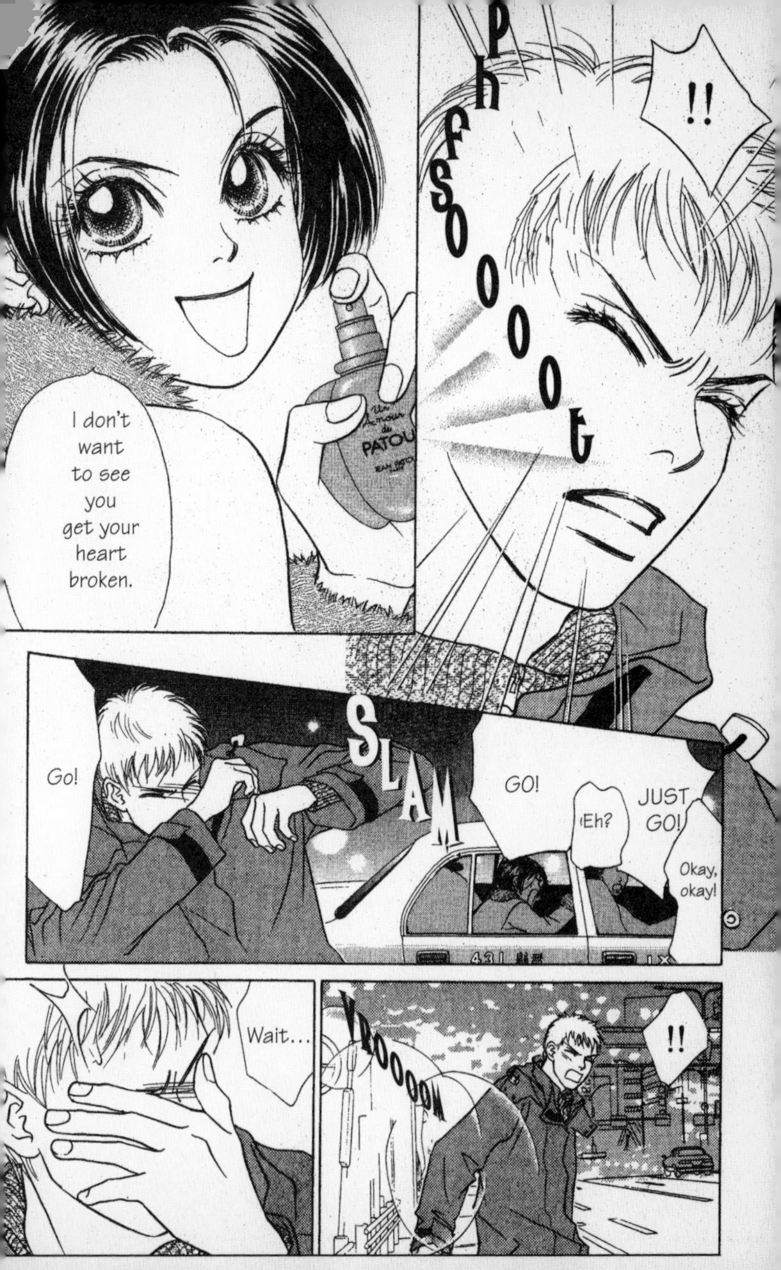
I don't want to see you get your heart broken.
!!
Phfsooooot
Go!
SLAM
GO!
Eh?
JUST GO!
Okay, okay!
Wait...
VROOOOOM
!!

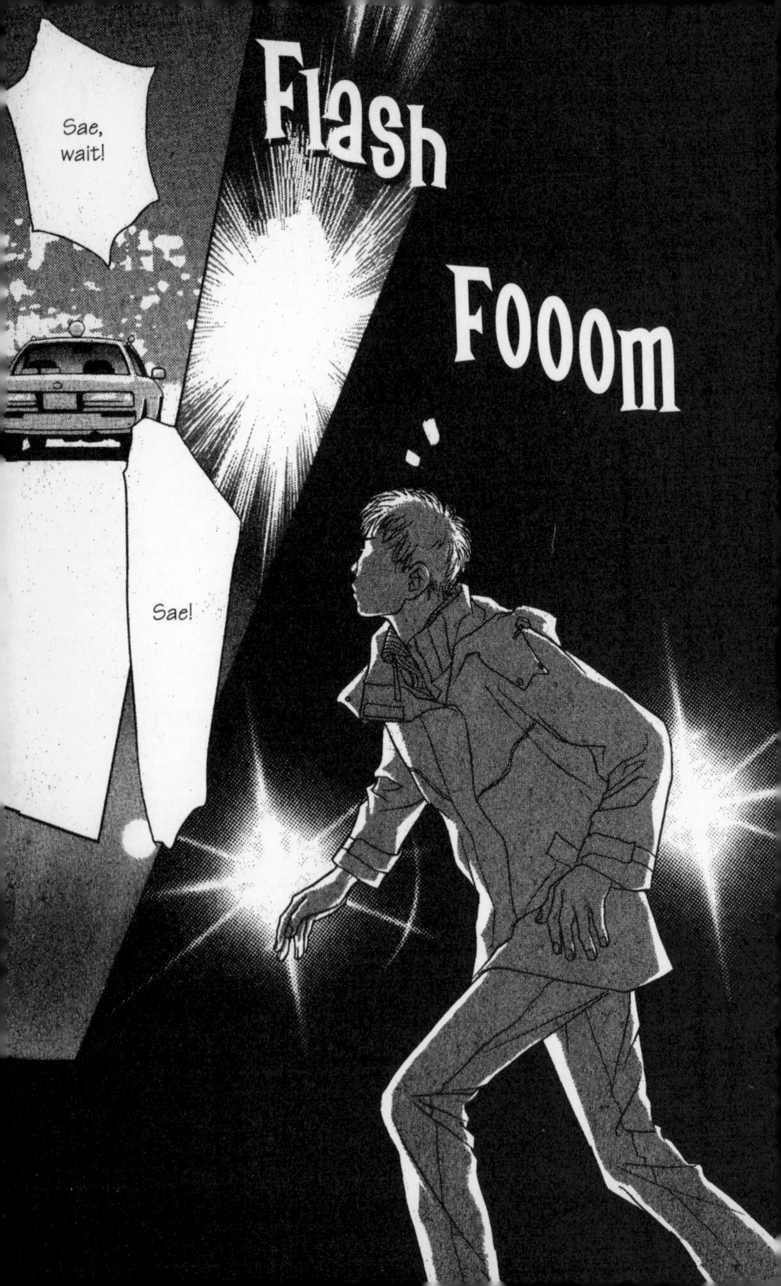
Flash
Fooom
Sae, wait!
Sae!

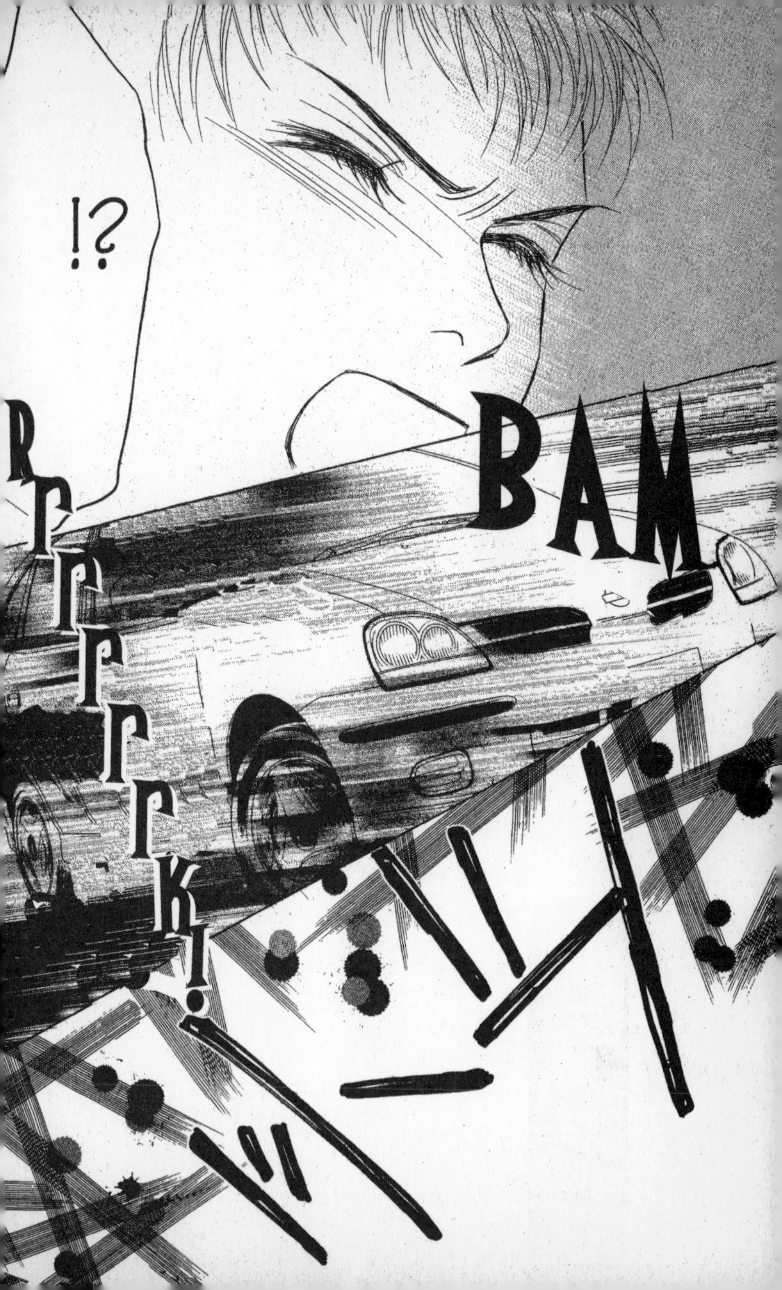
!?
BAM
Rrrrrrrrk!

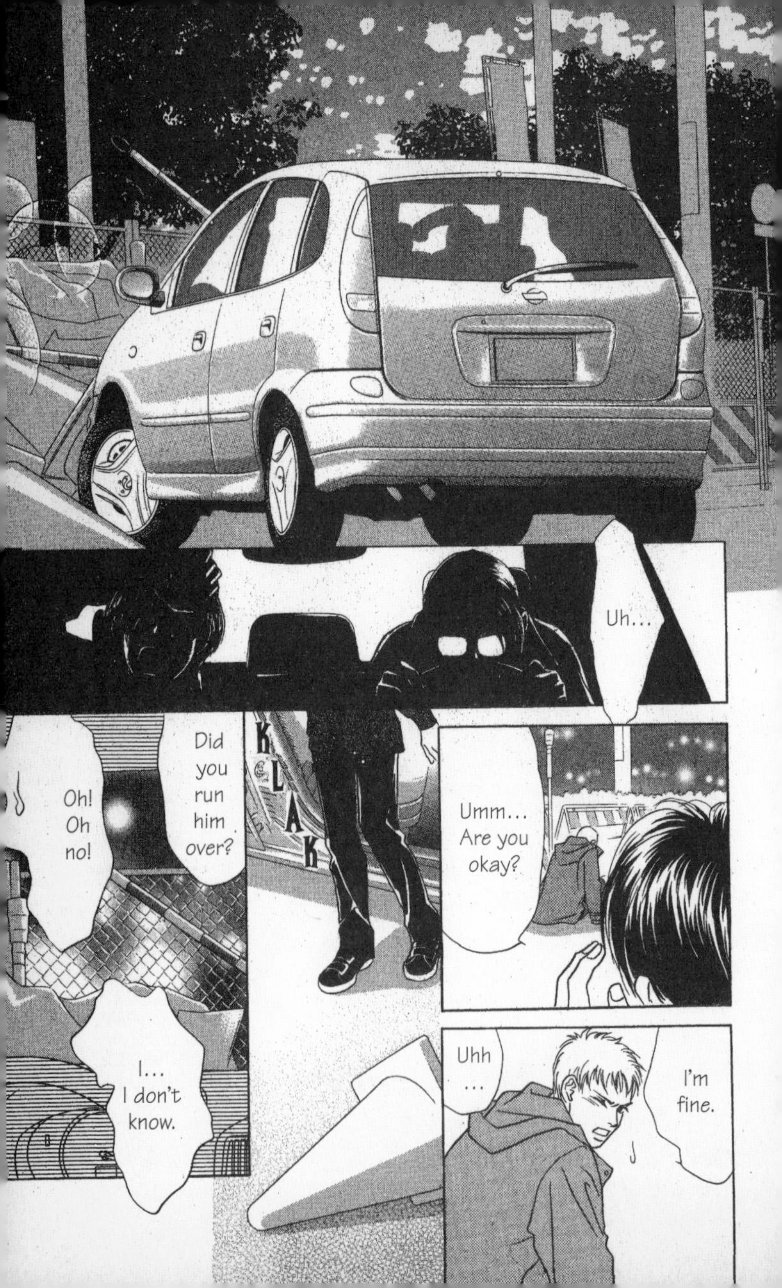
Uh...
Oh! Oh no!
Did you run him over?
I... I don't know.
KLAK
Umm... Are you okay?
Uhh...
I'm fine.

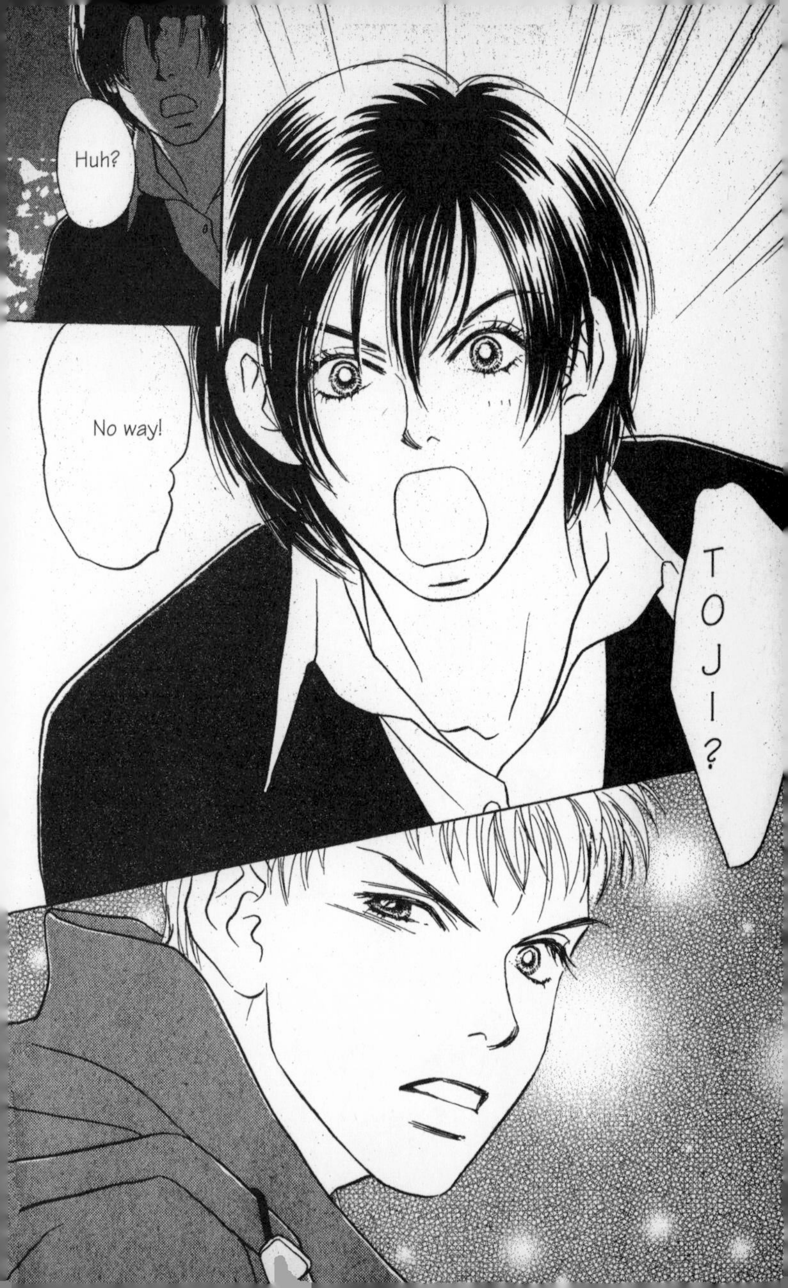
Huh?
No way!
TOJI?

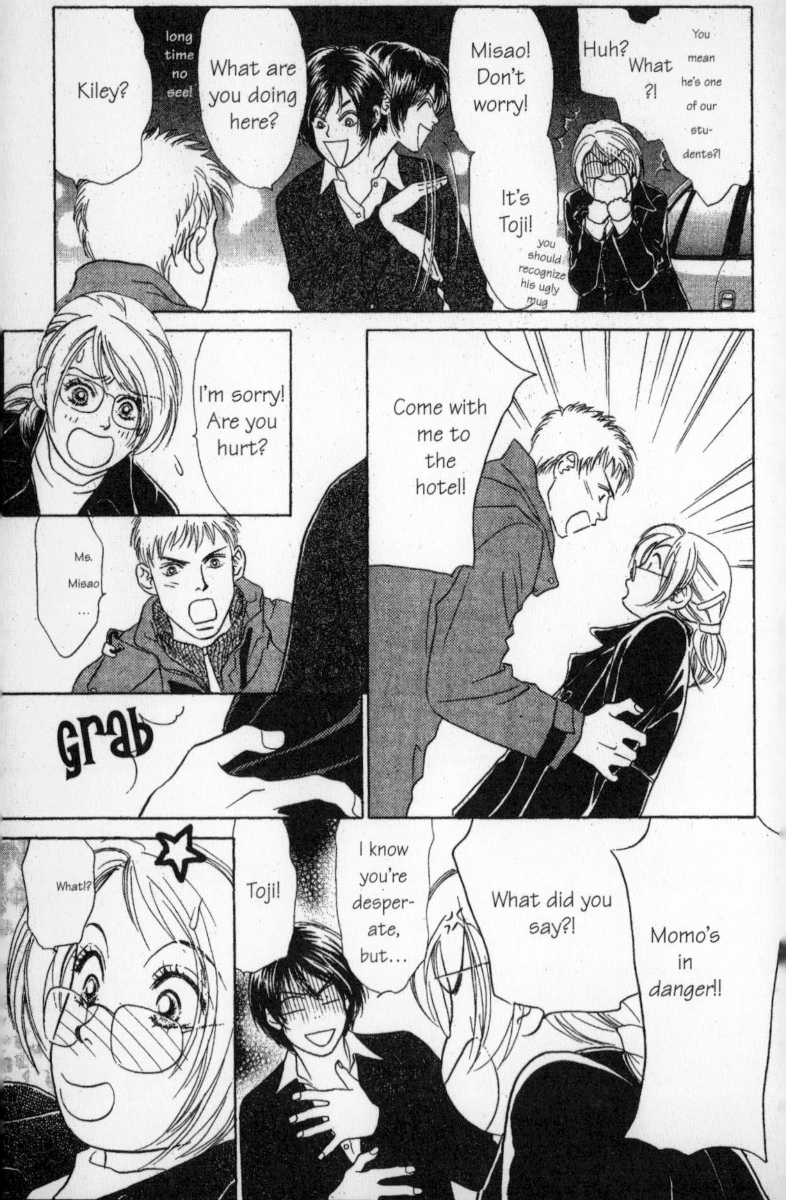
Kiley?
long time no see!
What are you doing here?
Misao! Don't worry!
It's Toji!
you should recognize his ugly mug
Huh?
What ?!
You mean he's one of our stu- dents?!
I'm sorry! Are you hurt?
Ms. Misao …
Grab
Come with me to the hotel!
What!?
Toji!
I know you're desper- ate, but…
What did you say?!
Momo's in danger!!

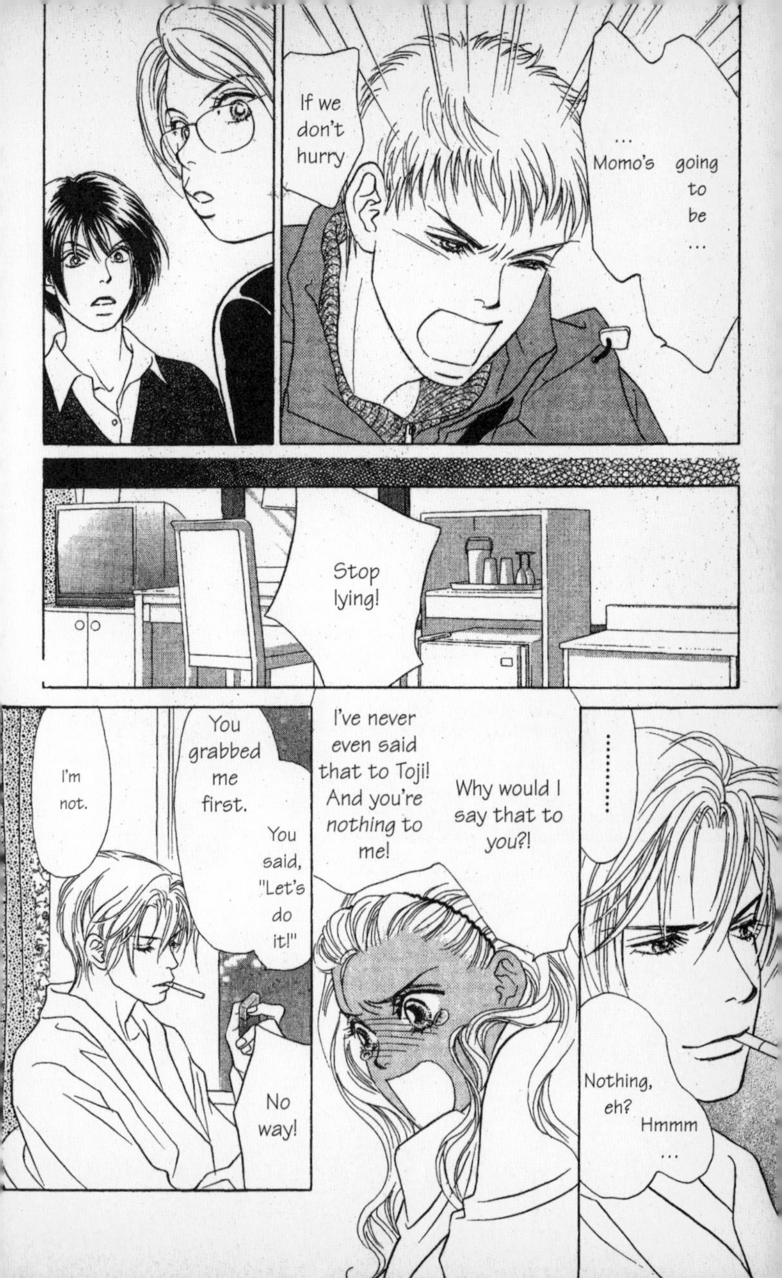
If we don't hurry
... Momo's going to be ...
Stop lying!
I'm not.
You grabbed me first.
You said, "Let's do it!"
No way!
I've never even said that to Toji! And you're nothing to me!
Why would I say that to you?!
....
Nothing, eh? Hmmm ...

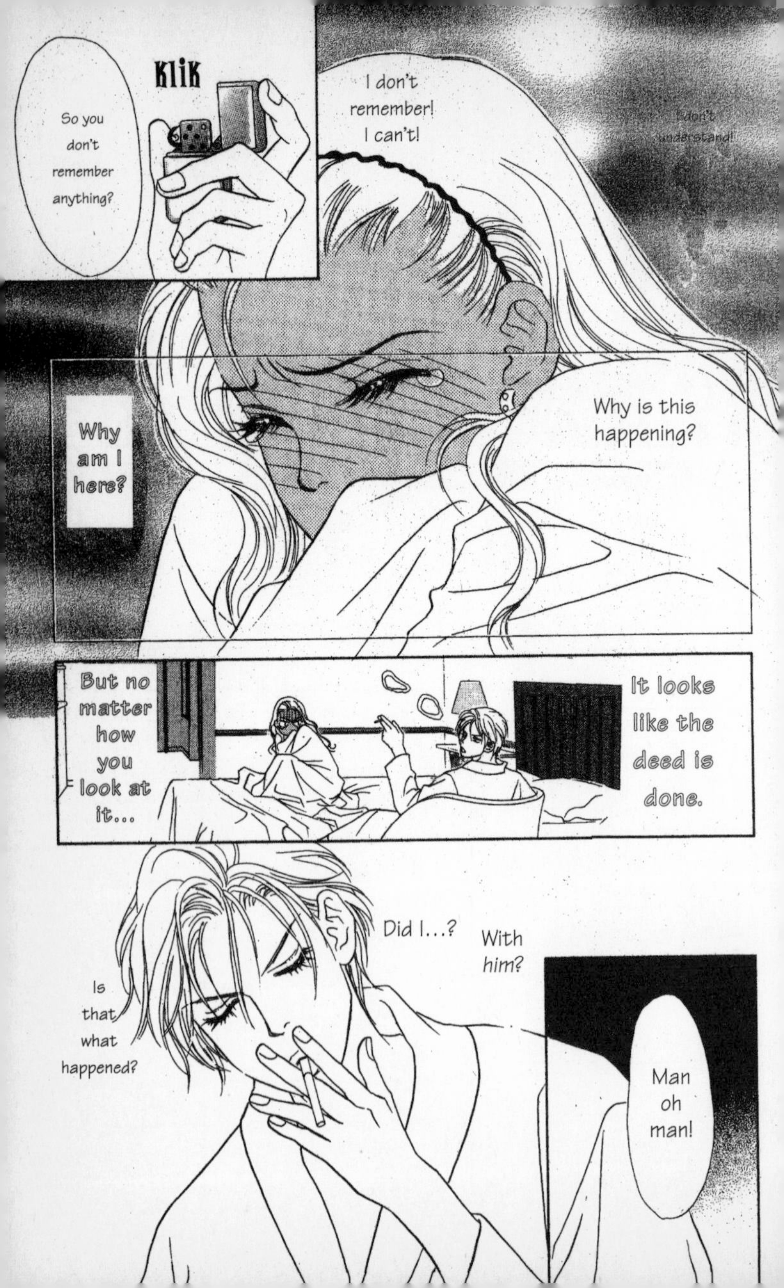
So you don't remember anything?
KLIK
I don't remember! I can't!
I don't understand!
Why am I here?
Why is this happening?
But no matter how you look at it...
It looks like the deed is done.
Is that what happened?
Did I...?
With him?
Man oh man!

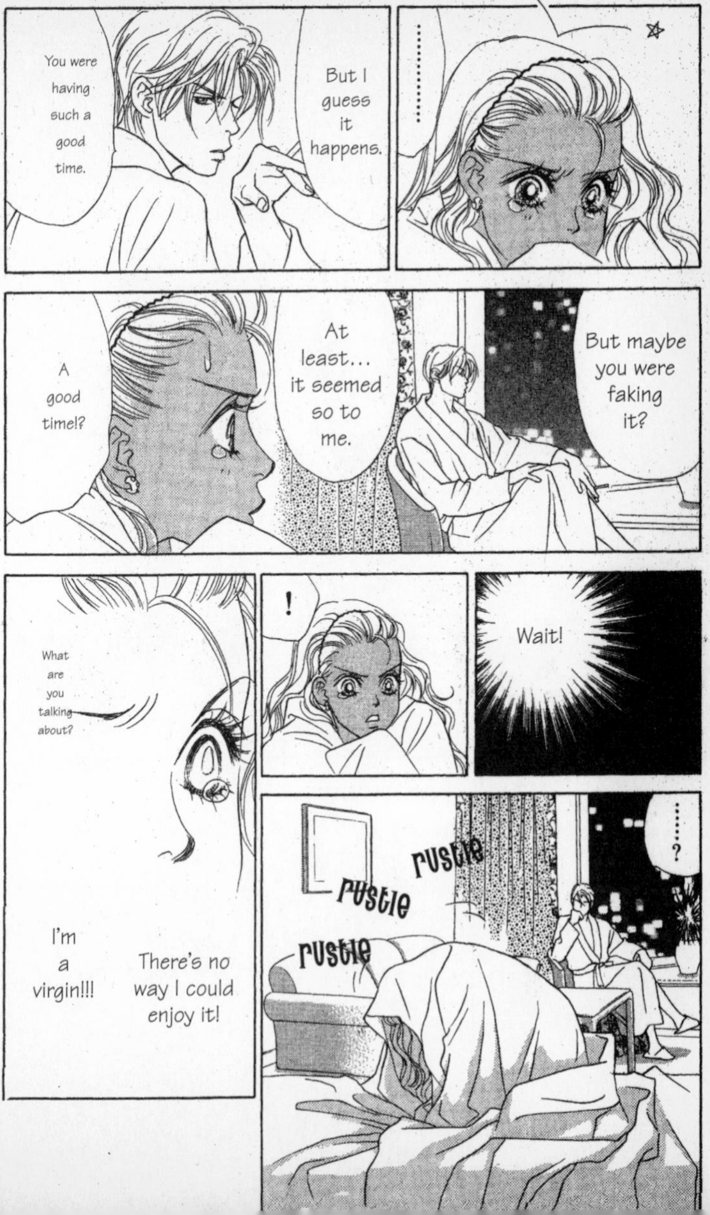
You were having such a good time.
But I guess it happens.
......
A good time!?
At least... it seemed so to me.
But maybe you were faking it?
What are you talking about?
I'm a virgin!!!
There's no way I could enjoy it!
!
Wait!
rustle
rustle
rustle
......?

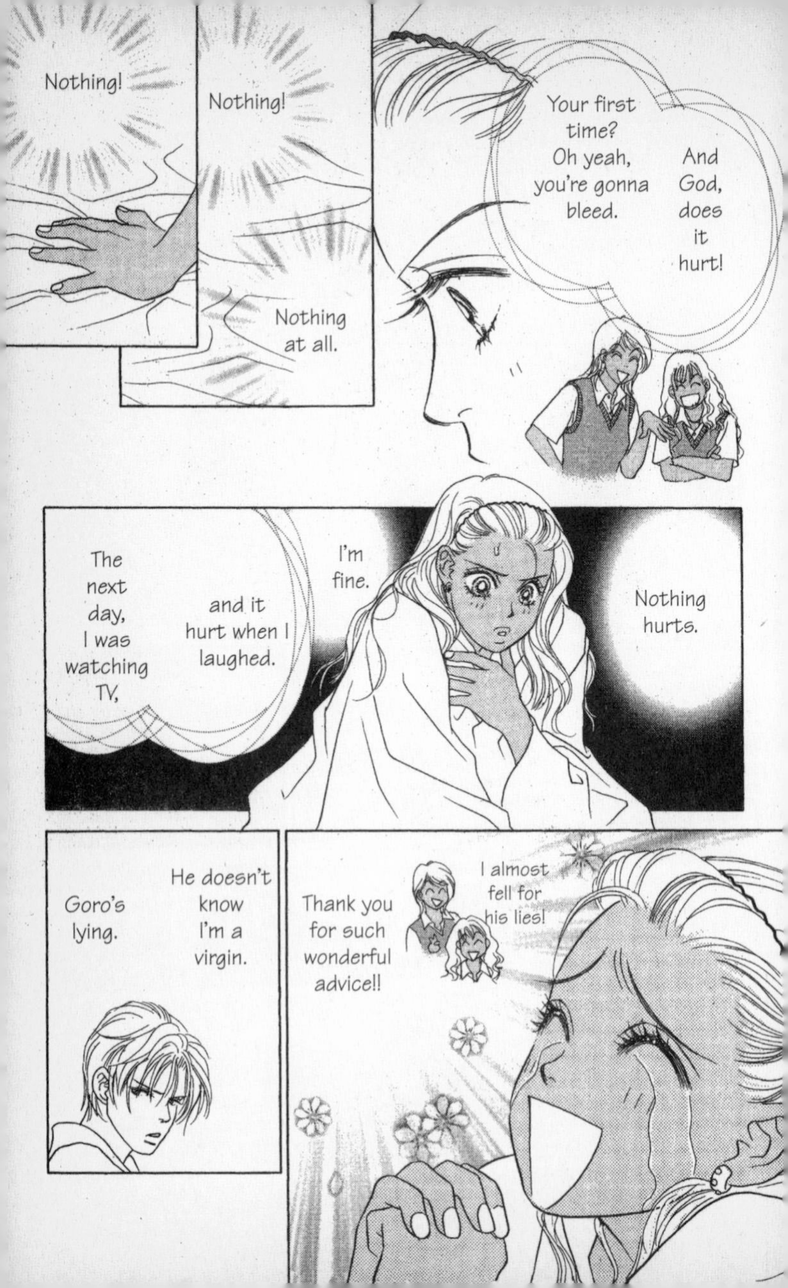
Nothing!
Nothing!
Nothing at all.
Your first time? Oh yeah, you're gonna bleed.
And God, does it hurt!
The next day, I was watching TV,
and it hurt when I laughed.
I'm fine.
Nothing hurts.
Goro's lying.
He doesn't know I'm a virgin.
Thank you for such wonderful advice!!
I almost fell for his lies!

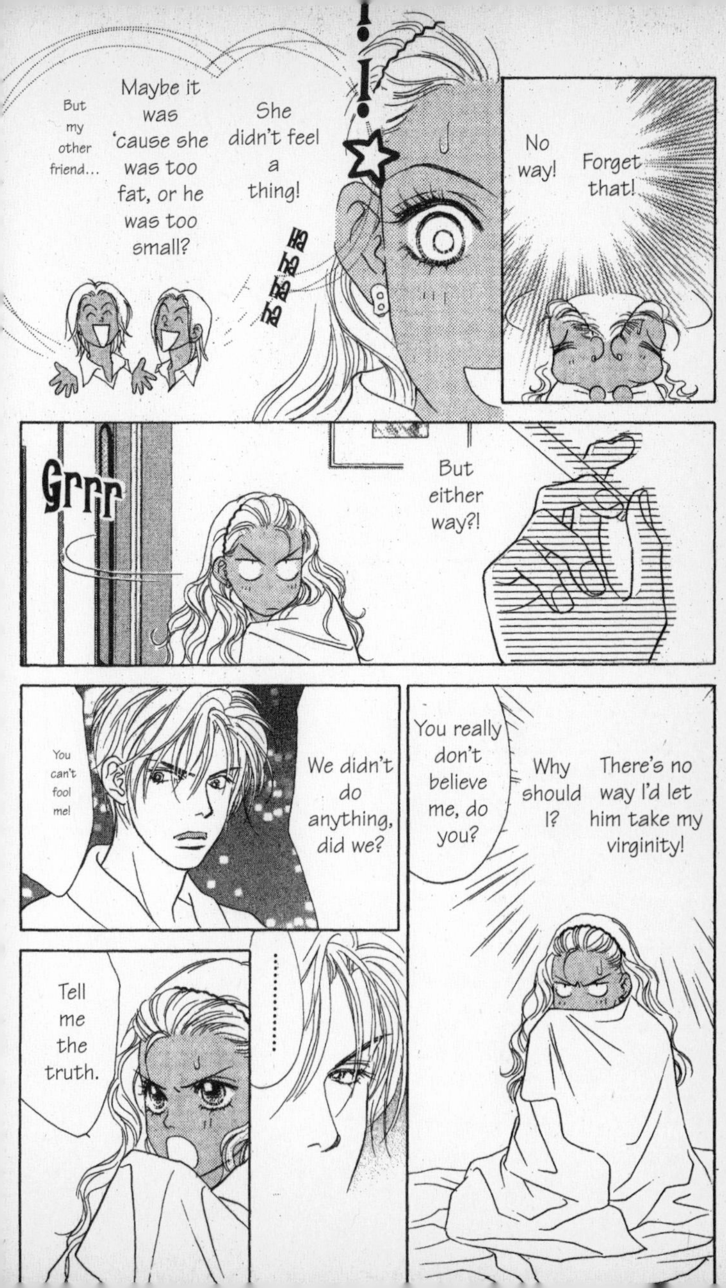
But my other friend...
Maybe it was 'cause she was too fat, or he was too small?
She didn't feel a thing!
HA HA HA HA HA
!
No way!
Forget that!
Grrr
But either way?!
You can't fool me!
We didn't do anything, did we?
Tell me the truth.
......
You really don't believe me, do you?
Why should I?
There's no way I'd let him take my virginity!

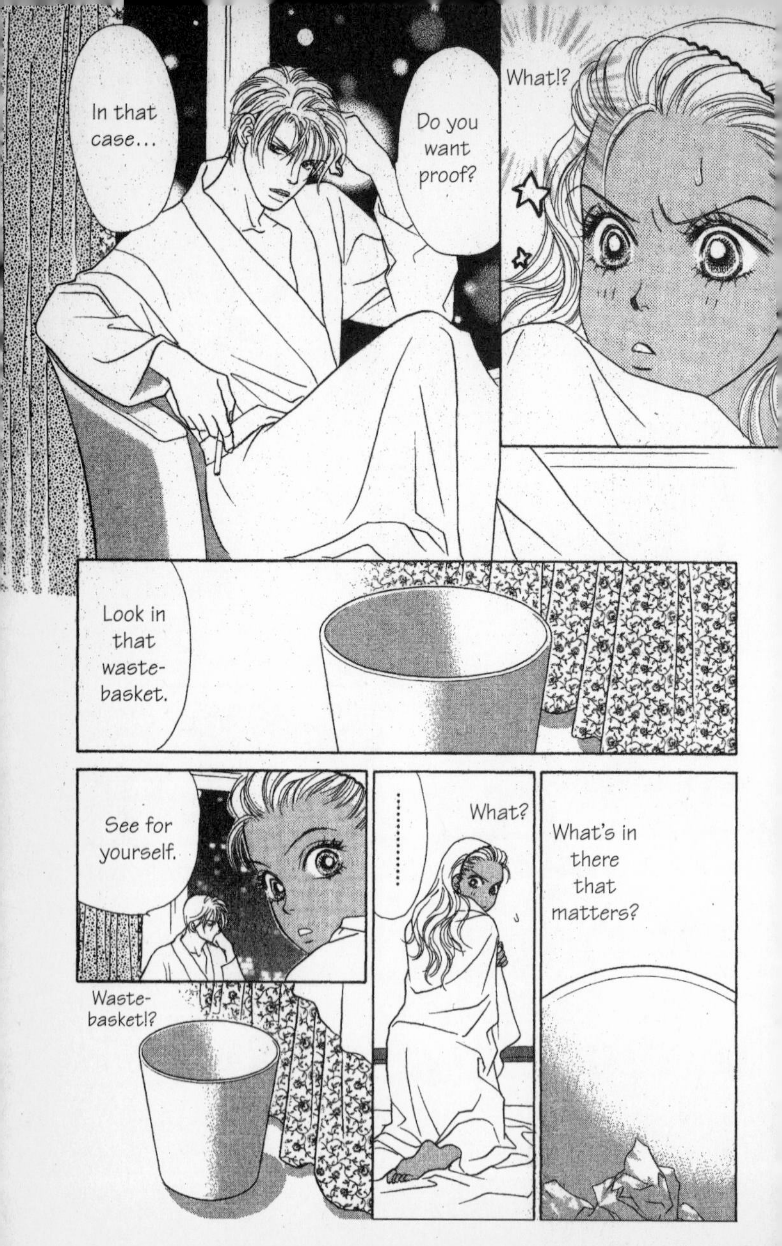
In that case...
Do you want proof?
What!?
Look in that waste-basket.
See for yourself.
Waste-basket!?
......
What?
What's in there that matters?

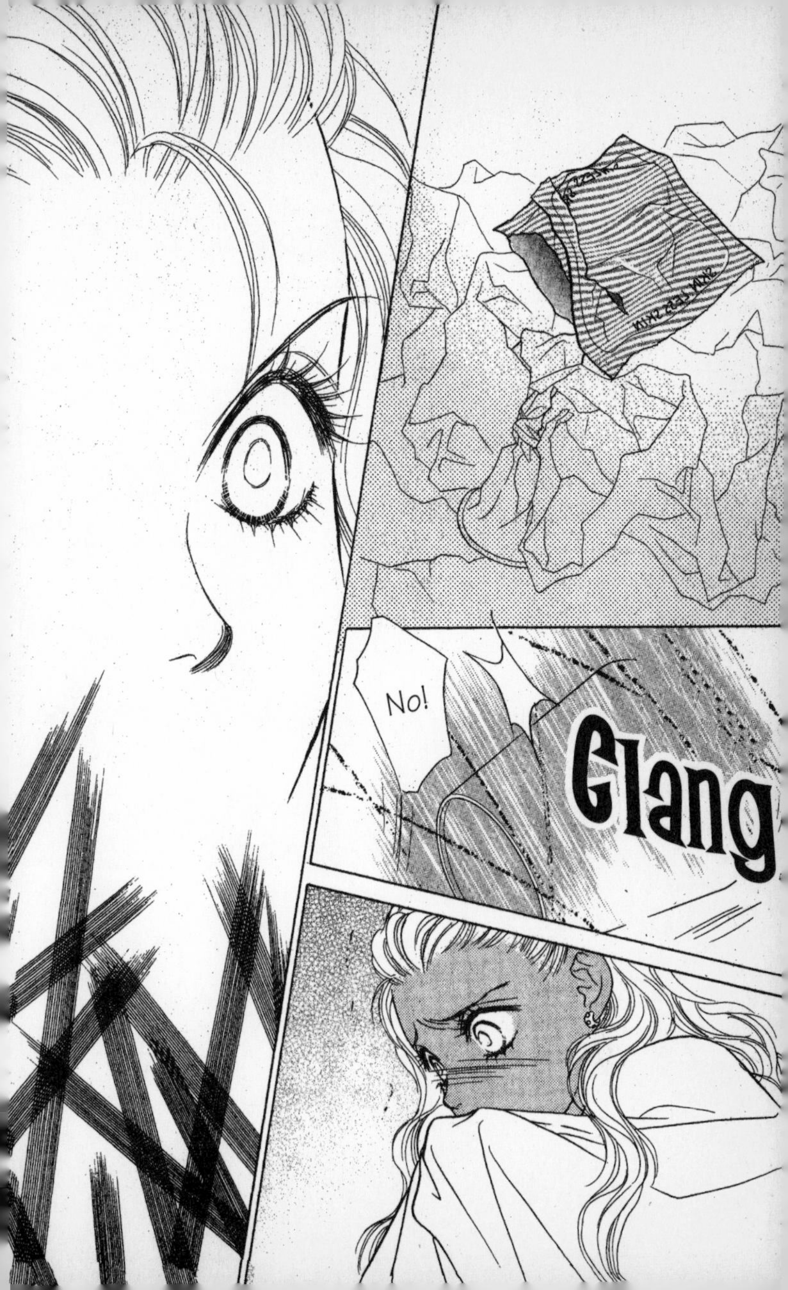
No!
Clang

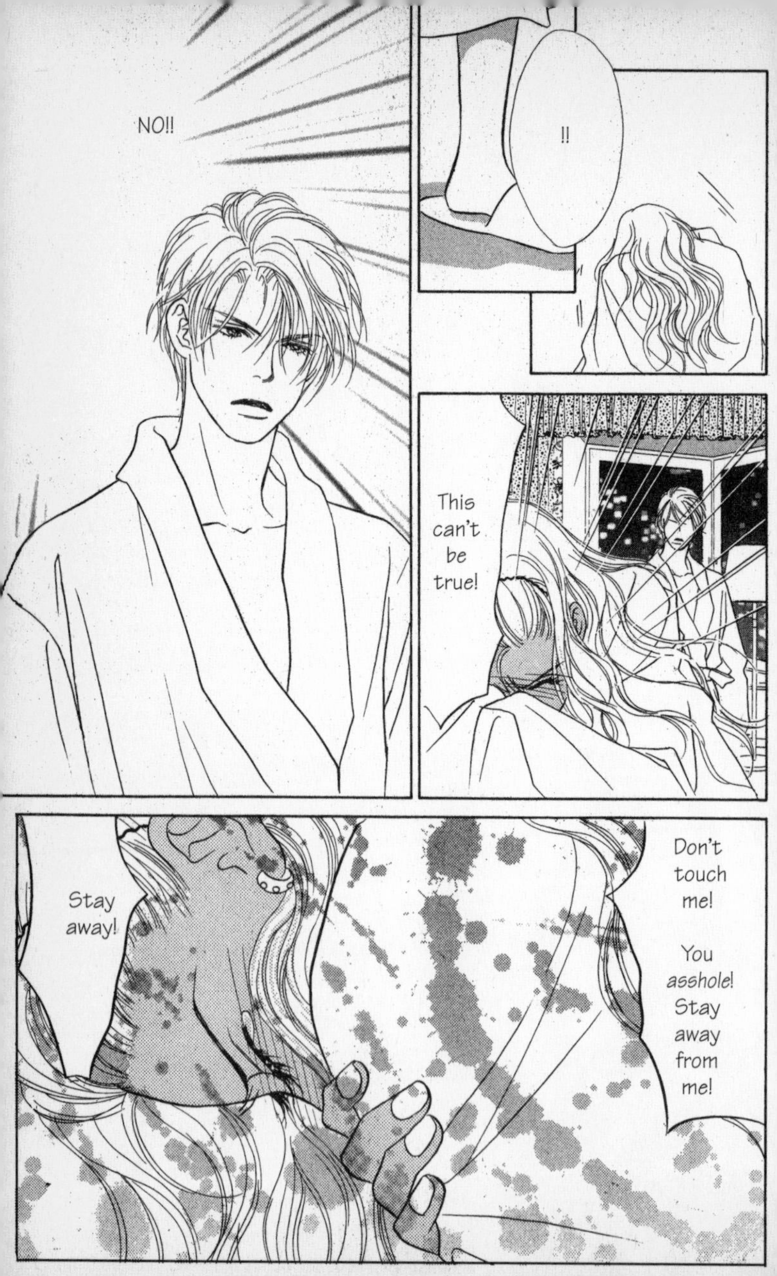
NO!!
!!
This can't be true!
Stay away!
Don't touch me!
You asshole! Stay away from me!

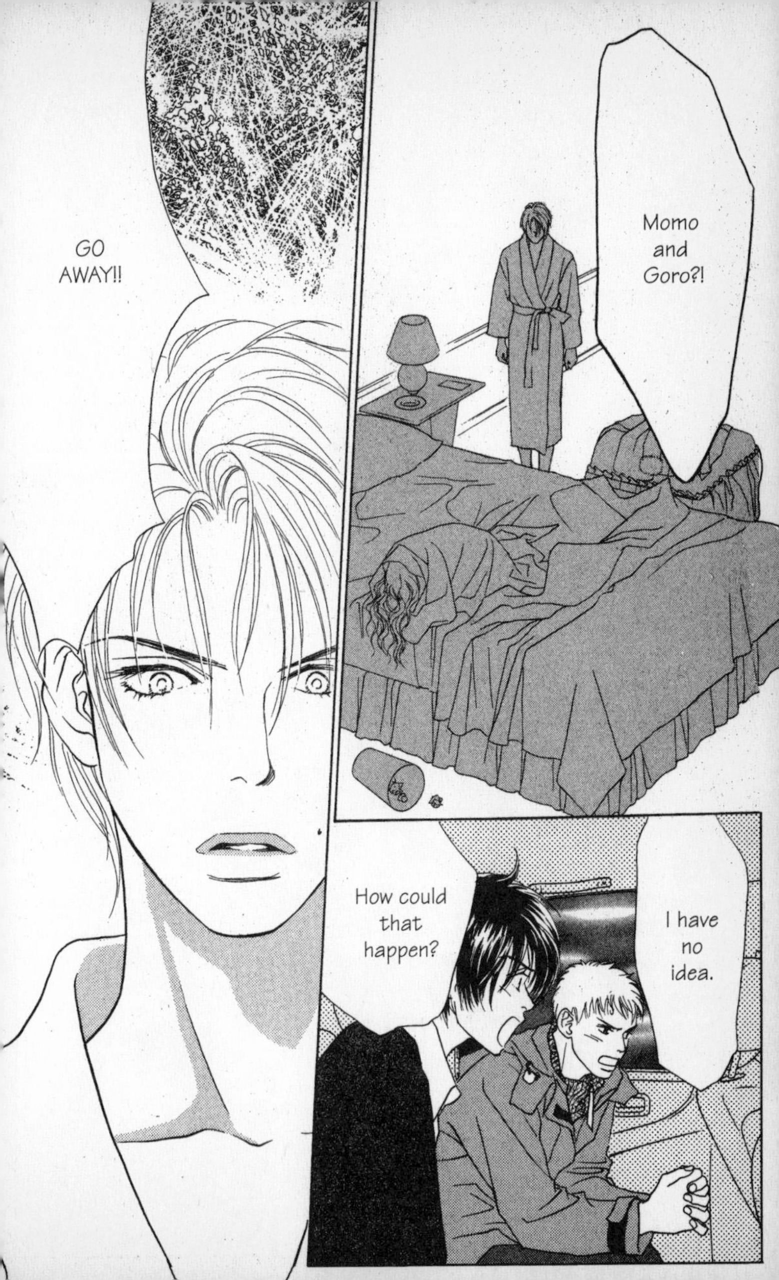
GO AWAY!!
Momo and Goro?!
How could that happen?
I have no idea.

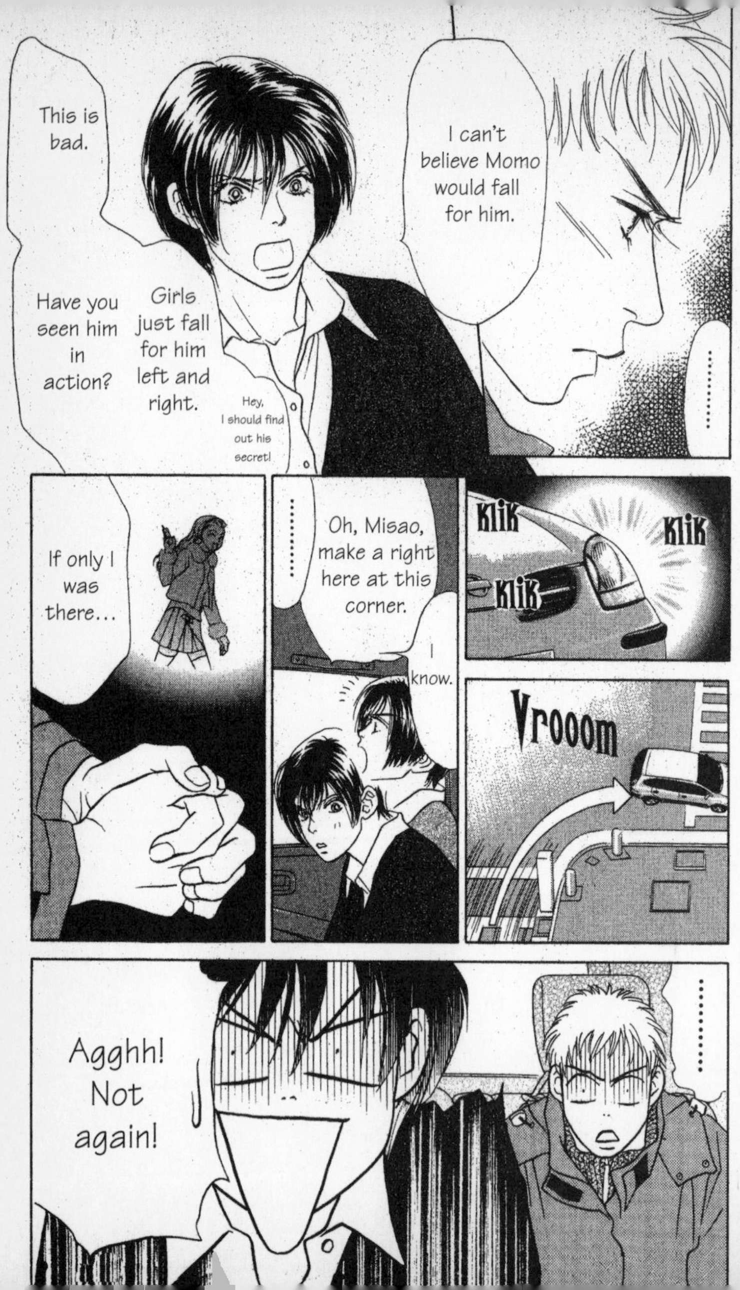
This is bad.
Have you seen him in action?
Girls just fall for him left and right.
Hey, I should find out his secret!
I can't believe Momo would fall for him.
......
If only I was there...
......
Oh, Misao, make a right here at this corner.
I know.
KliK
KliK
KliK
Vrooom
Agghh! Not again!
......

Didn't you just signal left?

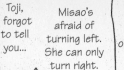

Toji, I forgot to tell you...

Misao's afraid of turning left. She can only turn right.

I can't help it! All that oncoming traffic is so scary!

don't ask me why...

So why did you turn right?

There's nothing to it. All you have to do is wait for the oncoming traffic to pass.

I know that! I tried!

But the last time, my car just stopped in the middle of the intersection!

Sorry to inconvenience you, but I can't help it!

I can't even figure out how you commute to work!

I know how to get to school only making right turns. So there!

Come on! Get in! We'll get a bite to eat.

We made so many right turns, I never made it home.

I remember when I bummed a ride from you once.

Don't worry! Traffic is getting light. I'll make it this time!

That's what you said the last time!

L...

Let me out of here!!!

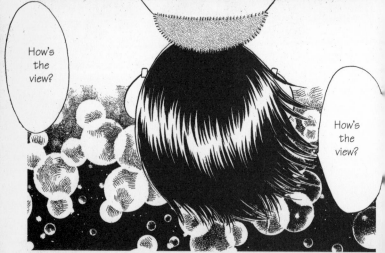

How's the view?

How's the view?

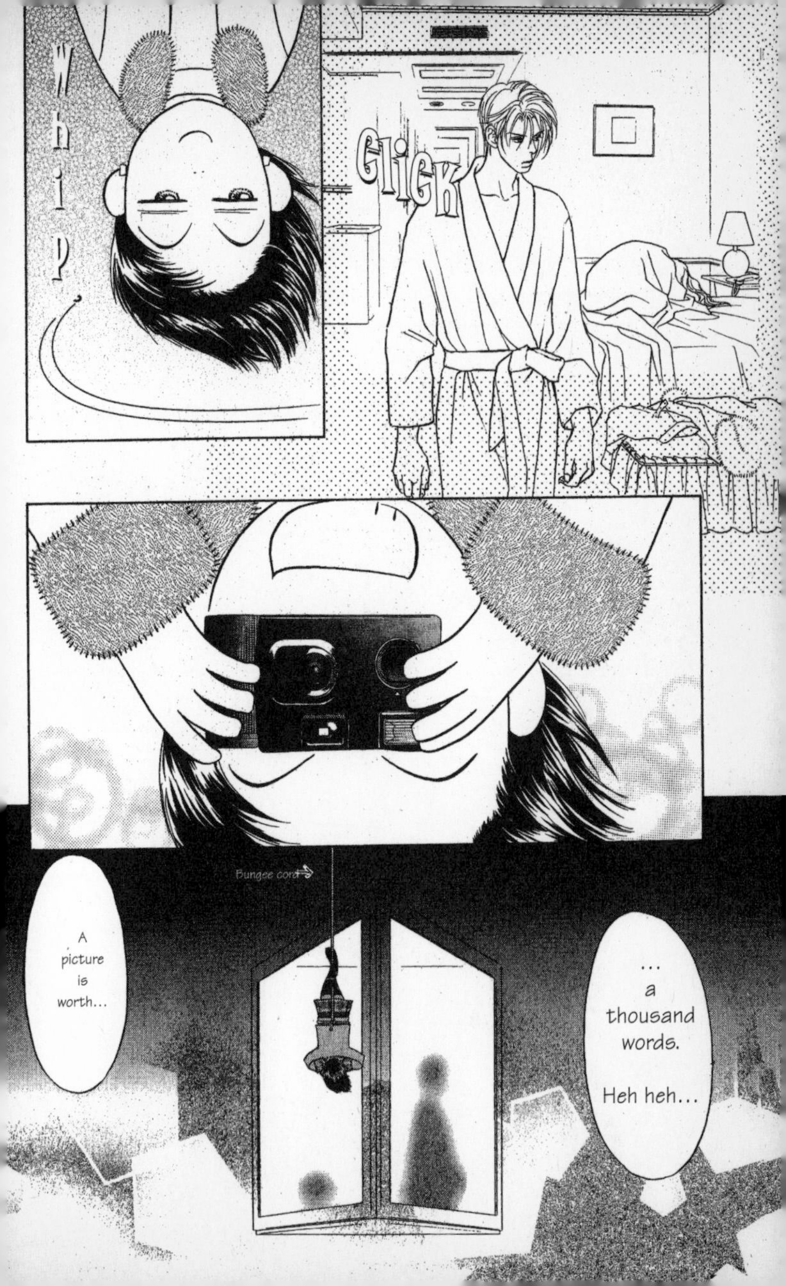
Whip
Click
Bungee cord
A picture is worth...
... a thousand words.
Heh heh...

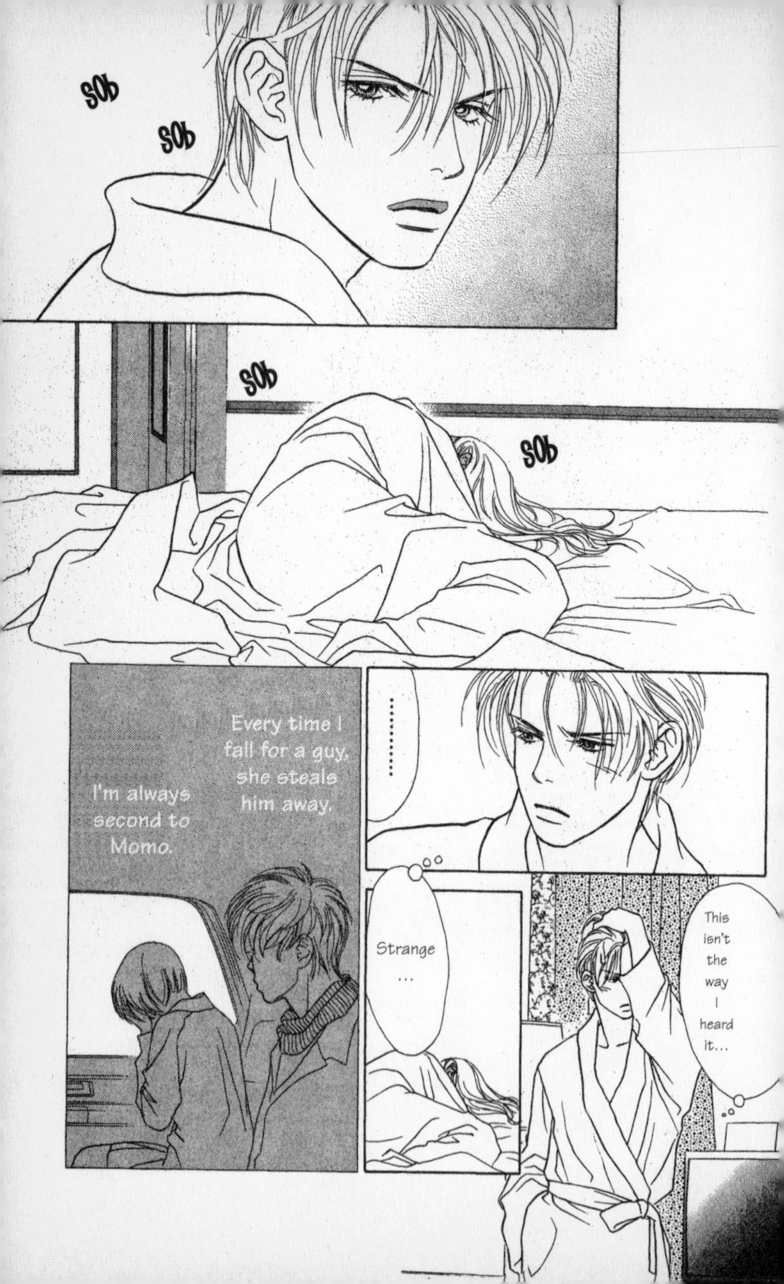
SOB
SOB
SOB
SOB
Every time I fall for a guy, she steals him away.
I'm always second to Momo.
....
Strange ...
This isn't the way I heard it...

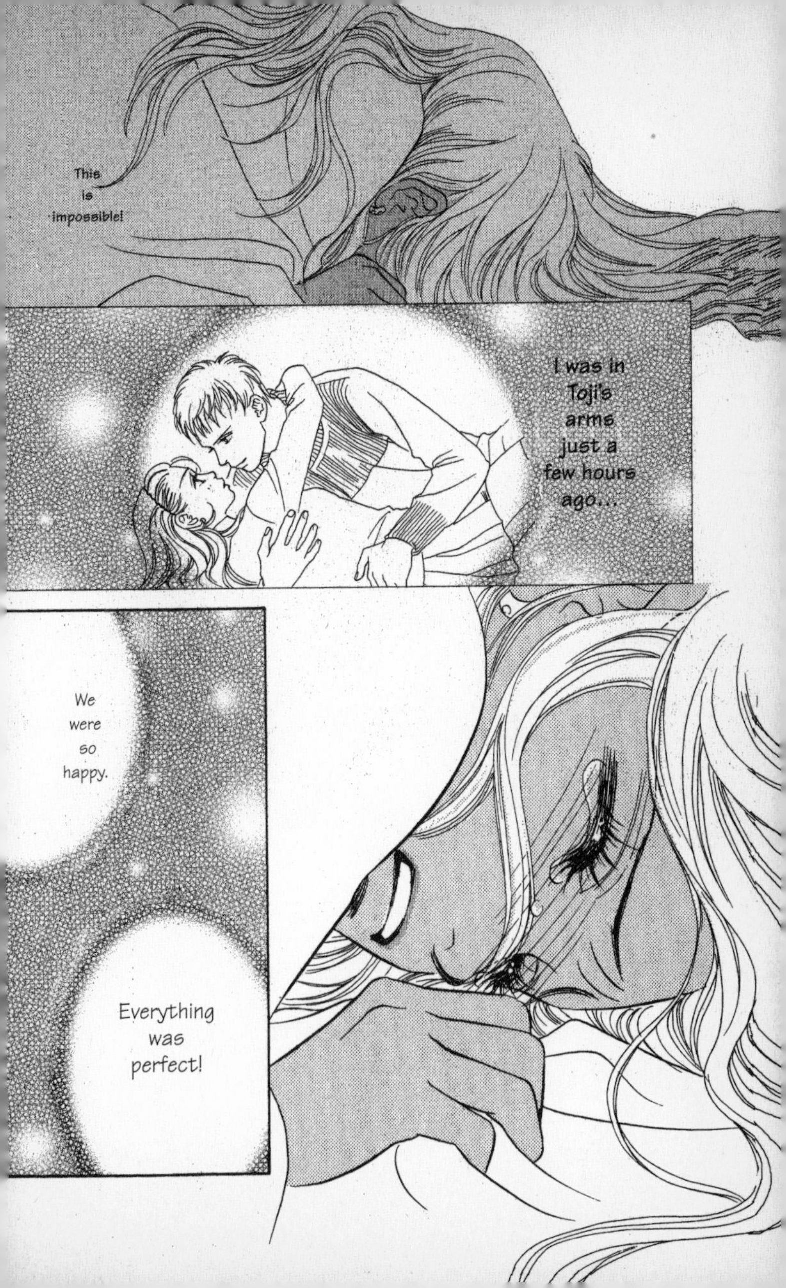
This is impossible!
I was in Toji's arms just a few hours ago...
We were so happy.
Everything was perfect!

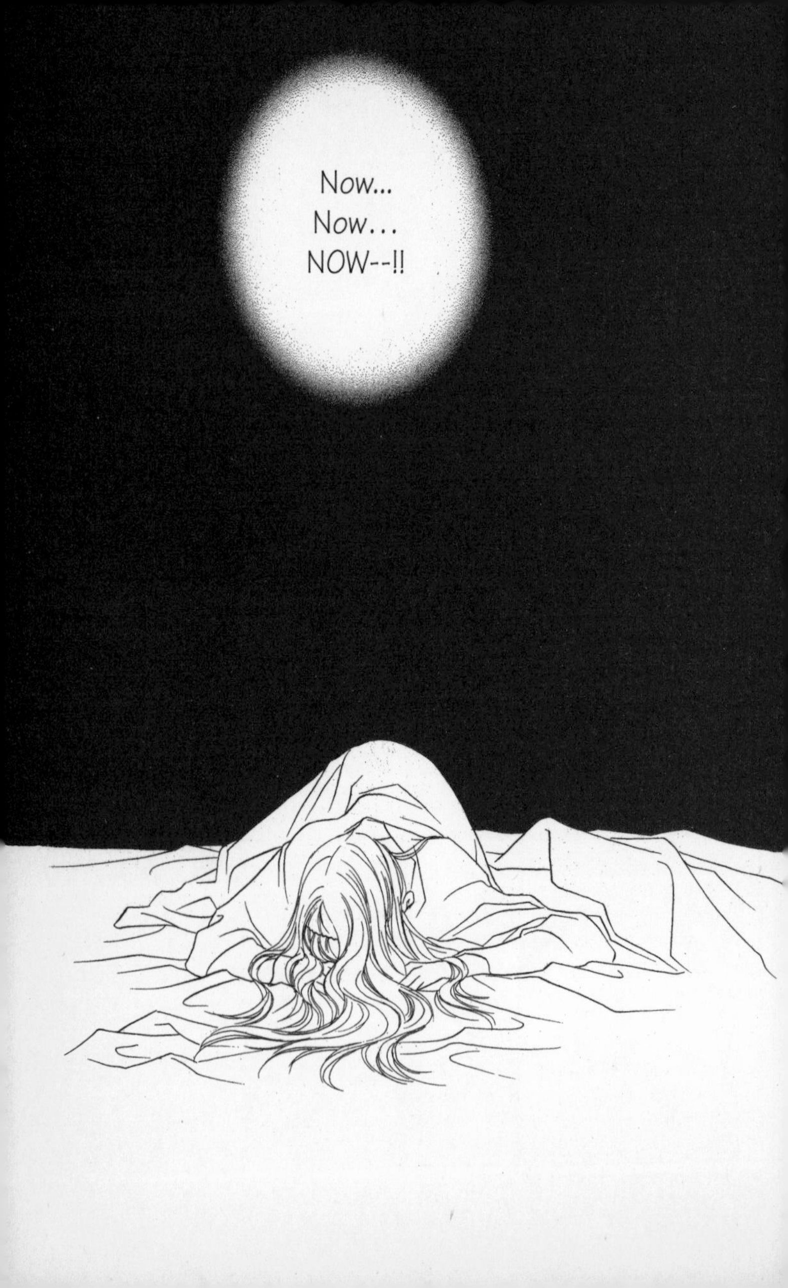
Now...
Now...
NOW--!!

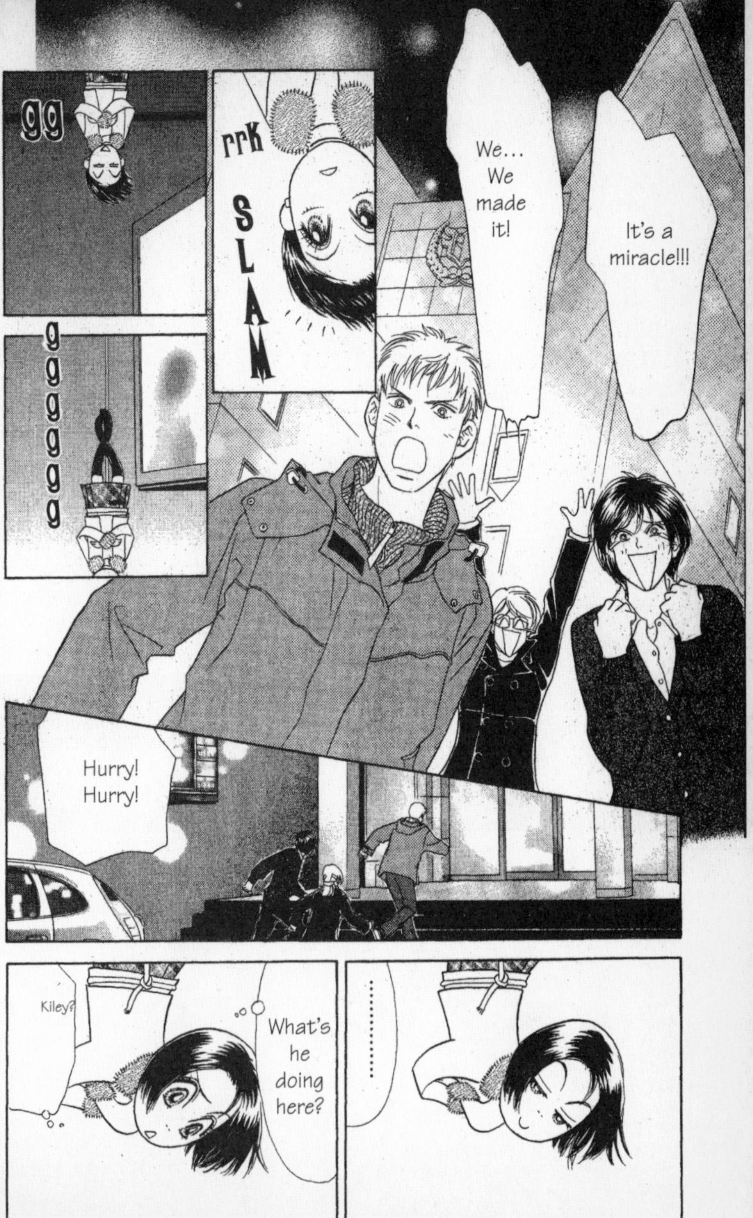
gg
gggggg
rrk
SLAM
We… We made it!
It's a miracle!!!
Hurry! Hurry!
Kiley?
What's he doing here?
……

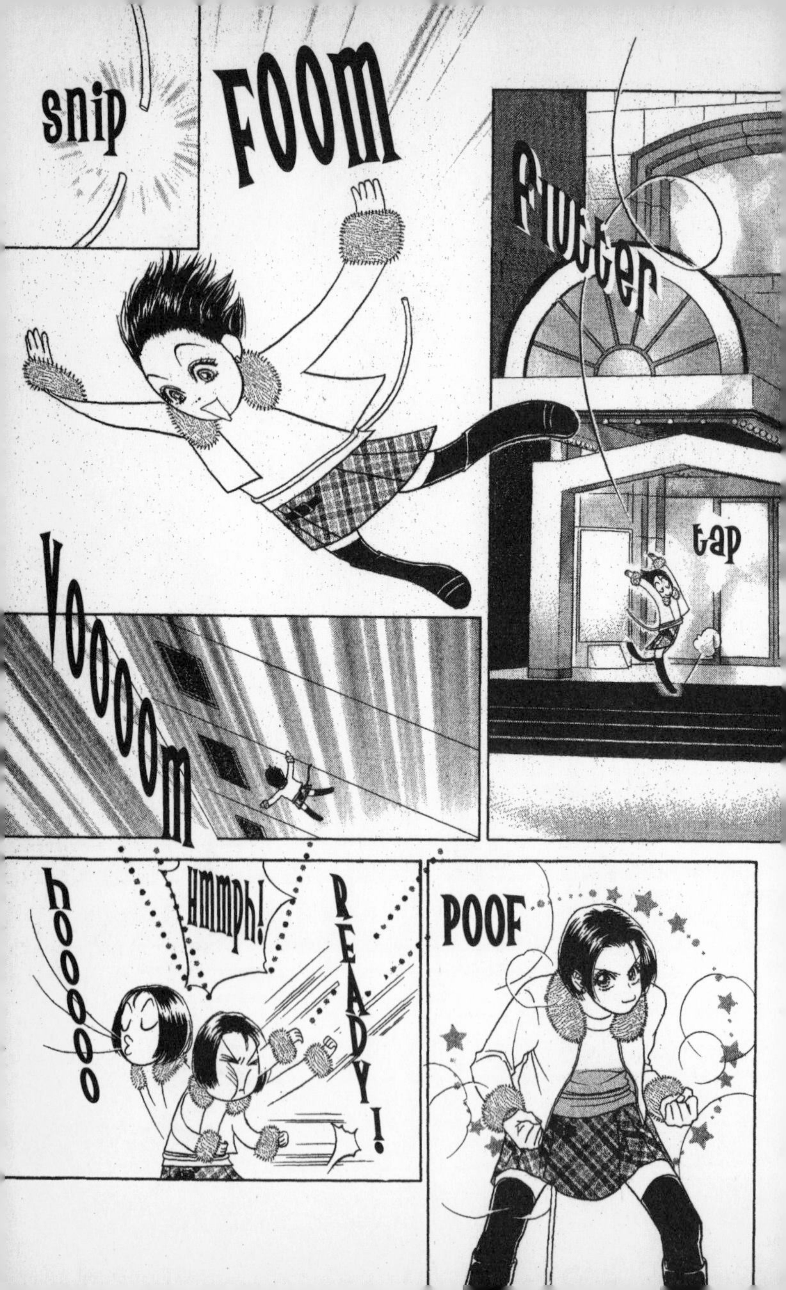
snip
FOOM
Flutter
tap
VOOOOOM
hooooo
HMMPh!
READY!
POOF

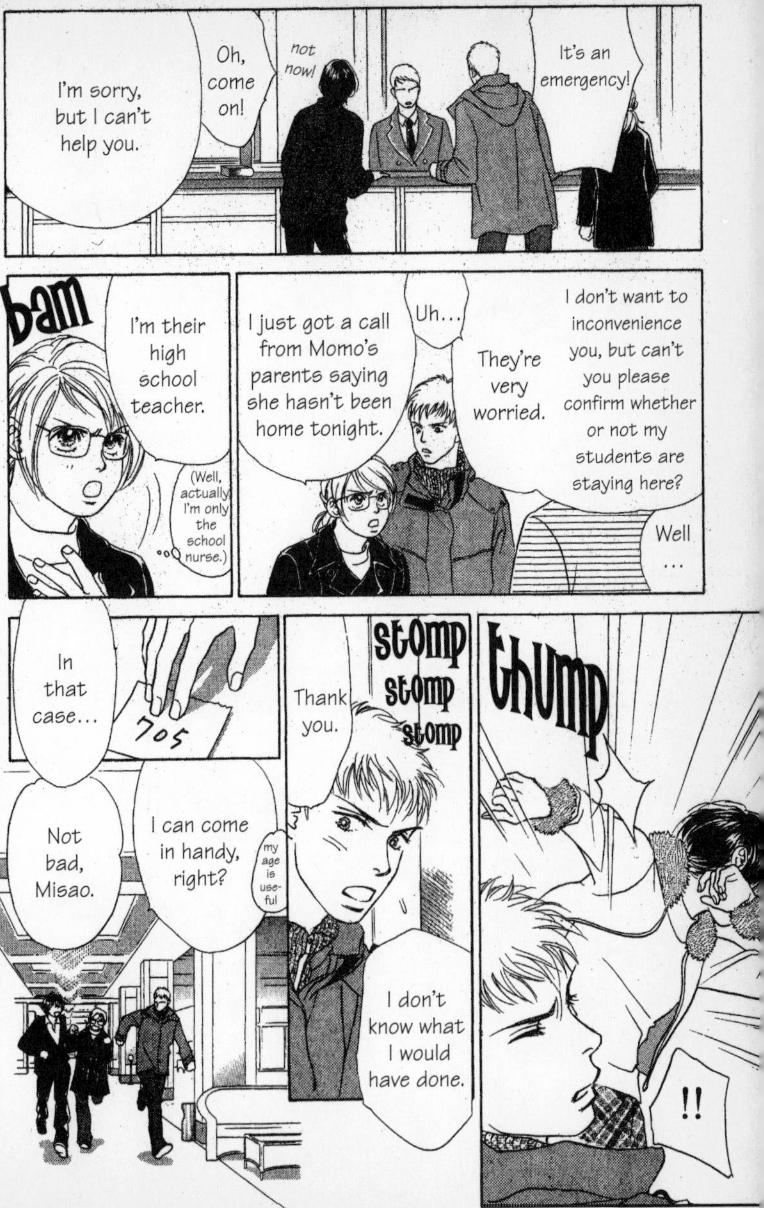
I'm sorry, but I can't help you.
Oh, come on!
not now!
It's an emergency!
bam
I'm their high school teacher.
(Well, actually I'm only the school nurse.)
I just got a call from Momo's parents saying she hasn't been home tonight.
Uh...
They're very worried.
I don't want to inconvenience you, but can't you please confirm whether or not my students are staying here?
Well ...
In that case...
705
Not bad, Misao.
I can come in handy, right?
my age is useful
Thank you.
stomp stomp stomp
I don't know what I would have done.
thump
!!

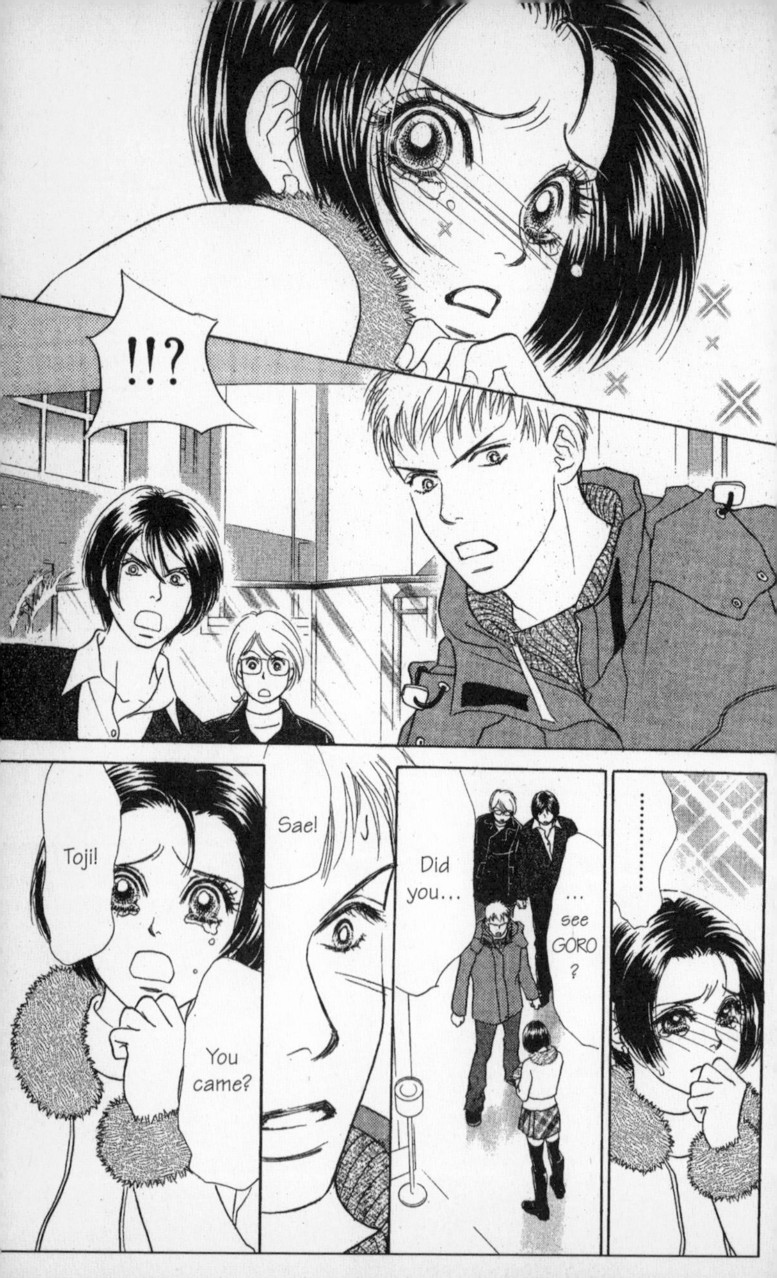

!!?
Toji!
You came?
Sae!
Did you...
... see GORO ?
......

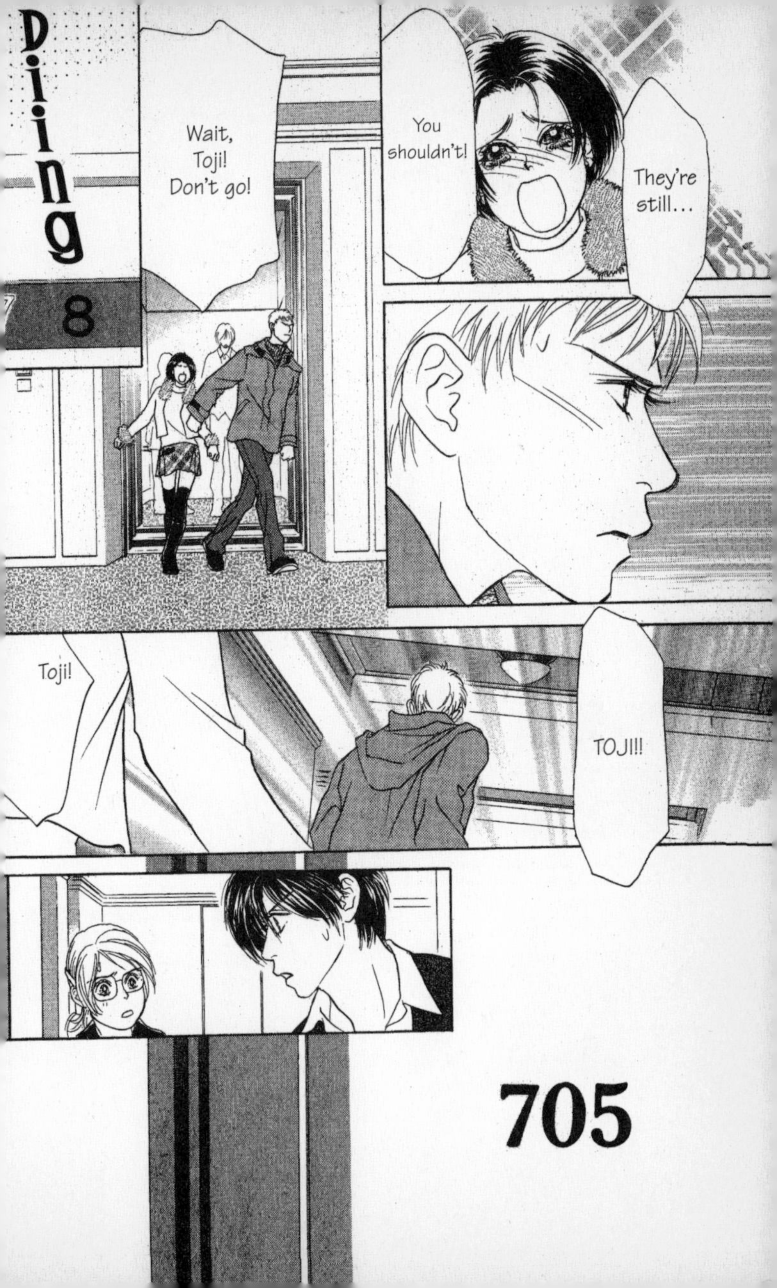
Ding
8
Wait, Toji! Don't go!
You shouldn't!
They're still...
Toji!
TOJI!!
705

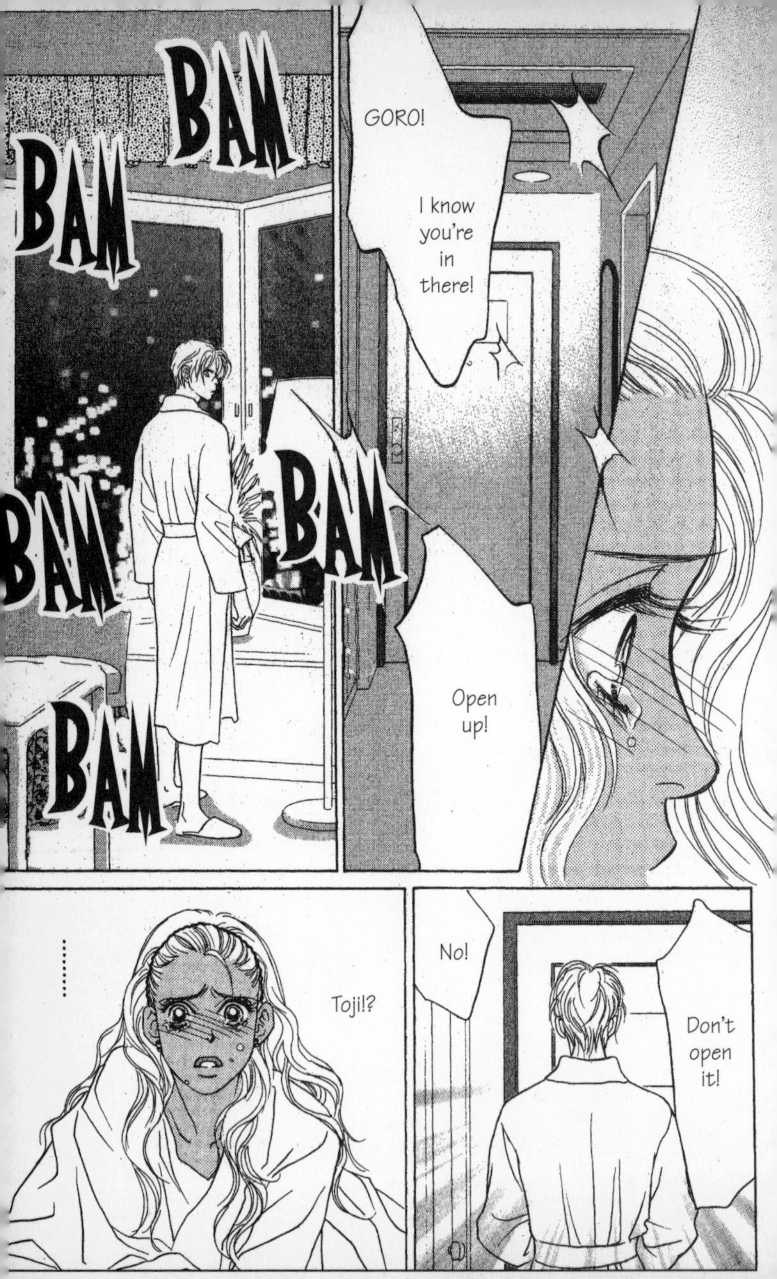
BAM
BAM
BAM
BAM
BAM
GORO!
I know you're in there!
Open up!
....
Toji!?
No!
Don't open it!

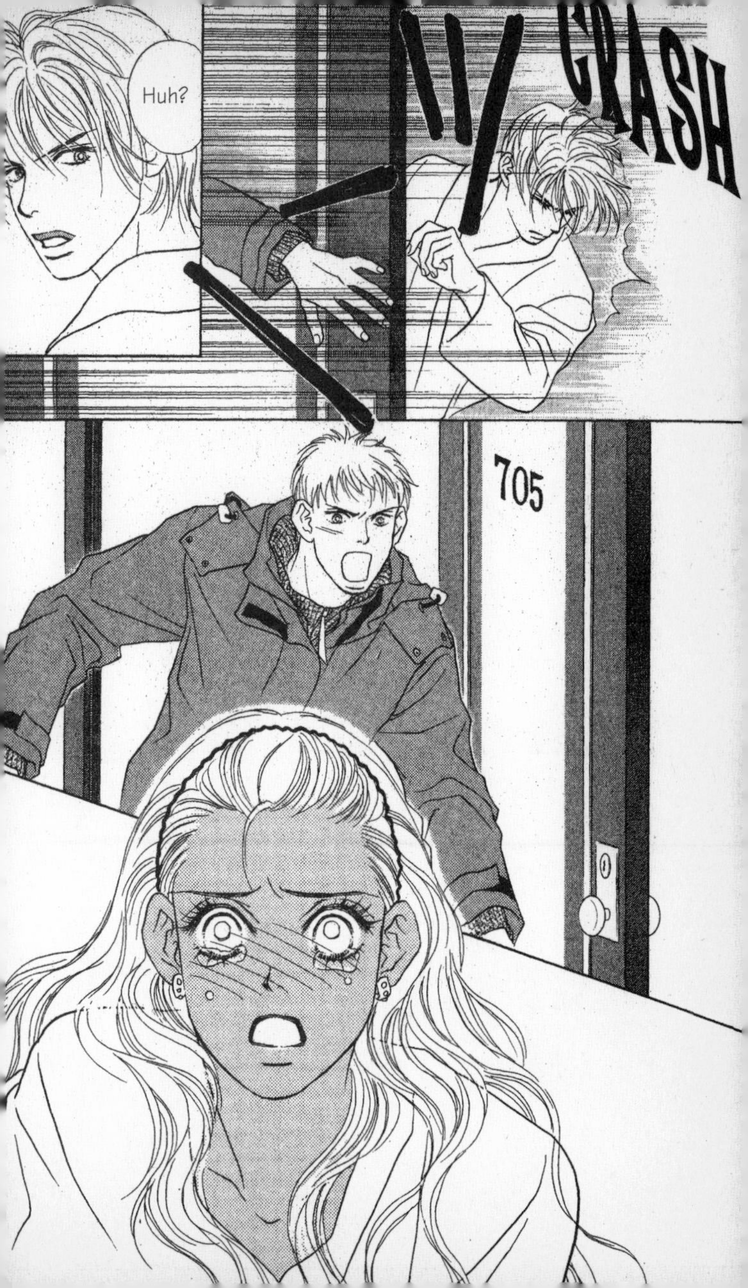
Huh?
CRASH
705

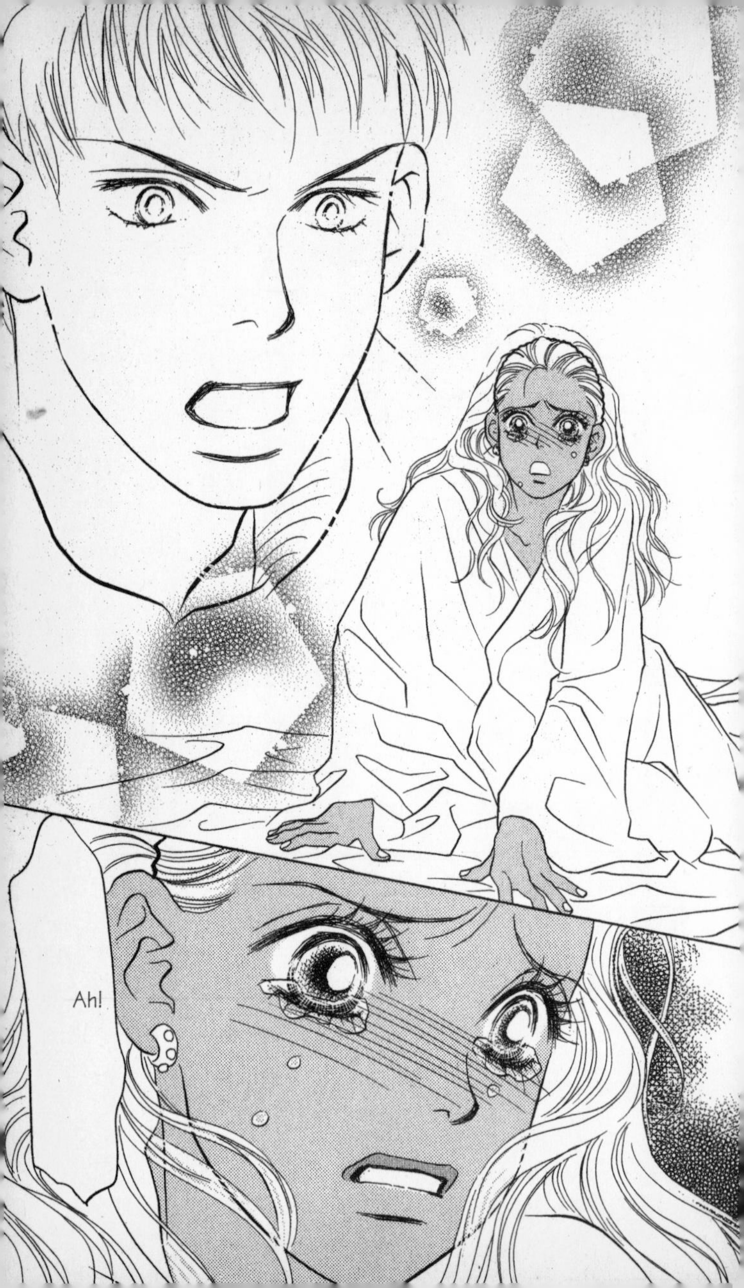
Ah!

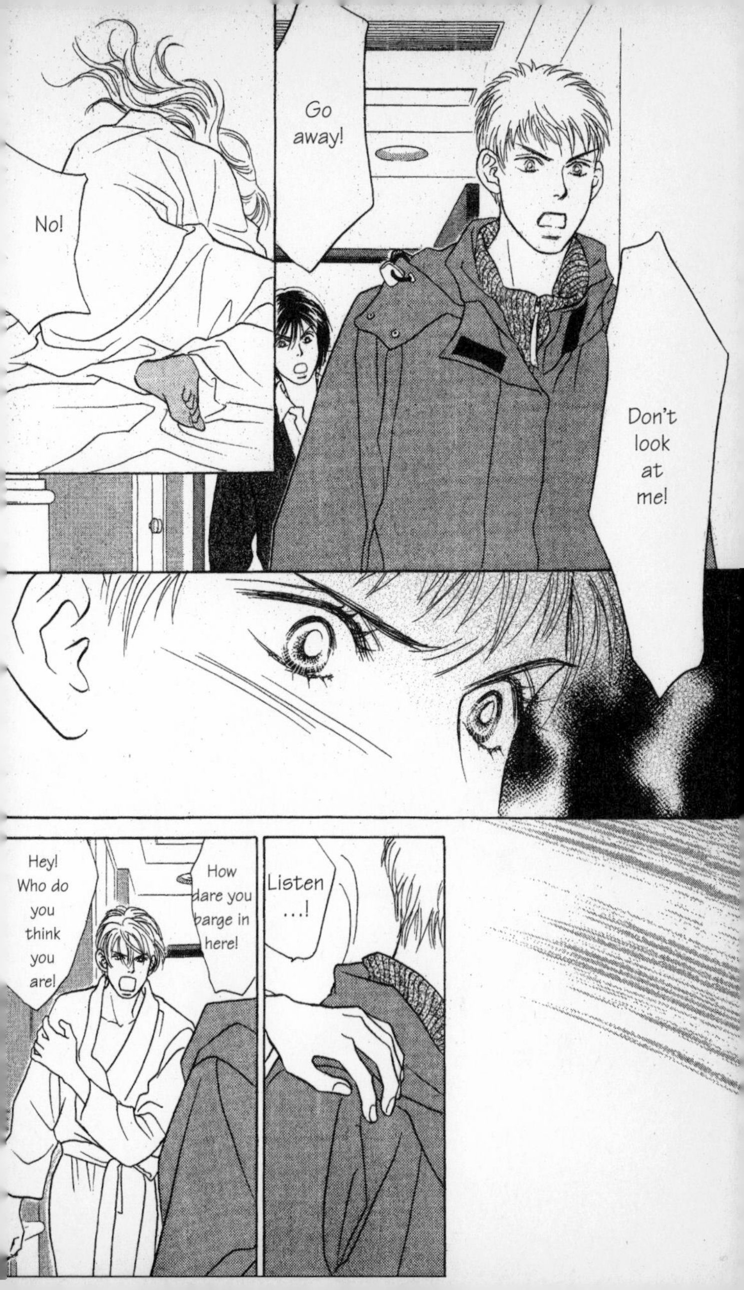
No!
Go away!
Don't look at me!
Hey! Who do you think you are!
How dare you barge in here!
Listen ...!

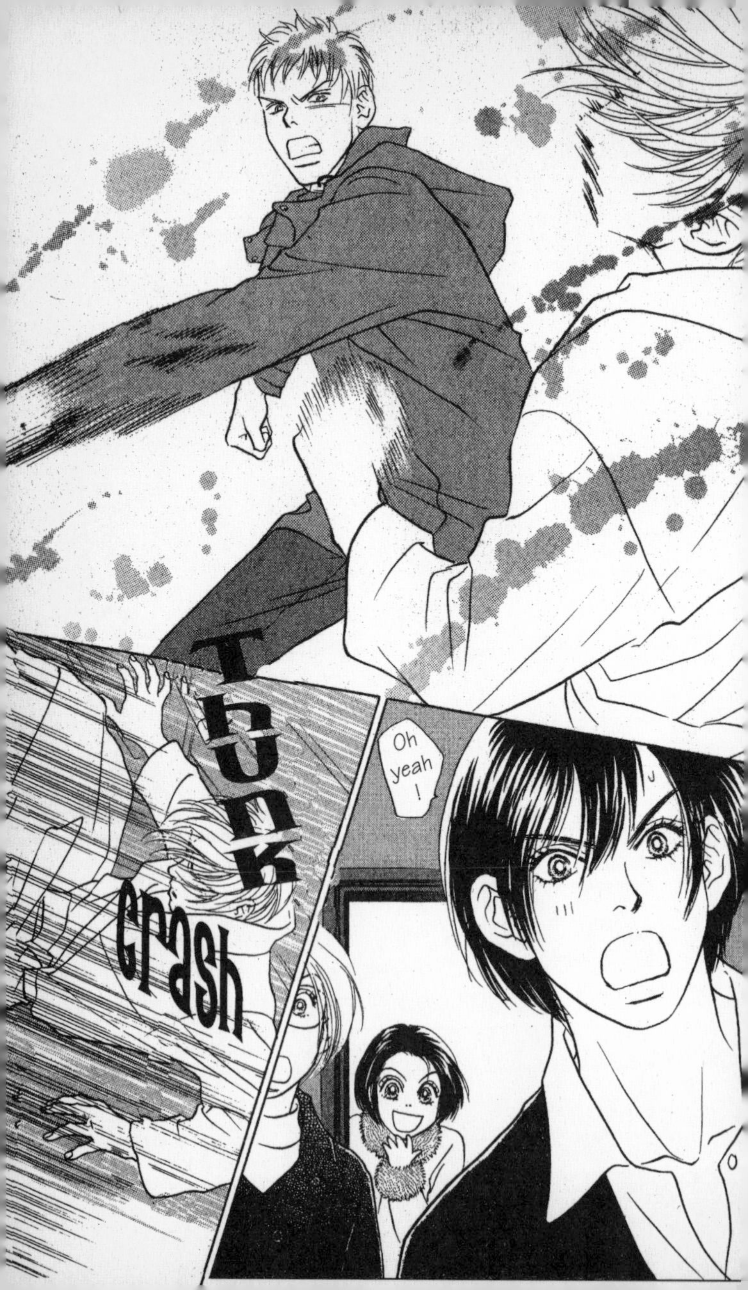
THUNK
crash
Oh yeah!

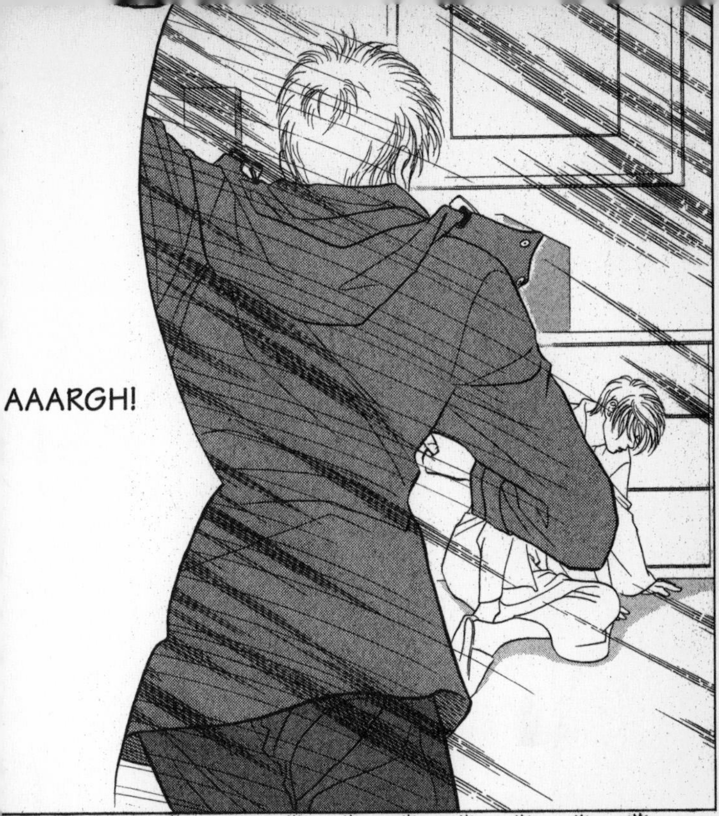
AAARGH!

PEACH CLUB

Hello everybody!
Thanks for reading Book 6!
I know it's old news now, but Peach Girl has won the Kodansha Comic Award for June, 1999. (If you read Book 5, you probably already know this.) I owe it all to my dearest fans. I'll continue to work hard, so thank you for your support! Let's make Peach Girl an even bigger hit!

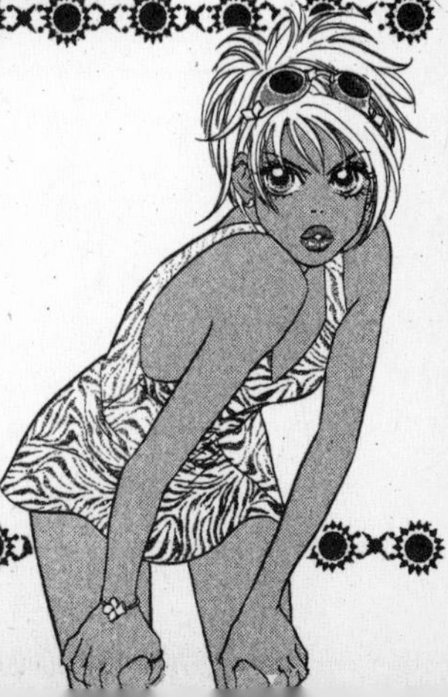

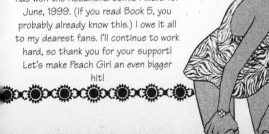

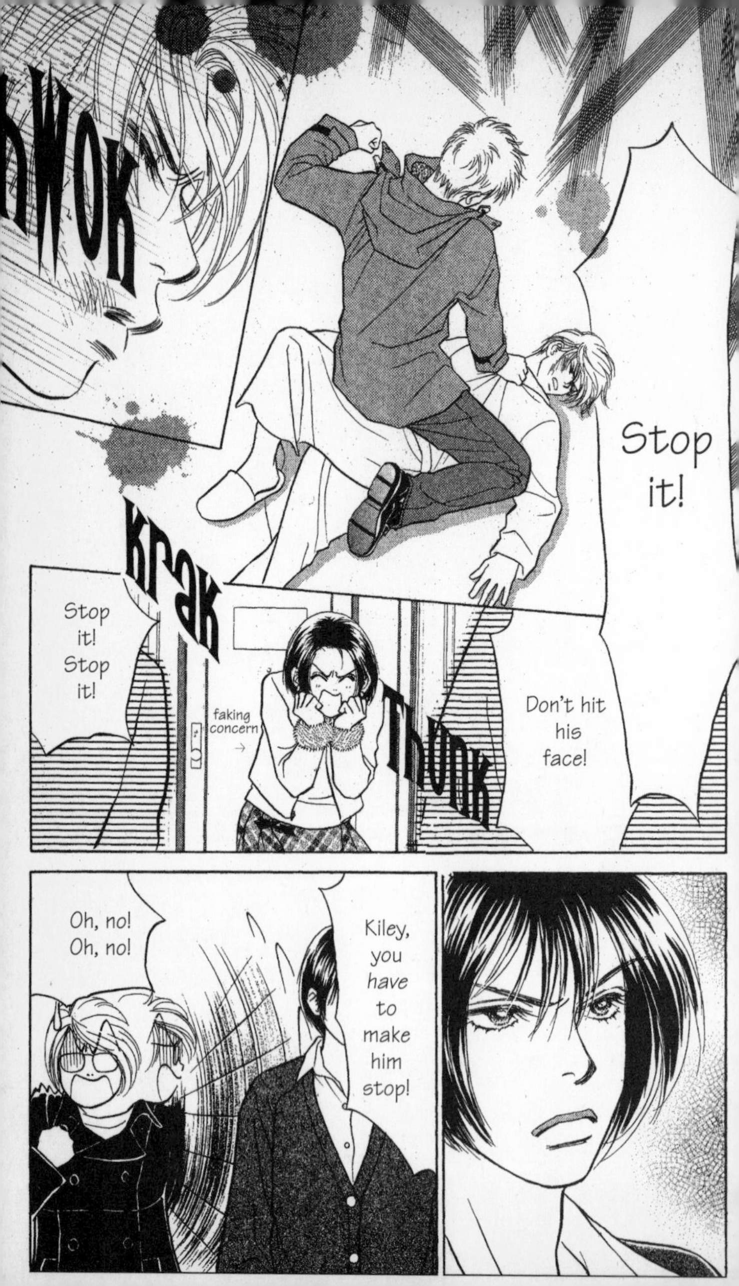

Stop it!
WOK
KRAK
Don't hit his face!
THUNK
faking concern →
Stop it! Stop it!
Kiley, you have to make him stop!
Oh, no! Oh, no!

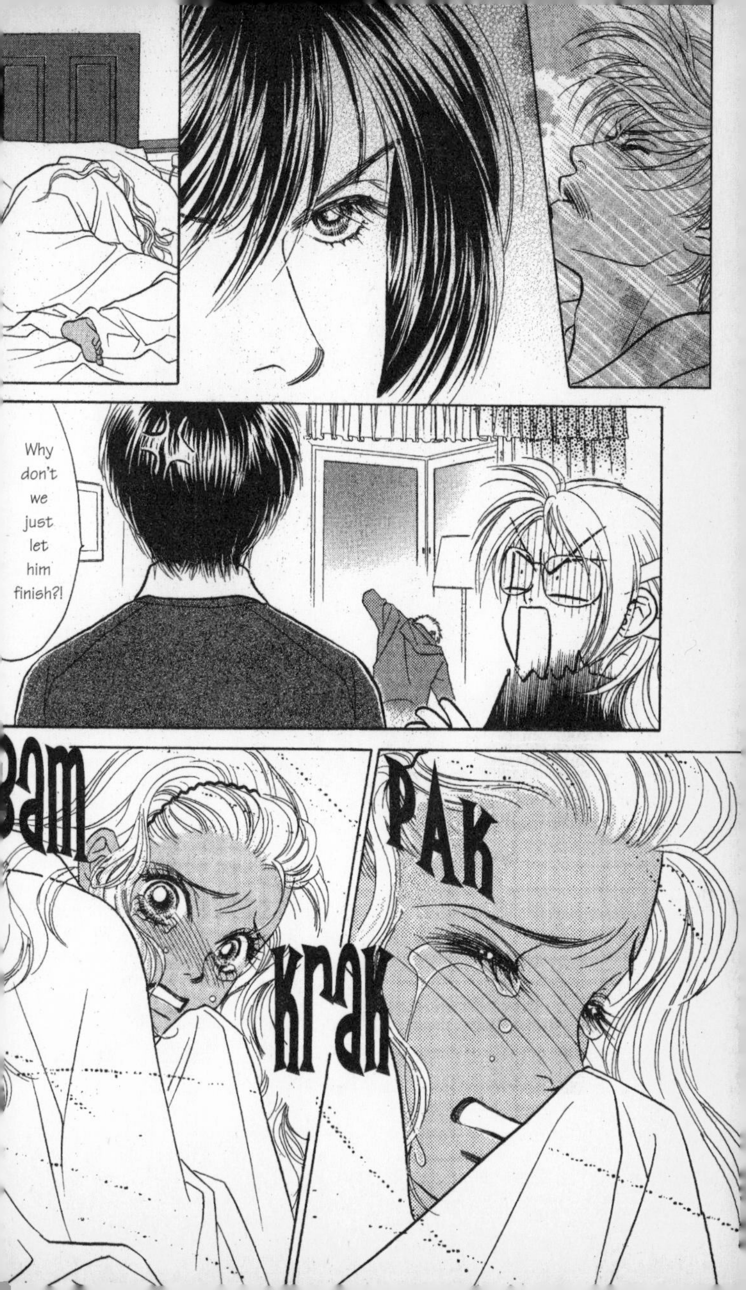
Why don't we just let him finish?!
Bam
PAK
Krak

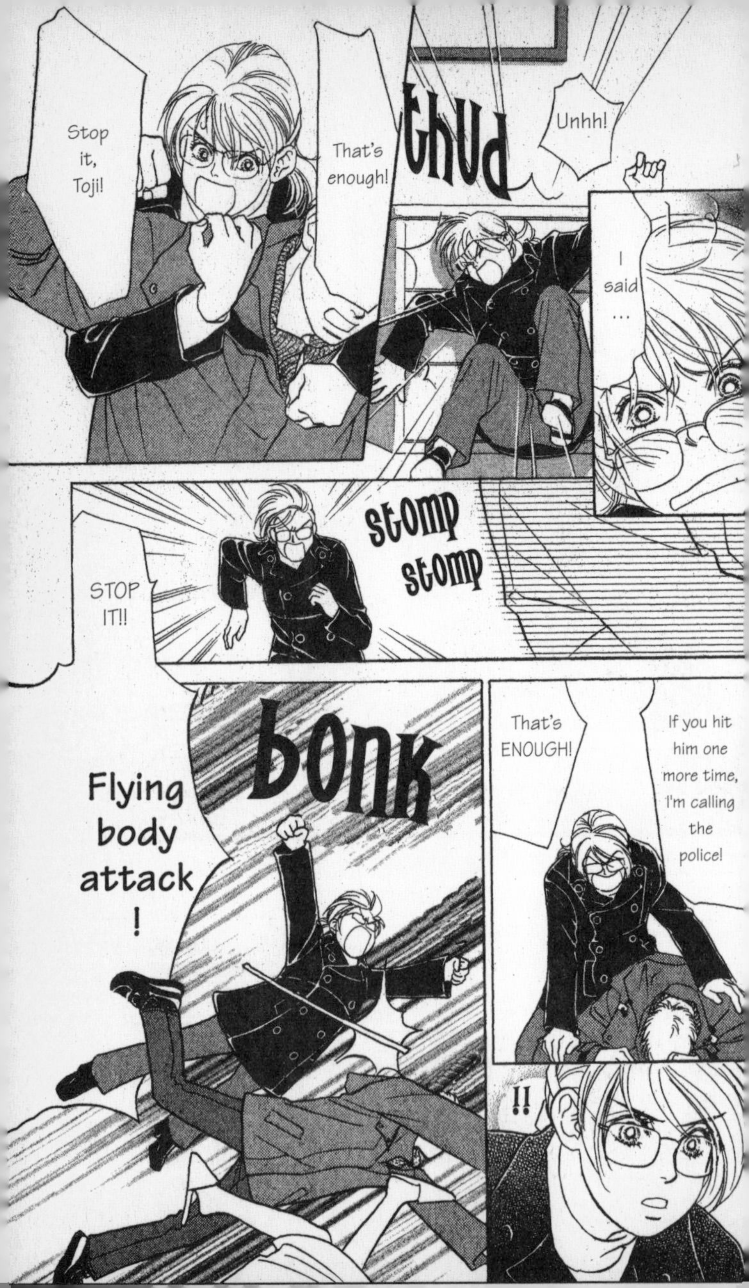
Stop it, Toji!
That's enough!
thud
Unhh!
I said ...
stomp stomp
STOP IT!!
That's ENOUGH!
If you hit him one more time, I'm calling the police!
!!
bonk
Flying body attack!

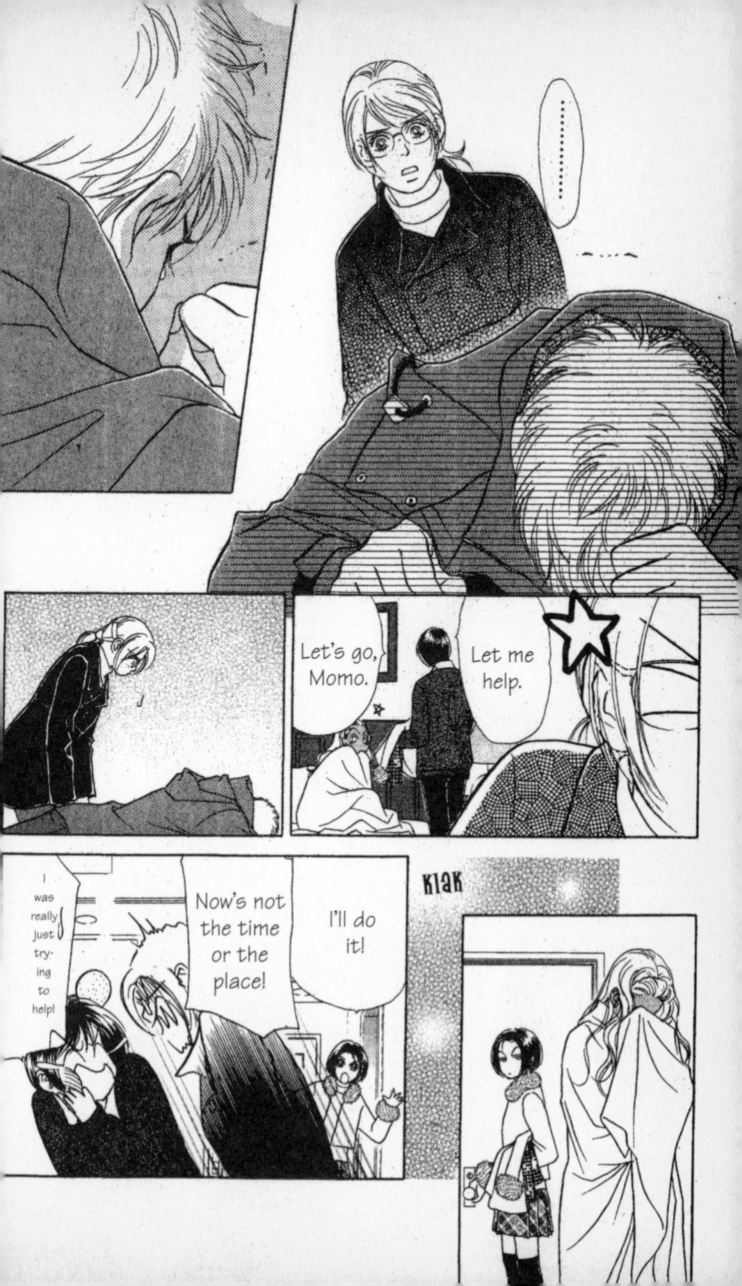
......
Let's go, Momo.
Let me help.
I was really just try-ing to help!
Now's not the time or the place!
I'll do it!
KlAK

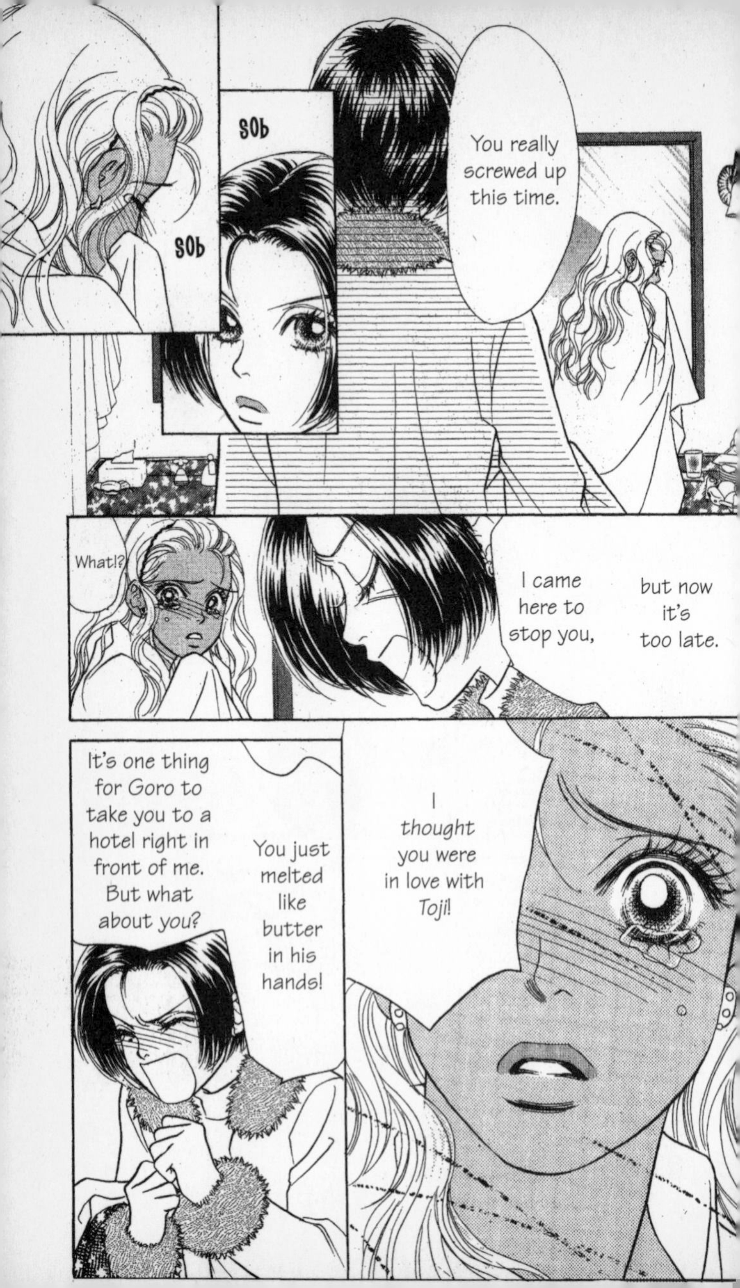
SOB
SOB
You really screwed up this time.
What!?
I came here to stop you,
but now it's too late.
It's one thing for Goro to take you to a hotel right in front of me. But what about you?
You just melted like butter in his hands!
I thought you were in love with Toji!

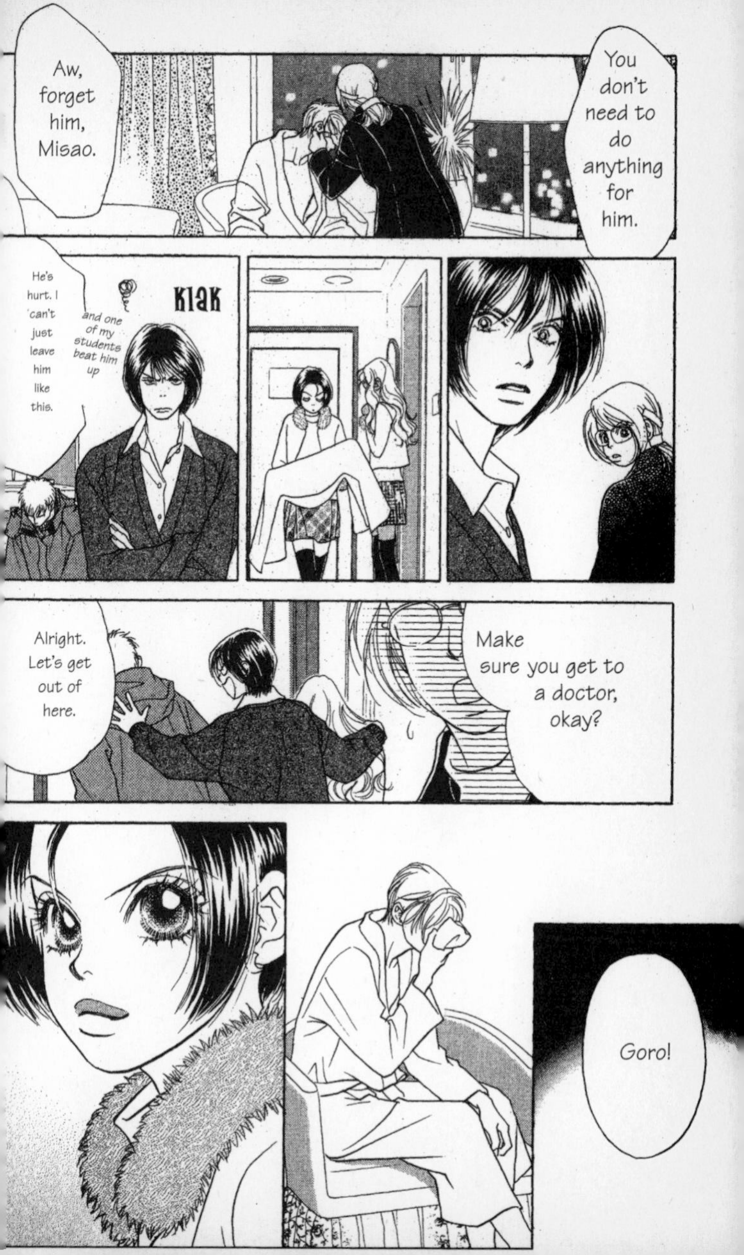
Aw, forget him, Misao.
You don't need to do anything for him.
He's hurt. I can't just leave him like this.
and one of my students beat him up
KLAK
Alright. Let's get out of here.
Make sure you get to a doctor, okay?
Goro!

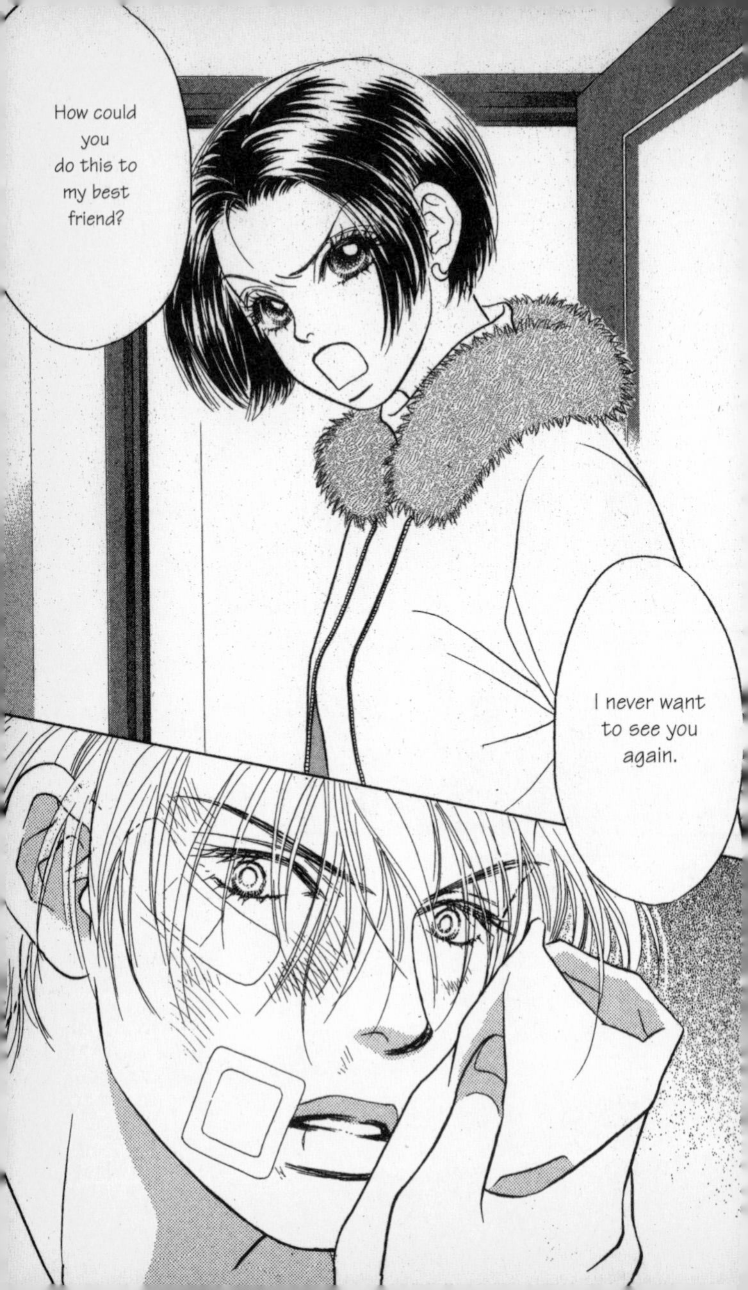
How could you do this to my best friend?
I never want to see you again.

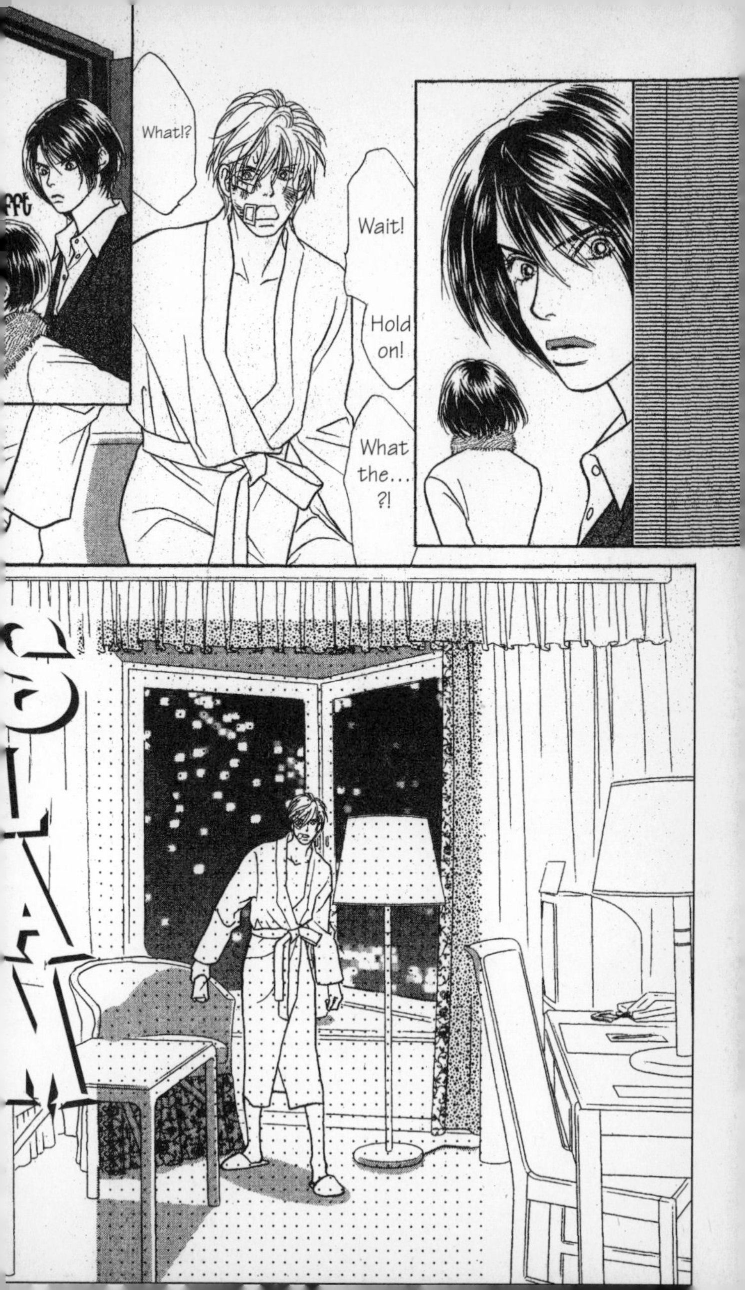
What!?
Wait!
Hold on!
What the... ?!
SLAM

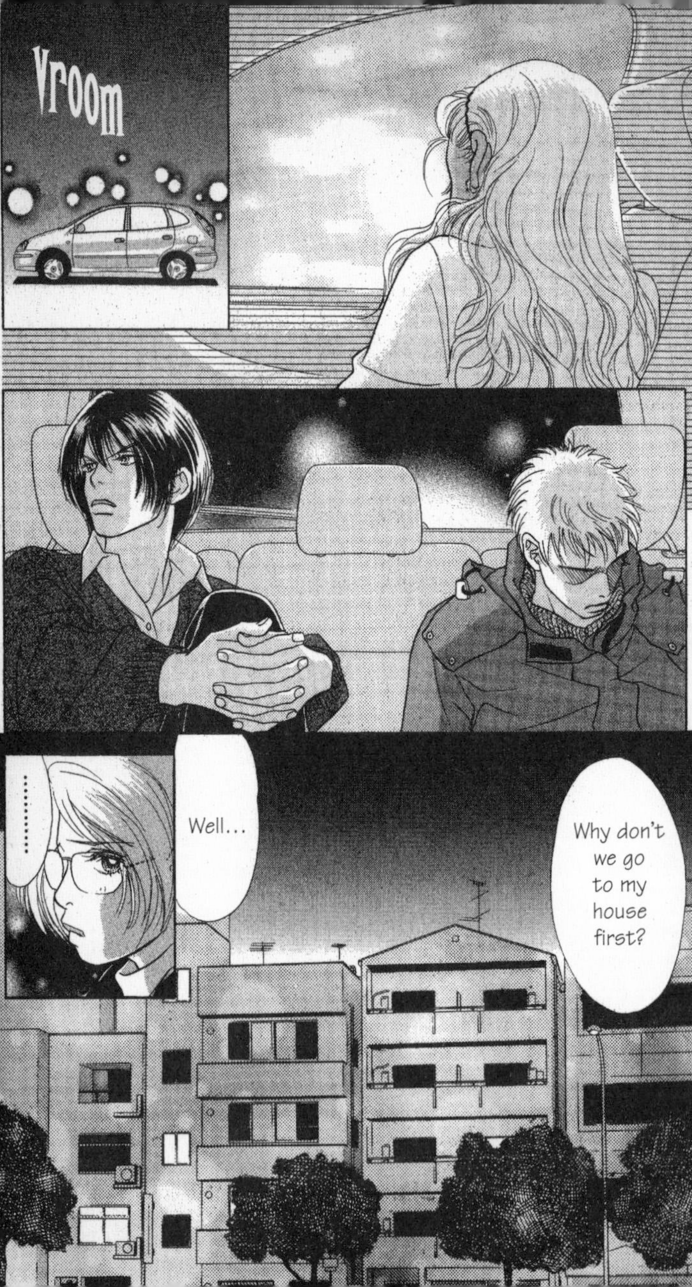
Vroom
....
Well...
Why don't we go to my house first?

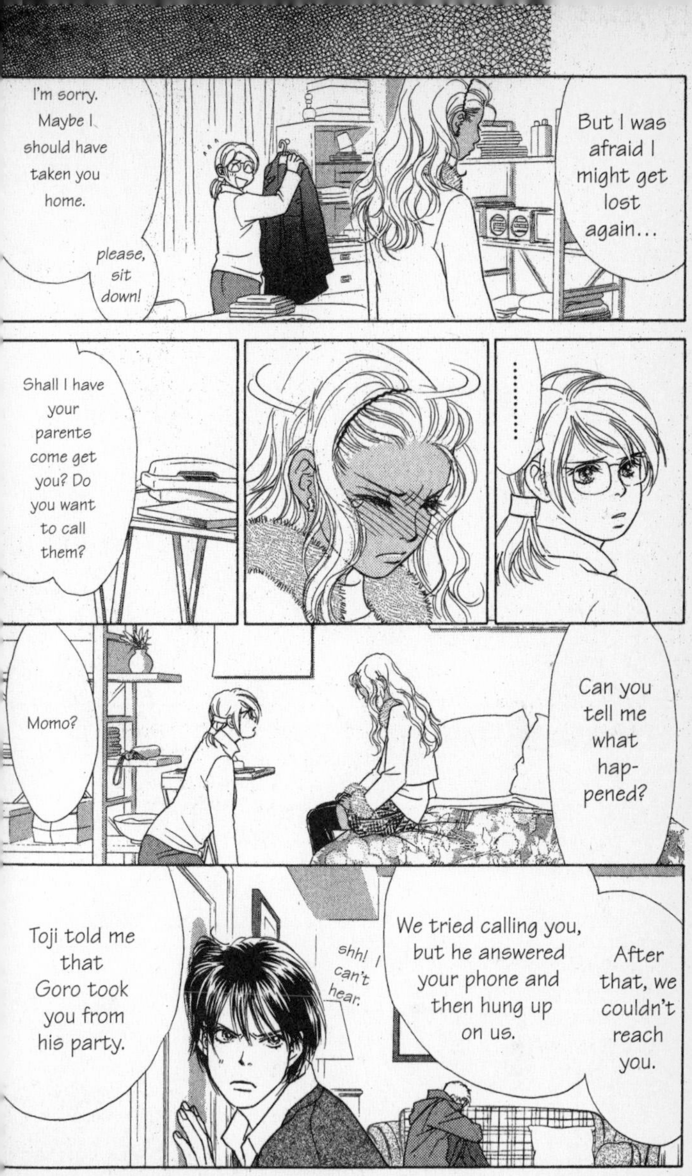
I'm sorry. Maybe I should have taken you home.
please, sit down!
But I was afraid I might get lost again...
Shall I have your parents come get you? Do you want to call them?
....
Momo?
Can you tell me what hap-pened?
Toji told me that Goro took you from his party.
shh! I can't hear.
We tried calling you, but he answered your phone and then hung up on us.
After that, we couldn't reach you.

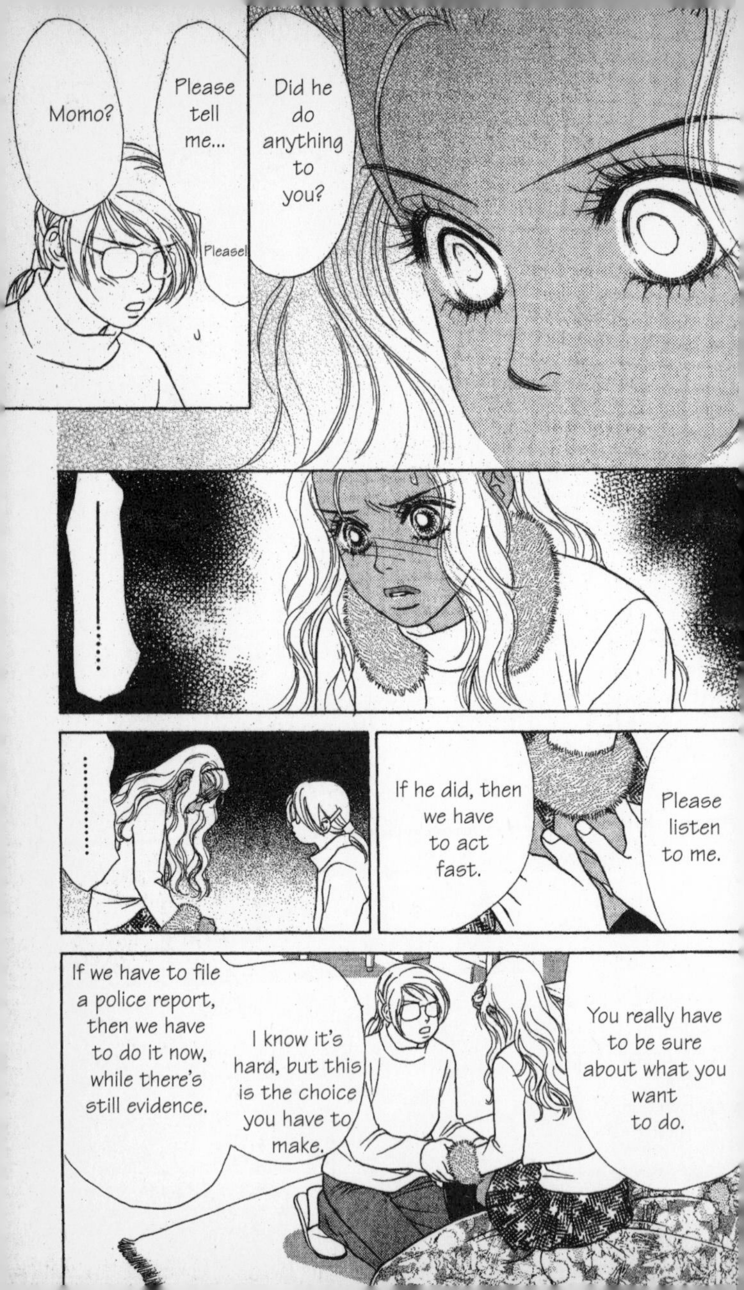
Momo?
Please tell me...
Please!
Did he do anything to you?
......
......
If he did, then we have to act fast.
Please listen to me.
If we have to file a police report, then we have to do it now, while there's still evidence.
I know it's hard, but this is the choice you have to make.
You really have to be sure about what you want to do.

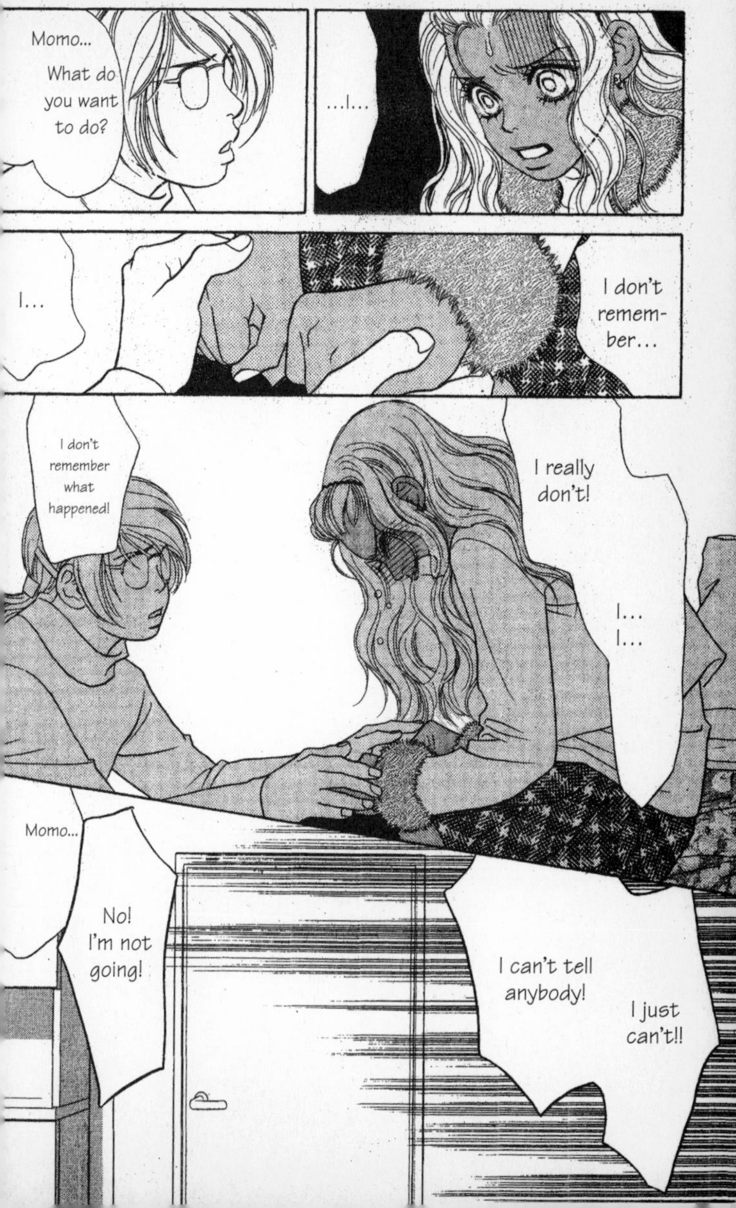
Momo... What do you want to do?
...I...
I...
I don't remember...
I don't remember what happened!
I really don't!
I... I...
Momo...
No! I'm not going!
I can't tell anybody!
I just can't!!

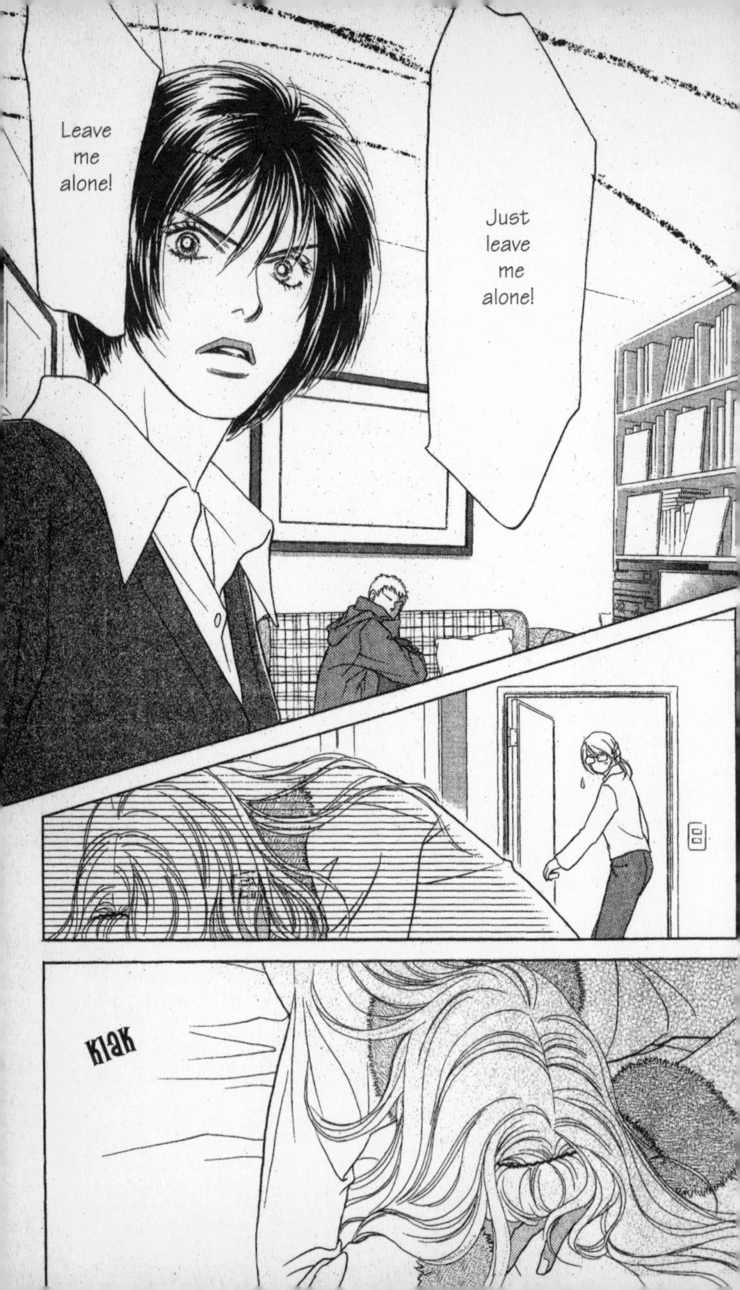

Leave me alone!
Just leave me alone!
KLAK

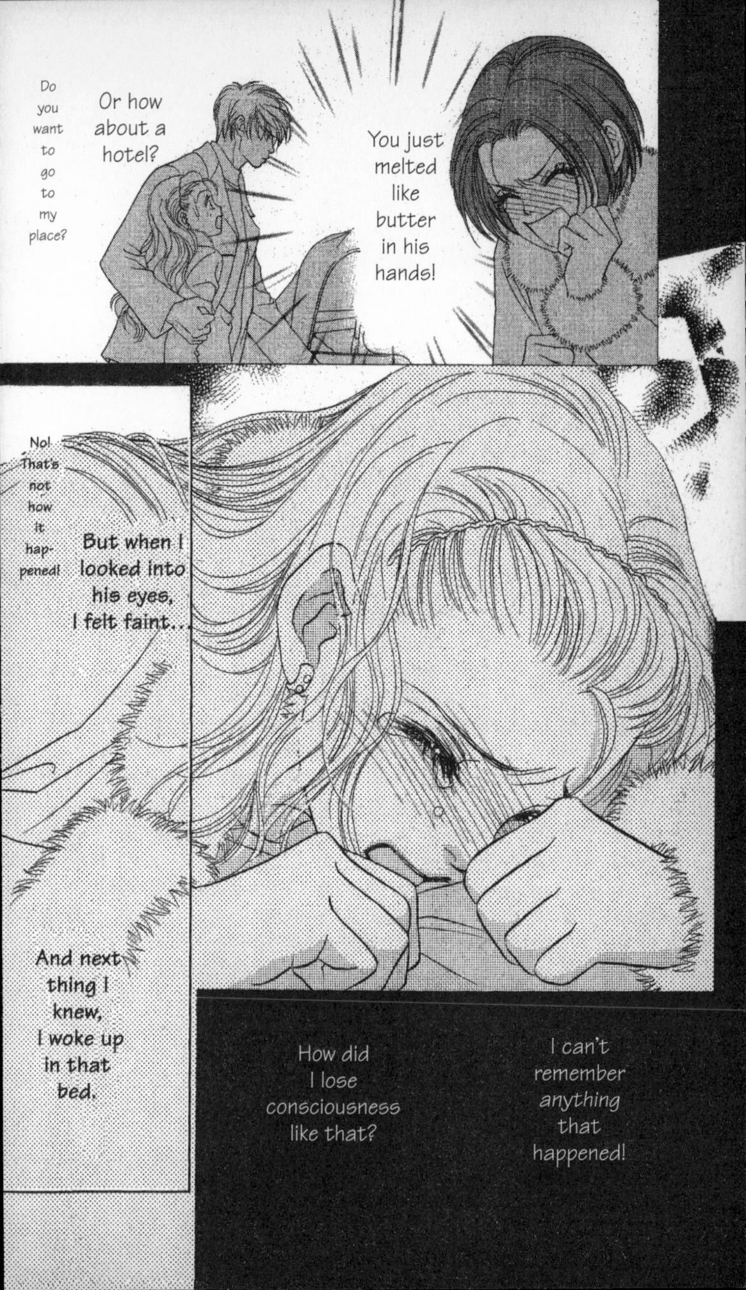
Do you want to go to my place?
Or how about a hotel?
You just melted like butter in his hands!
No! That's not how it hap-pened!
But when I looked into his eyes, I felt faint...
And next thing I knew, I woke up in that bed.
How did I lose consciousness like that?
I can't remember anything that happened!

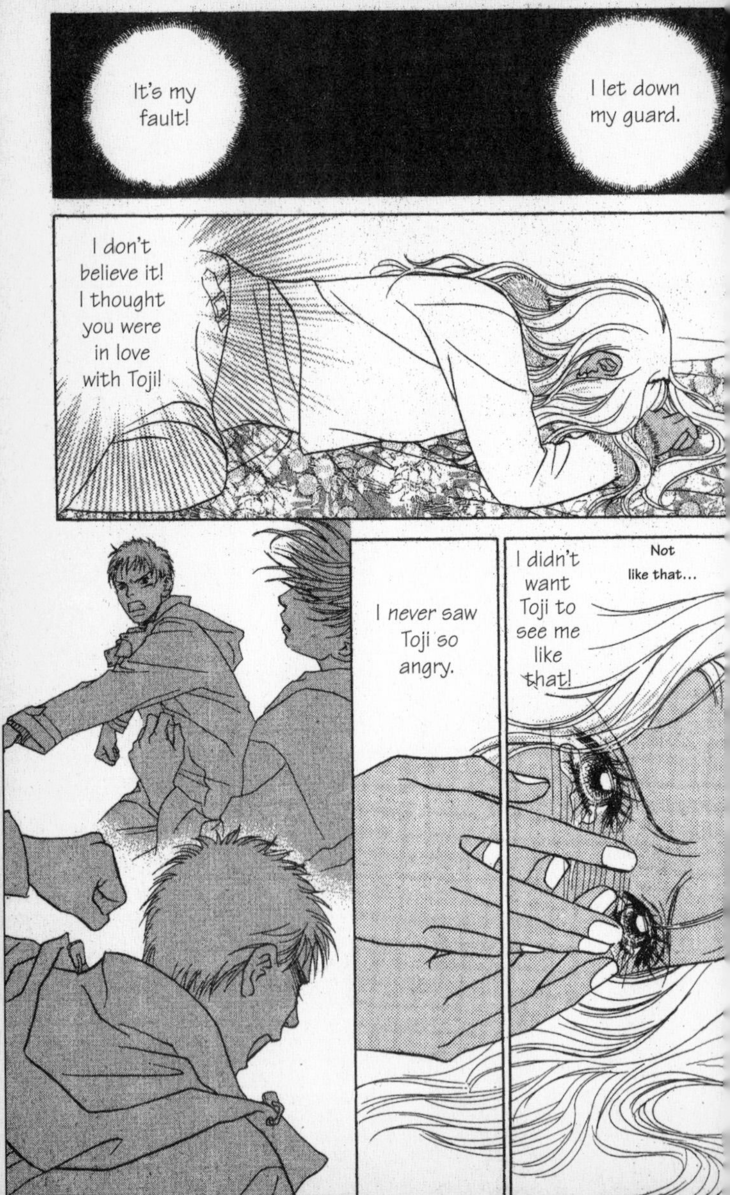
It's my fault!
I let down my guard.
I don't believe it! I thought you were in love with Toji!
I never saw Toji so angry.
I didn't want Toji to see me like that!
Not like that...

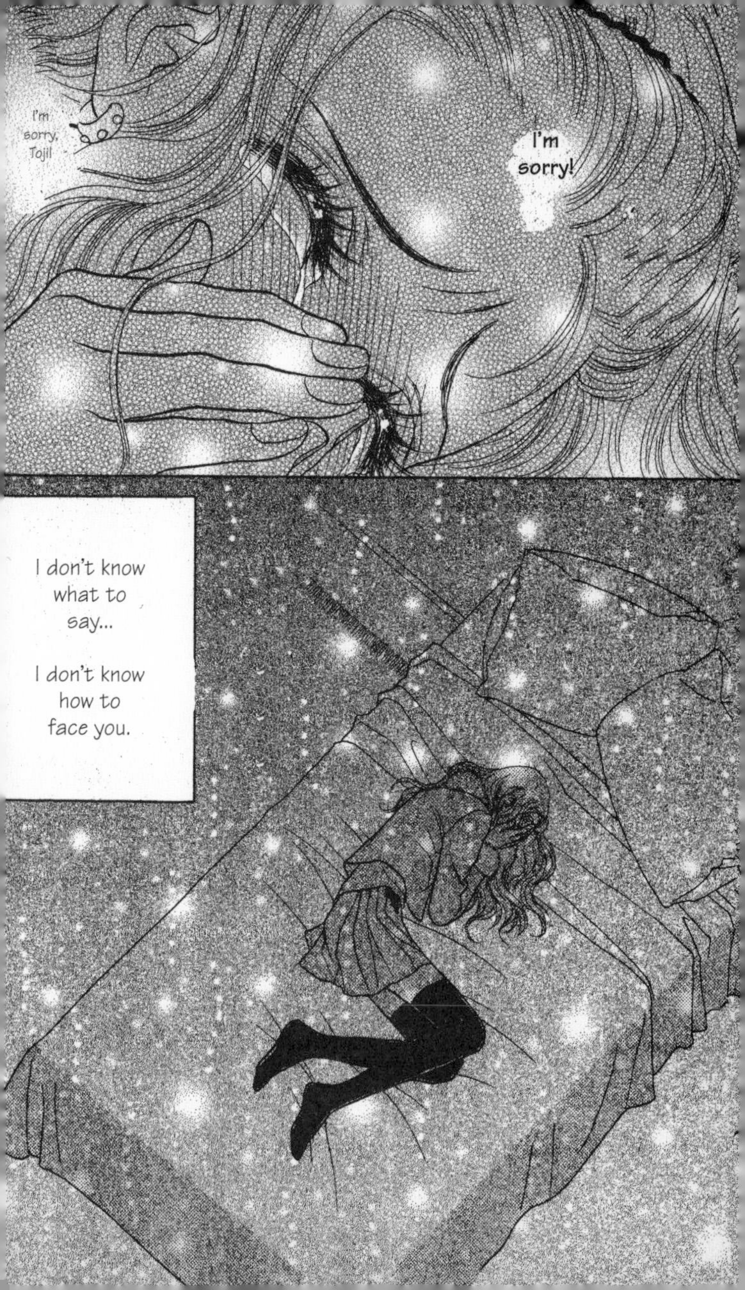

I'm sorry, Toji!
I'm sorry!
I don't know what to say...
I don't know how to face you.

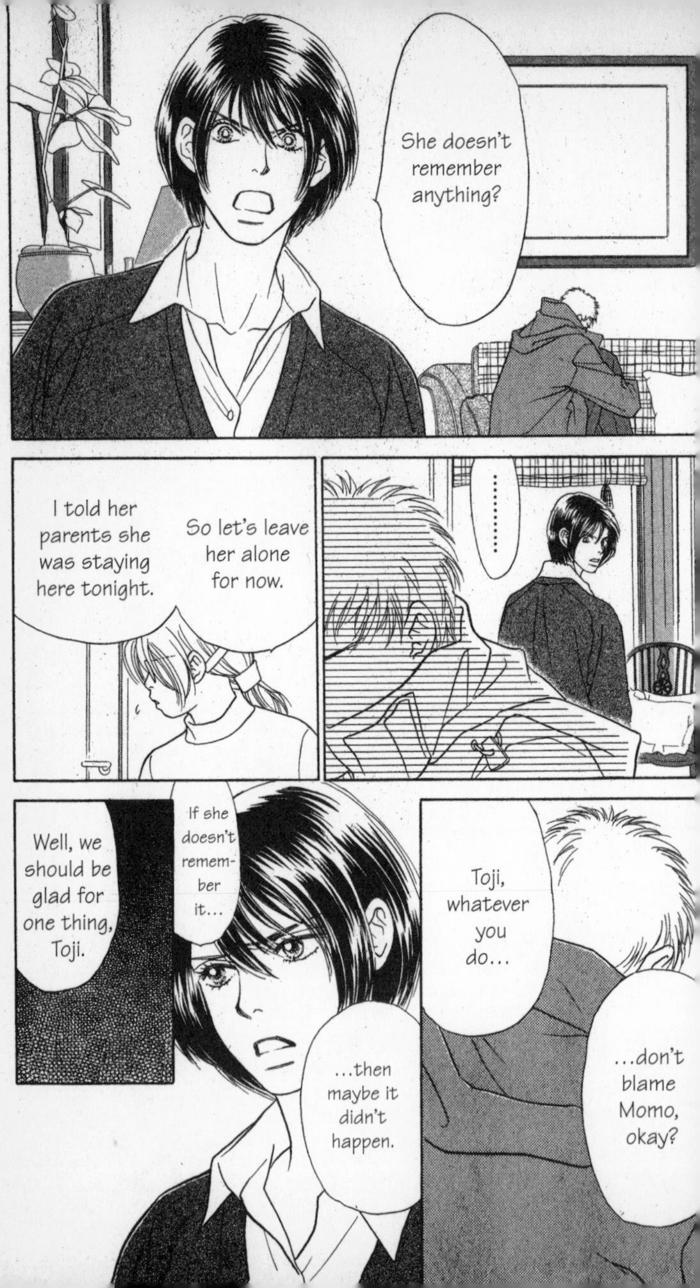
She doesn't remember anything?
I told her parents she was staying here tonight.
So let's leave her alone for now.
......
Well, we should be glad for one thing, Toji.
If she doesn't remember it...
...then maybe it didn't happen.
Toji, whatever you do...
...don't blame Momo, okay?

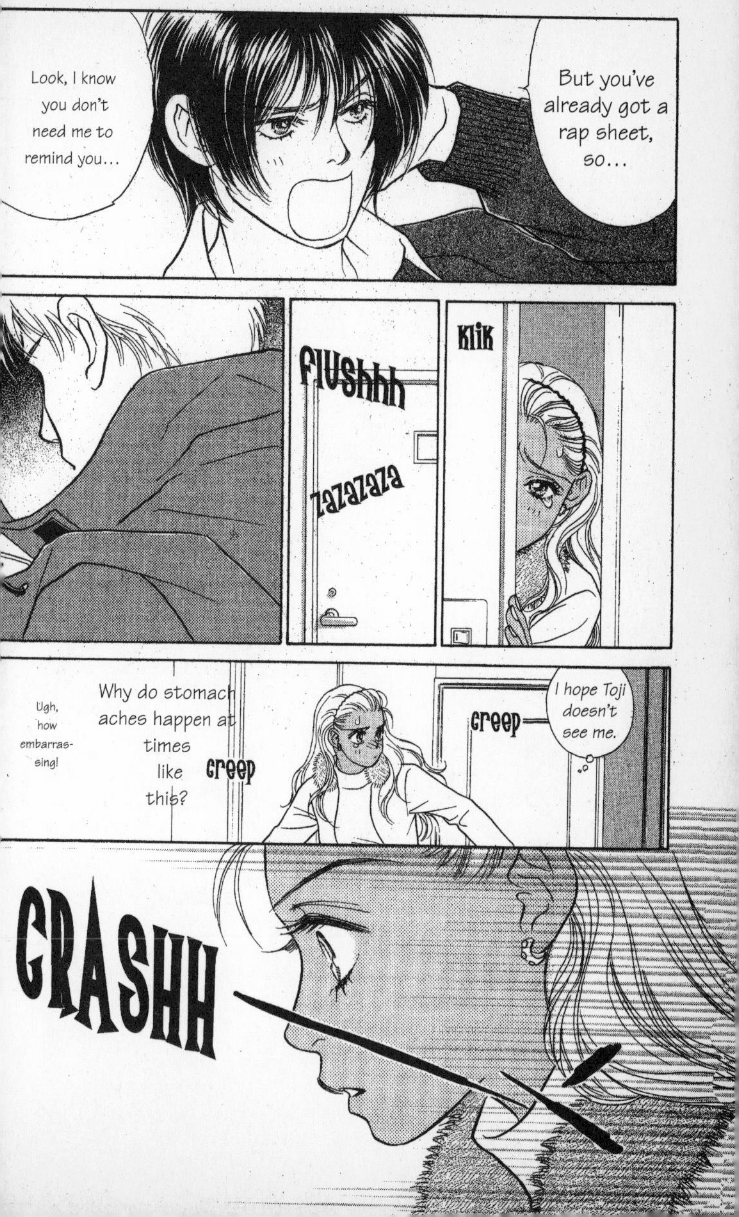
Look, I know you don't need me to remind you...
But you've already got a rap sheet, so...
FLUSHHH
ZAZAZAZA
KLIK
Ugh, how embarras-sing!
Why do stomach aches happen at times like this?
CREEP
CREEP
I hope Toji doesn't see me.
CRASHH

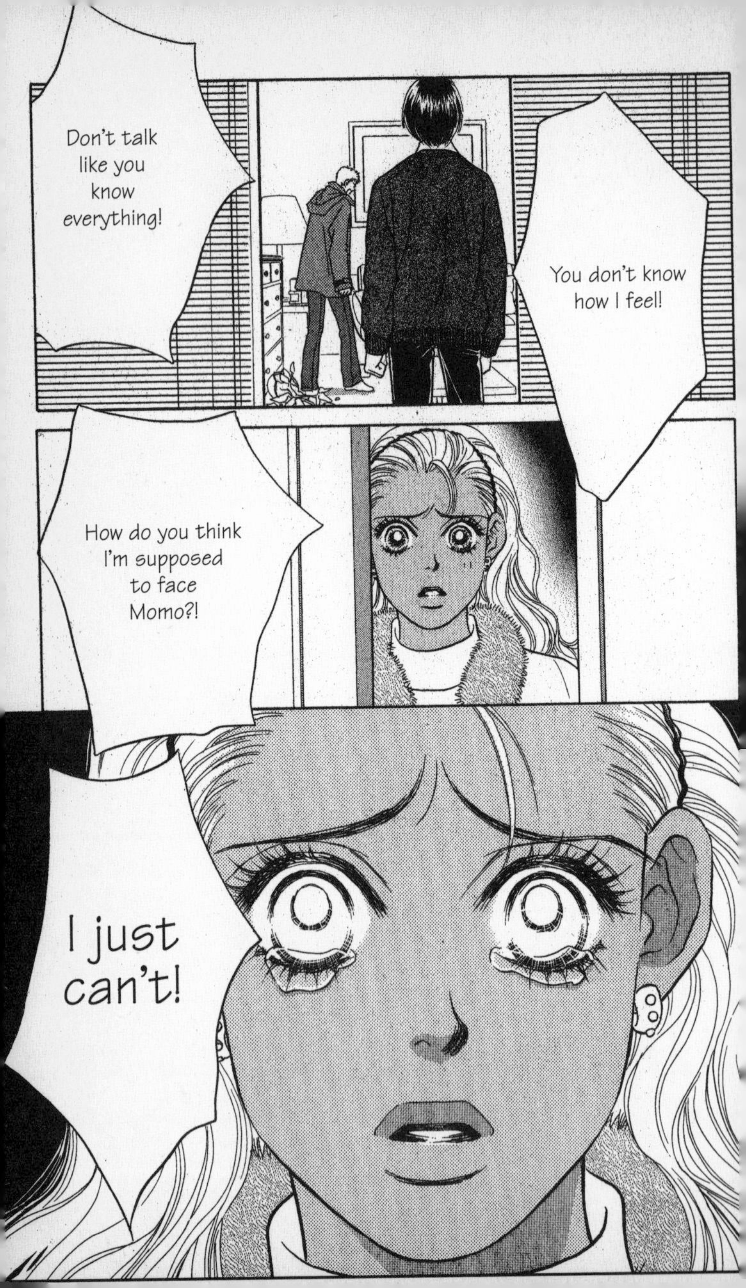
Don't talk like you know everything!
You don't know how I feel!
How do you think I'm supposed to face Momo?!
I just can't!

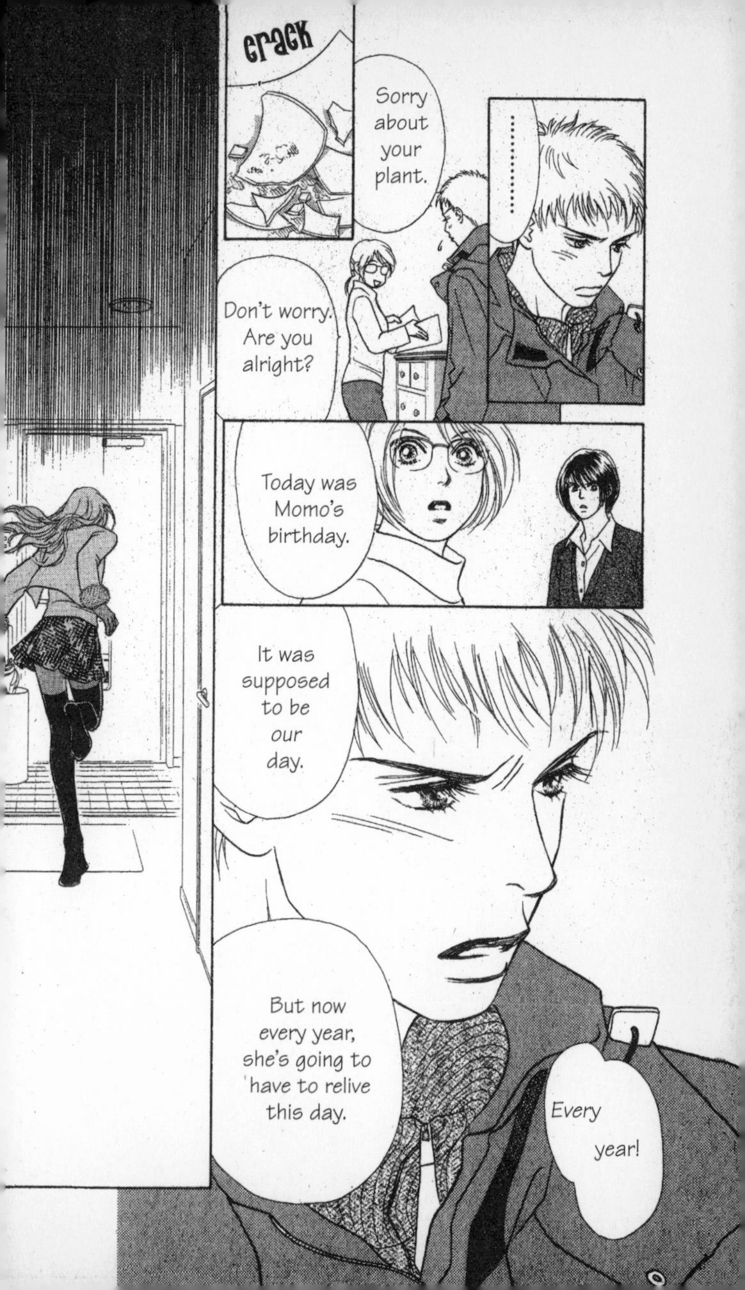
crack
Sorry about your plant.
Don't worry. Are you alright?
......
Today was Momo's birthday.
It was supposed to be our day.
But now every year, she's going to have to relive this day.
Every year!

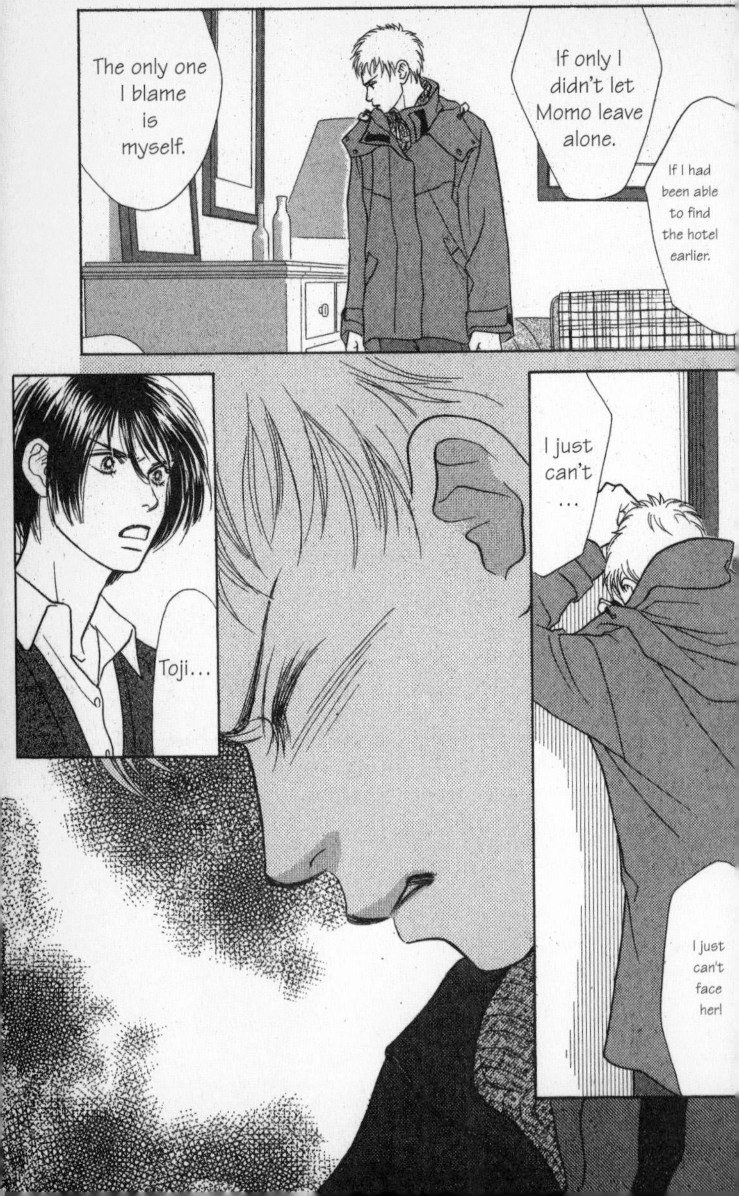
The only one I blame is myself.
If only I didn't let Momo leave alone.
If I had been able to find the hotel earlier.
Toji...
I just can't ...
I just can't face her!

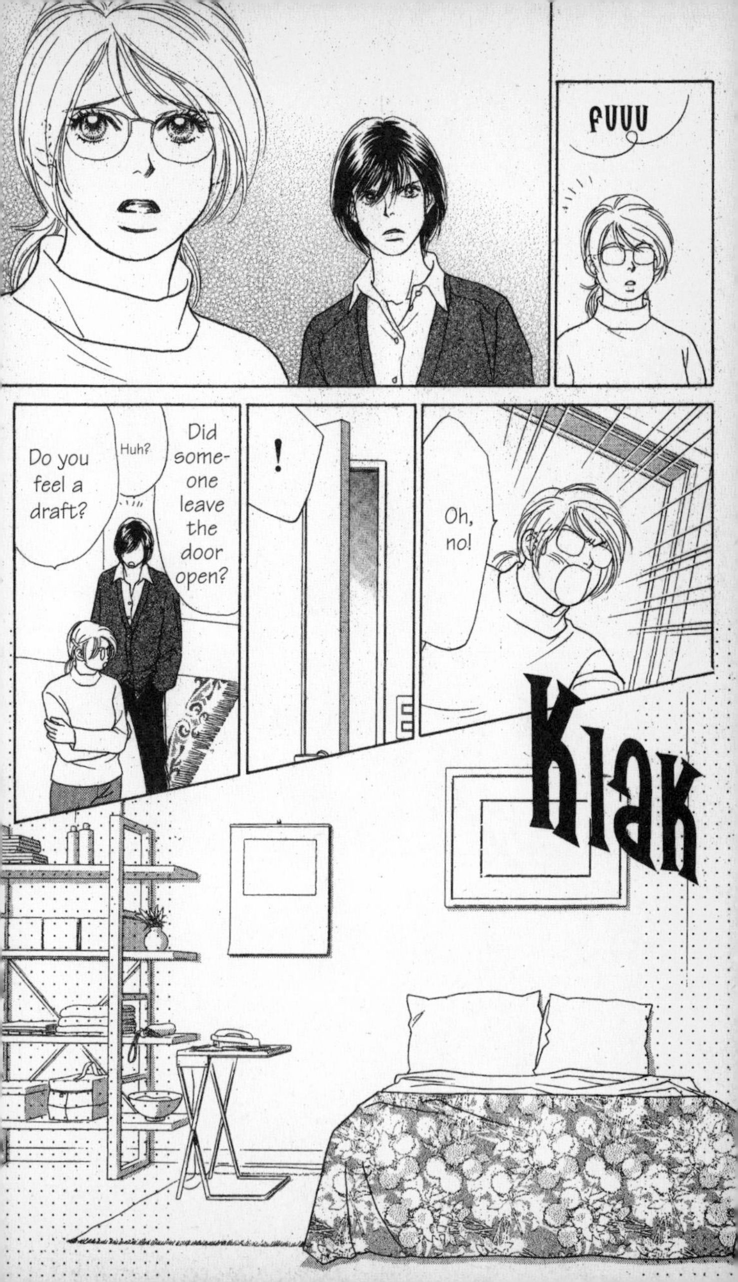
FUUU
Do you feel a draft?
Huh?
Did someone leave the door open?
!
Oh, no!
KLAK

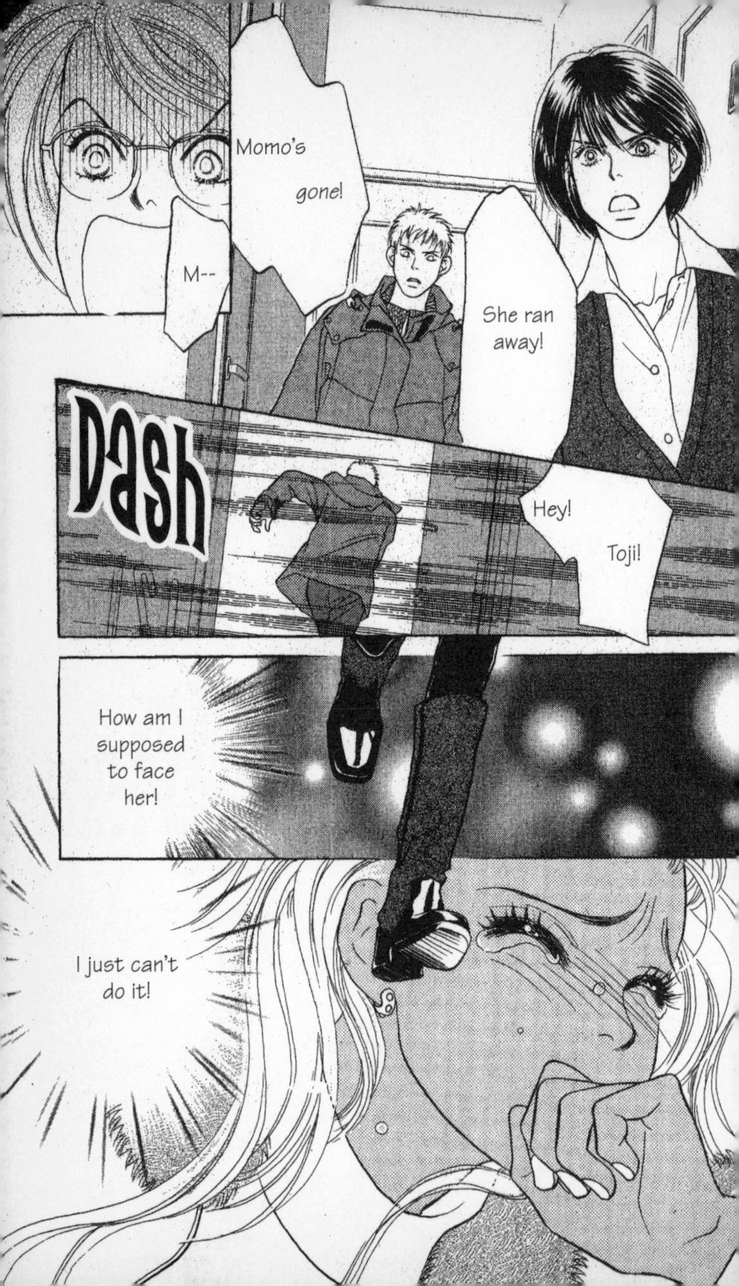
M--
Momo's gone!
She ran away!
Dash
Hey! Toji!
How am I supposed to face her!
I just can't do it!

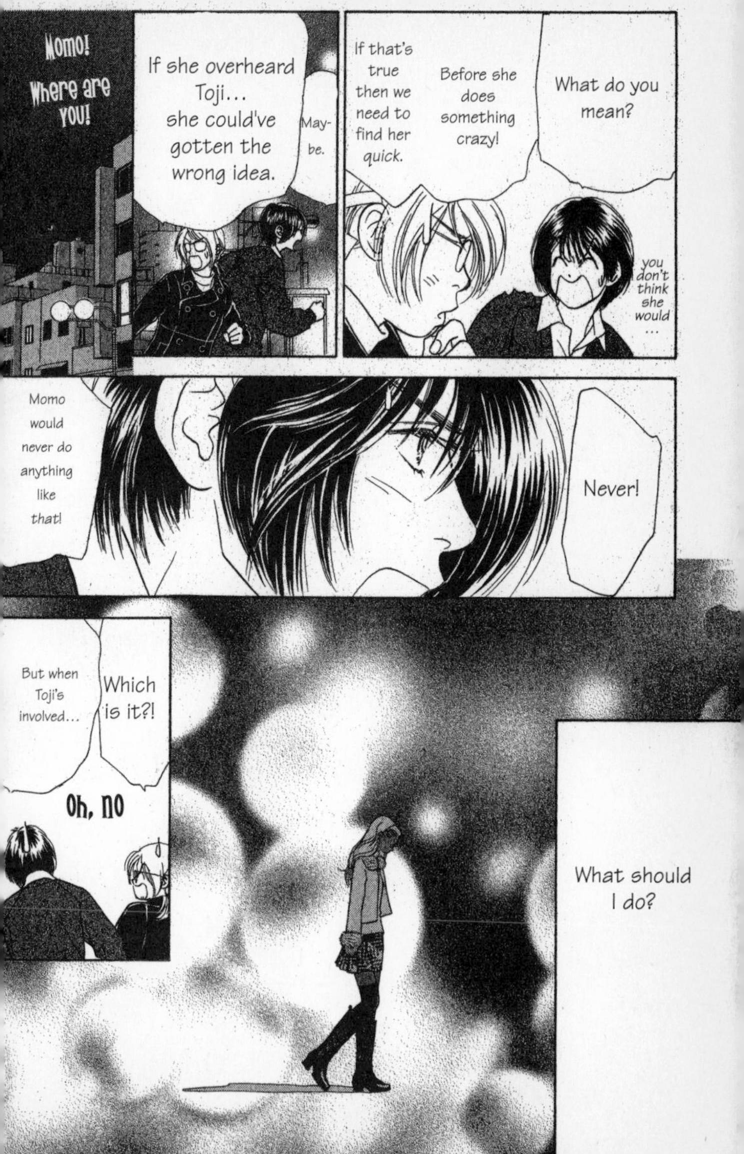
Momo! Where are you!
If she overheard Toji… she could've gotten the wrong idea.
Maybe.
If that's true then we need to find her quick.
Before she does something crazy!
What do you mean?
you don't think she would…
Momo would never do anything like that!
Never!
But when Toji's involved…
Which is it?!
Oh, no
What should I do?

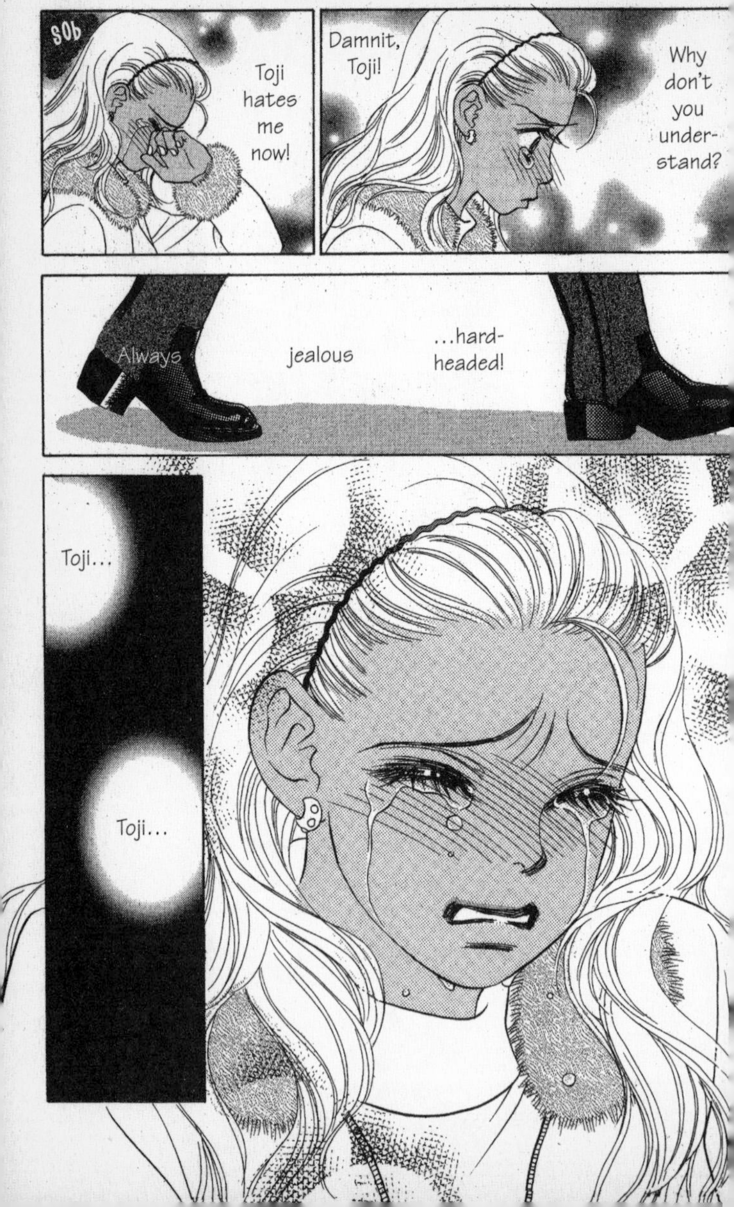
SOb
Toji hates me now!
Damnit, Toji!
Why don't you under-stand?
Always
jealous
...hard-headed!
Toji...
Toji...

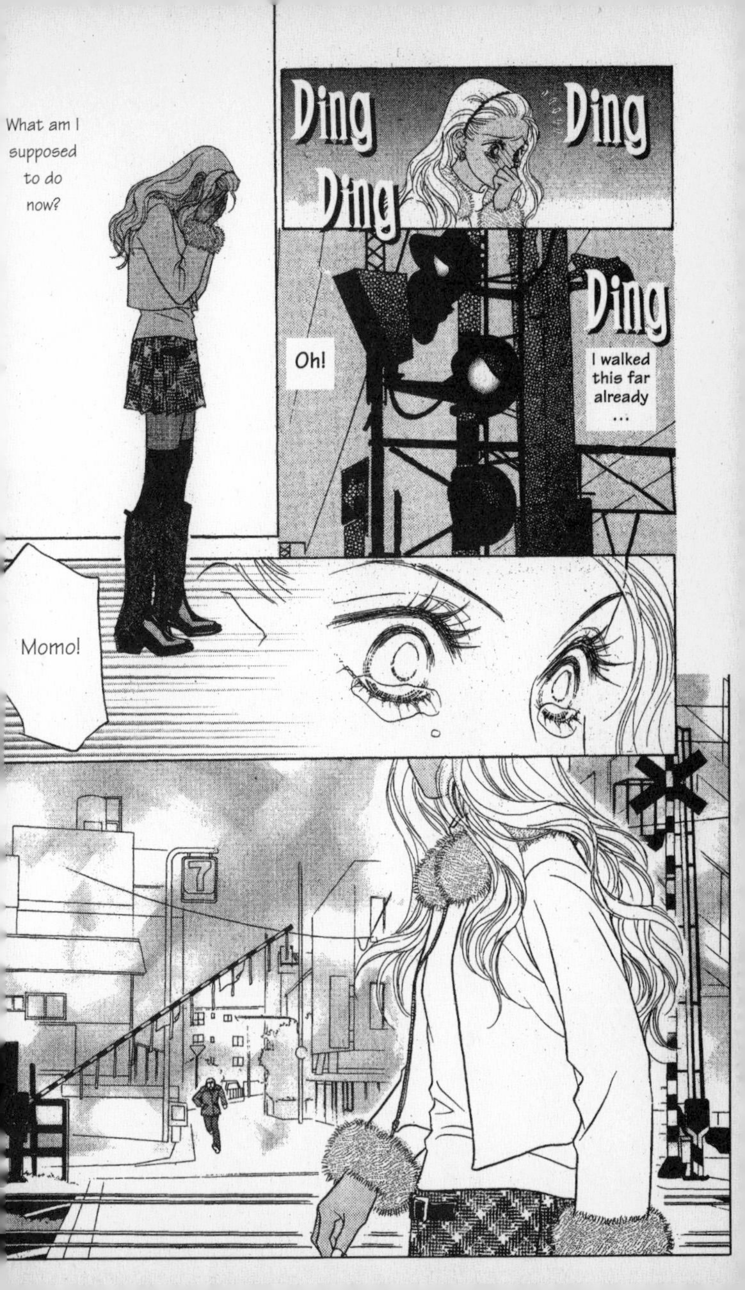
What am I supposed to do now?
Ding
Ding
Ding
Oh!
Ding
I walked this far already ...
Momo!

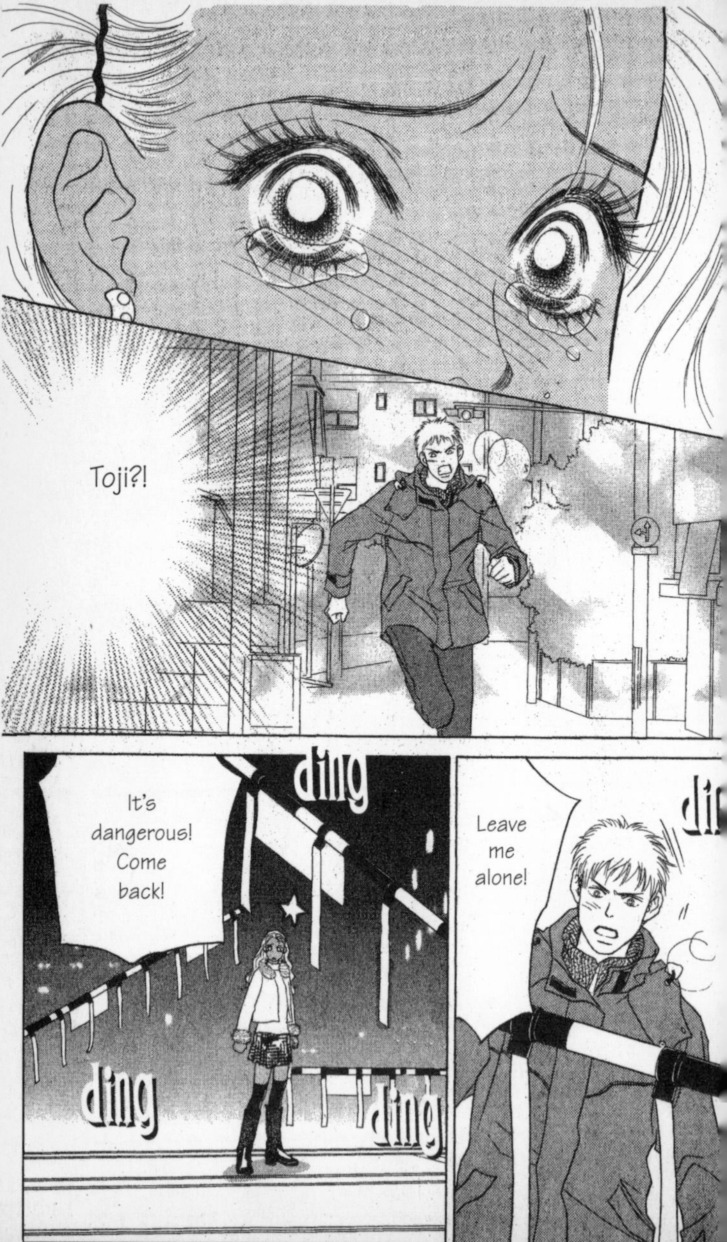
Toji?!
It's dangerous! Come back!
ding
ding
ding
Leave me alone!

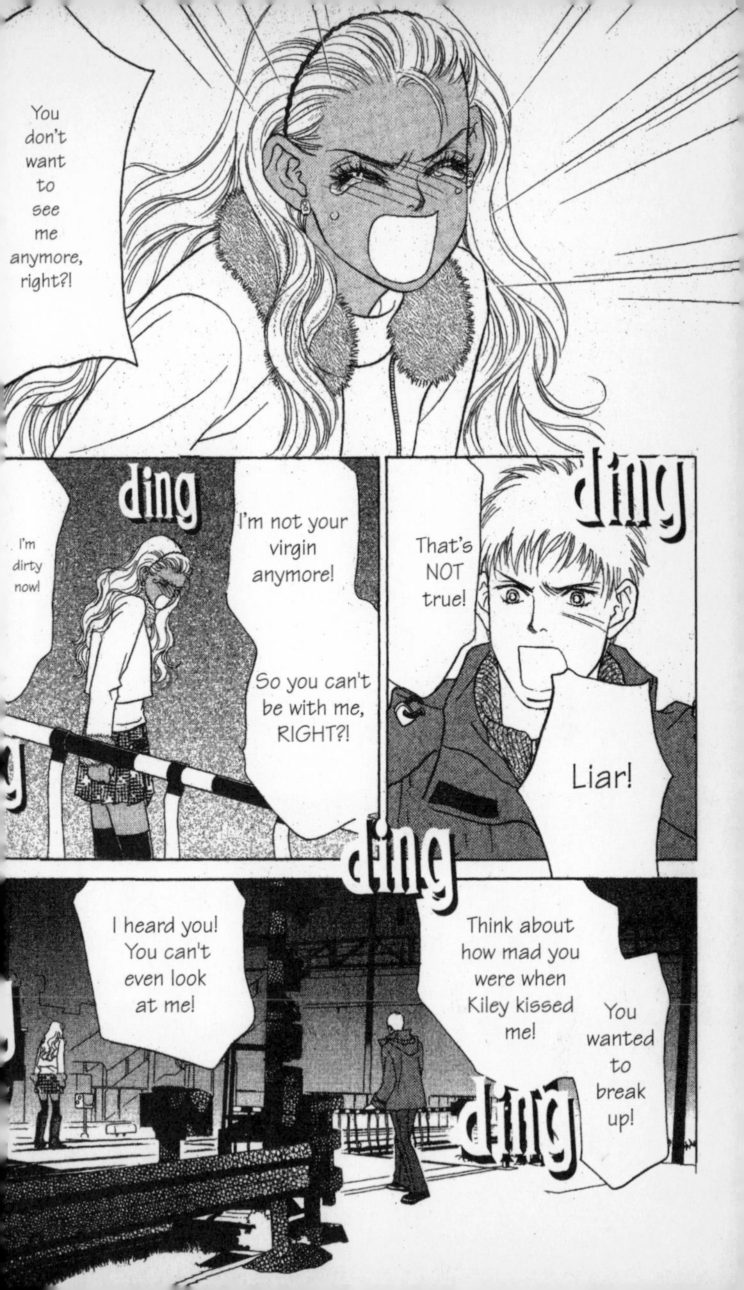
You don't want to see me anymore, right?!
ding
I'm dirty now!
I'm not your virgin anymore!
So you can't be with me, RIGHT?!
ding
That's NOT true!
Liar!
ding
I heard you! You can't even look at me!
Think about how mad you were when Kiley kissed me!
You wanted to break up!
ding

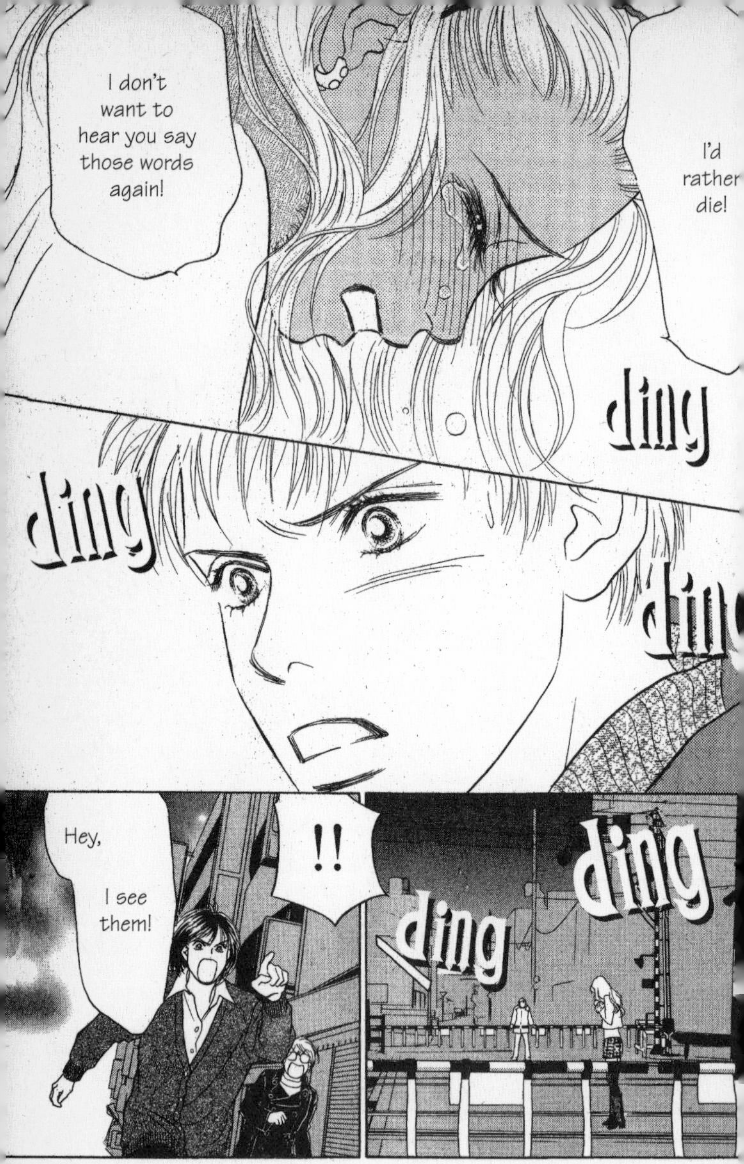
I don't want to hear you say those words again!
I'd rather die!
ding
ding
ding
Hey,
I see them!
!!
ding
ding

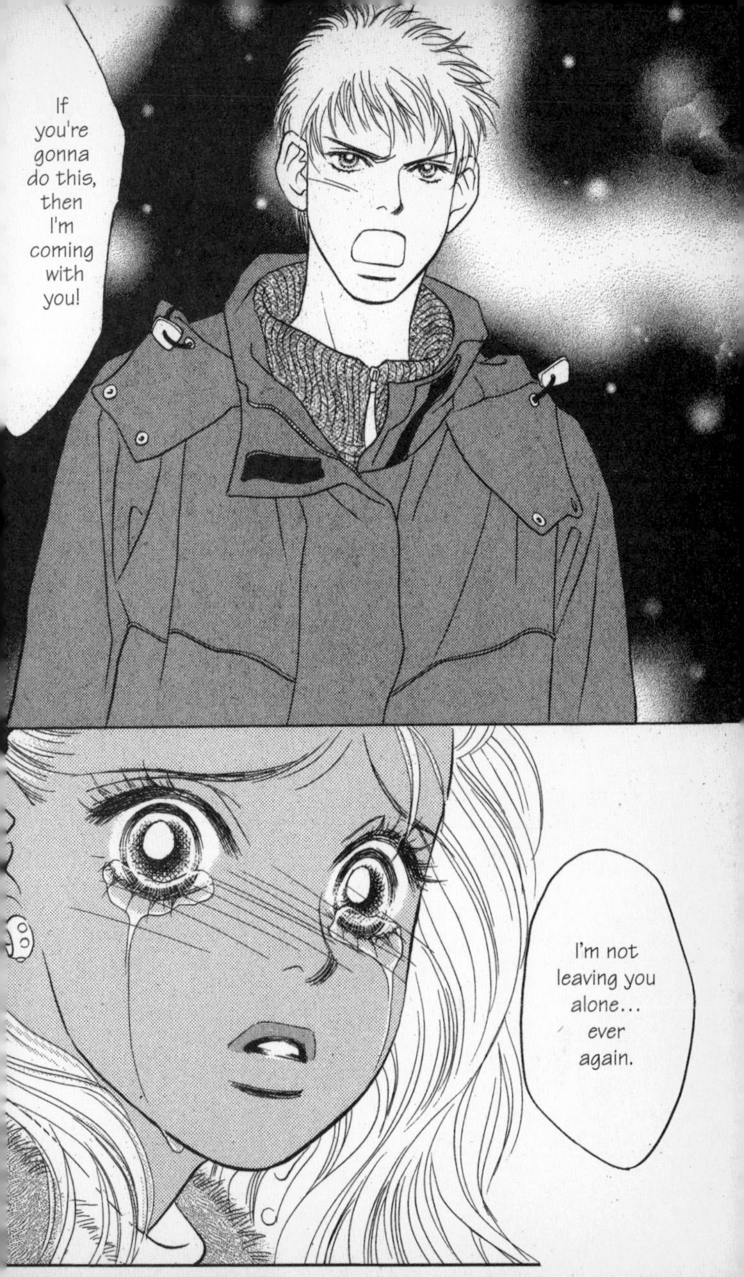
If you're gonna do this, then I'm coming with you!
I'm not leaving you alone... ever again.

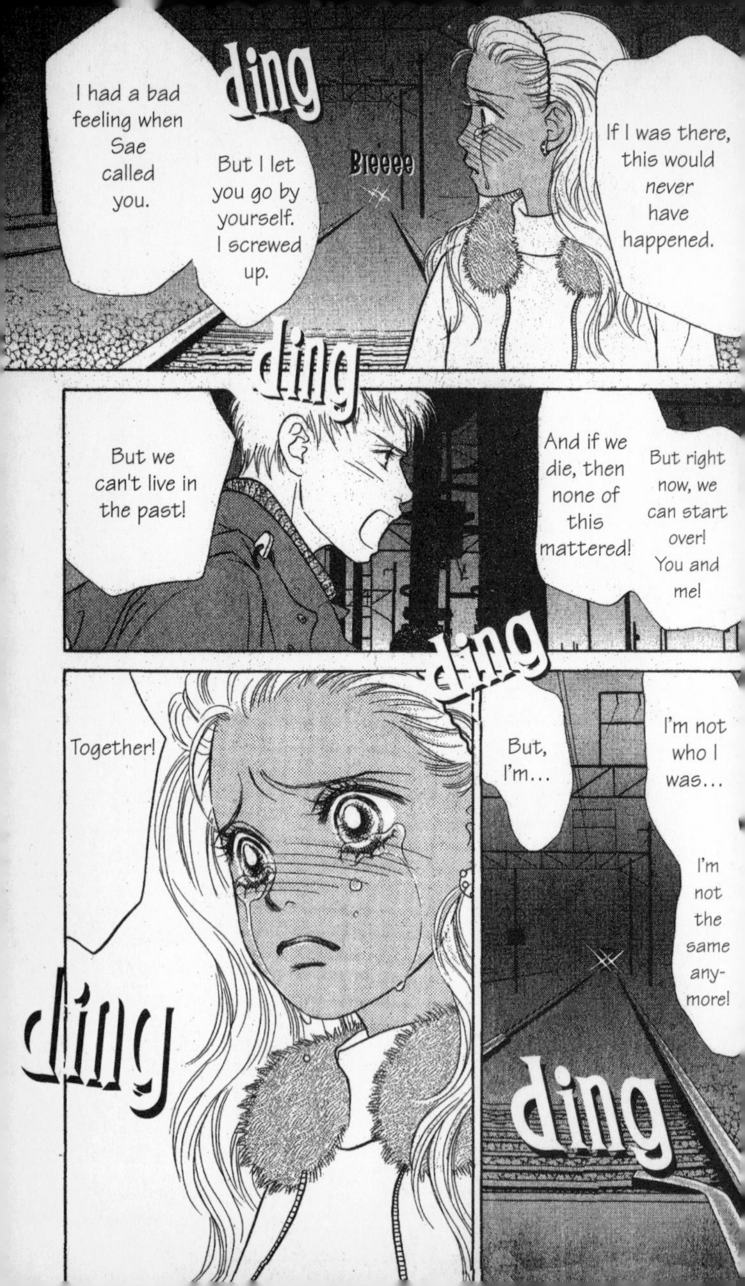
I had a bad feeling when Sae called you.
ding
But I let you go by yourself. I screwed up.
Bleeeee
If I was there, this would never have happened.
ding
But we can't live in the past!
And if we die, then none of this mattered!
But right now, we can start over! You and me!
ding
Together!
ding
But, I'm...
I'm not who I was...
I'm not the same any-more!
ding

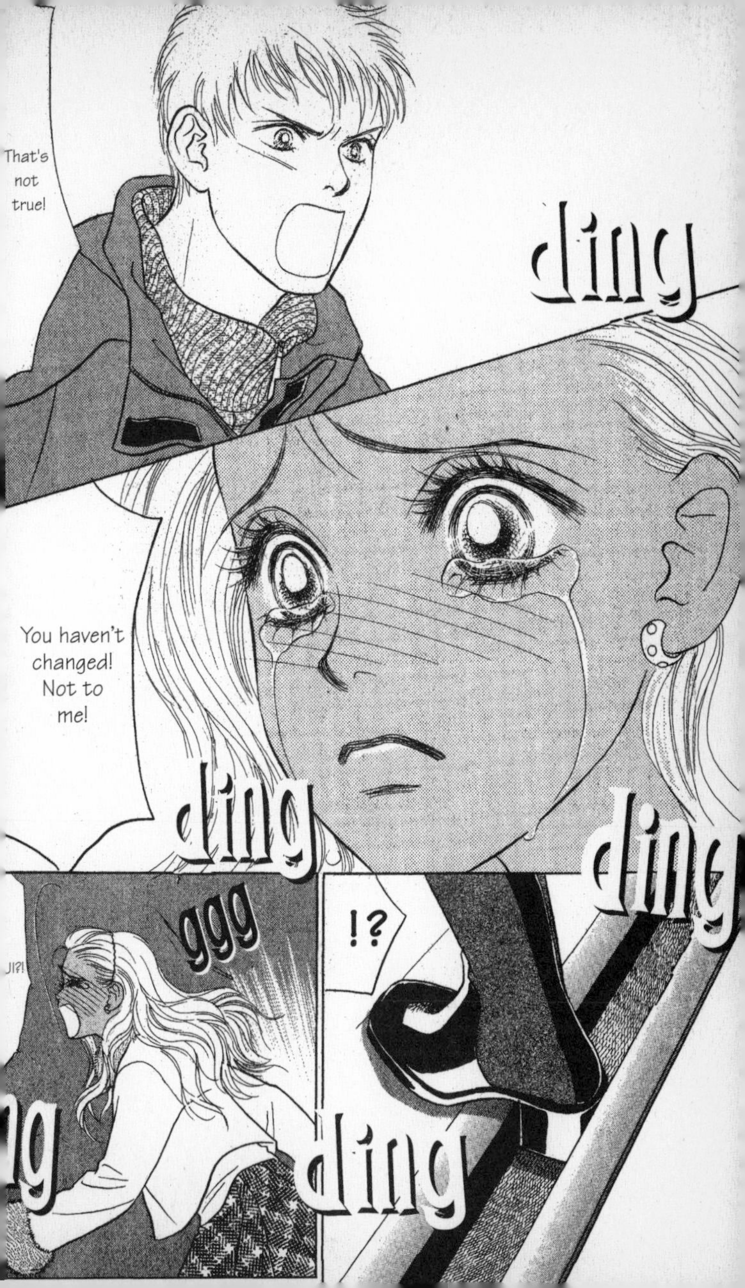
That's not true!
ding
You haven't changed! Not to me!
ding
ding
JI?!
ggg
ng
!?
ding

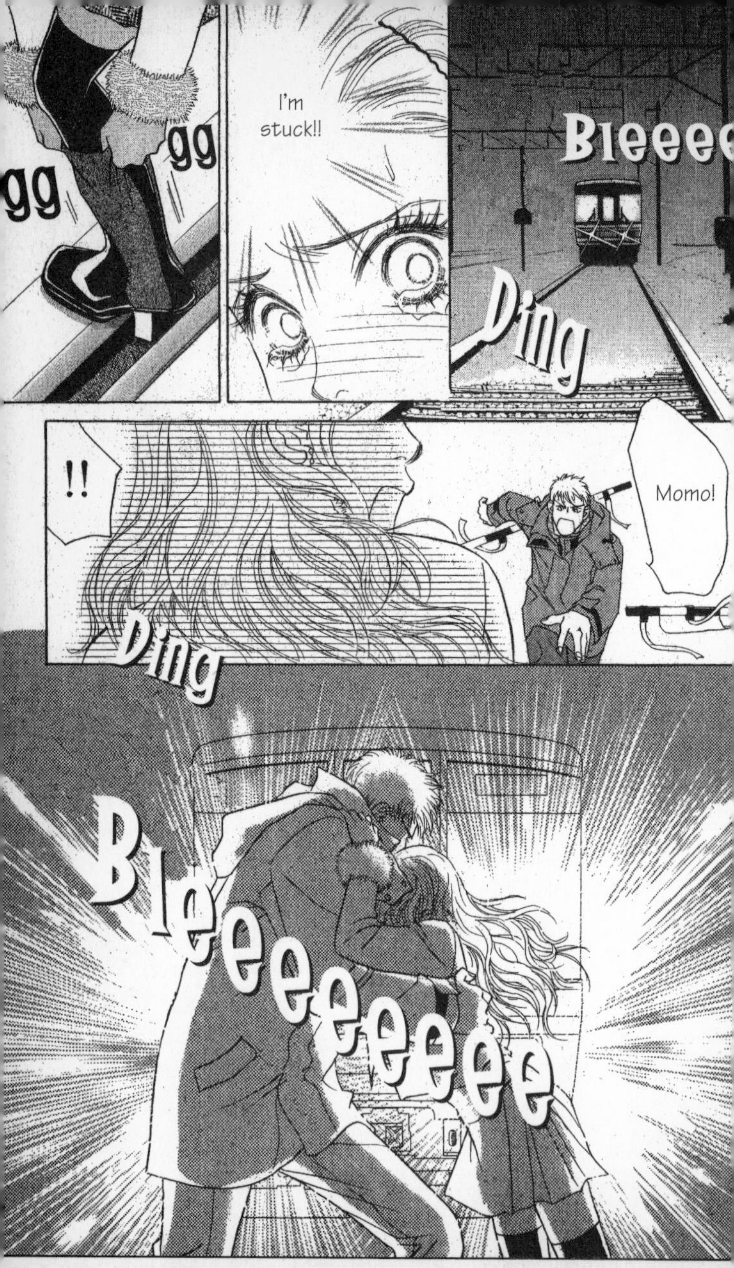
Bleeee
Ding
I'm stuck!!
gg
gg
Momo!
!!
Ding
Bleeeeeeee

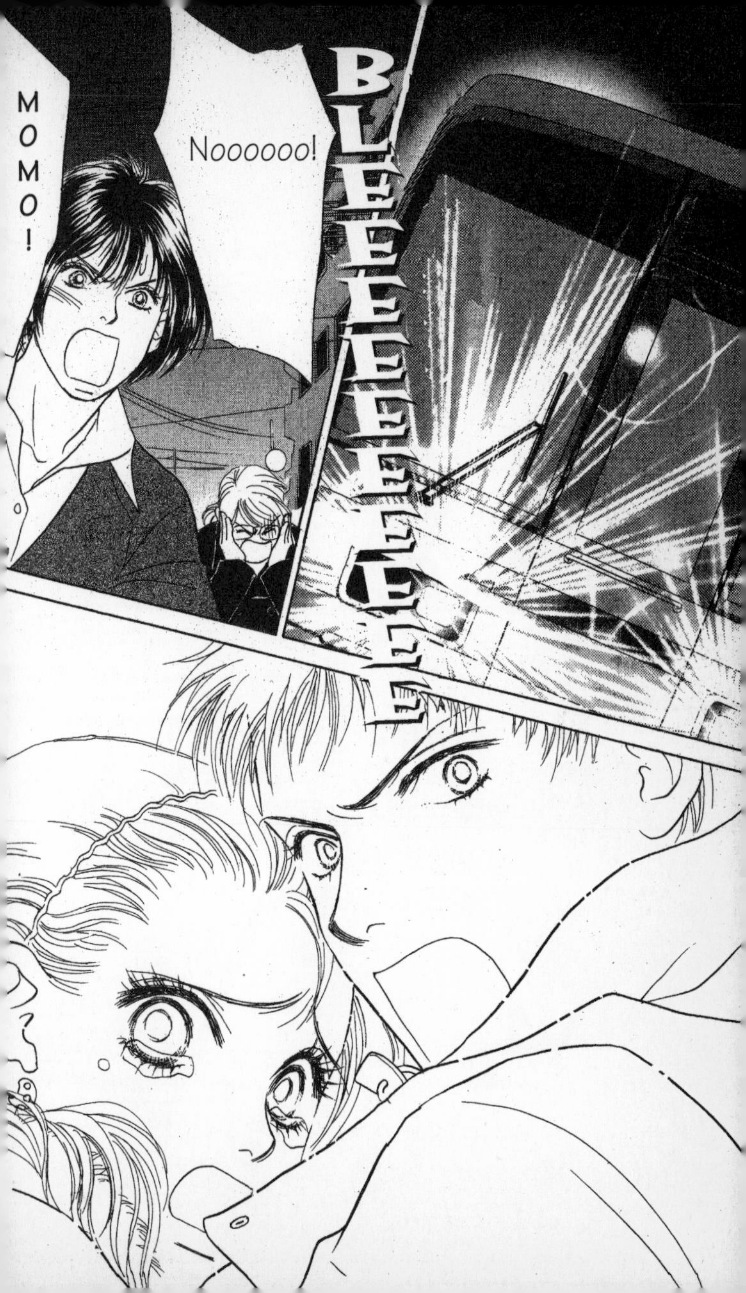
MOMO!
Noooooo!
BLEEEEEEEEEEEE

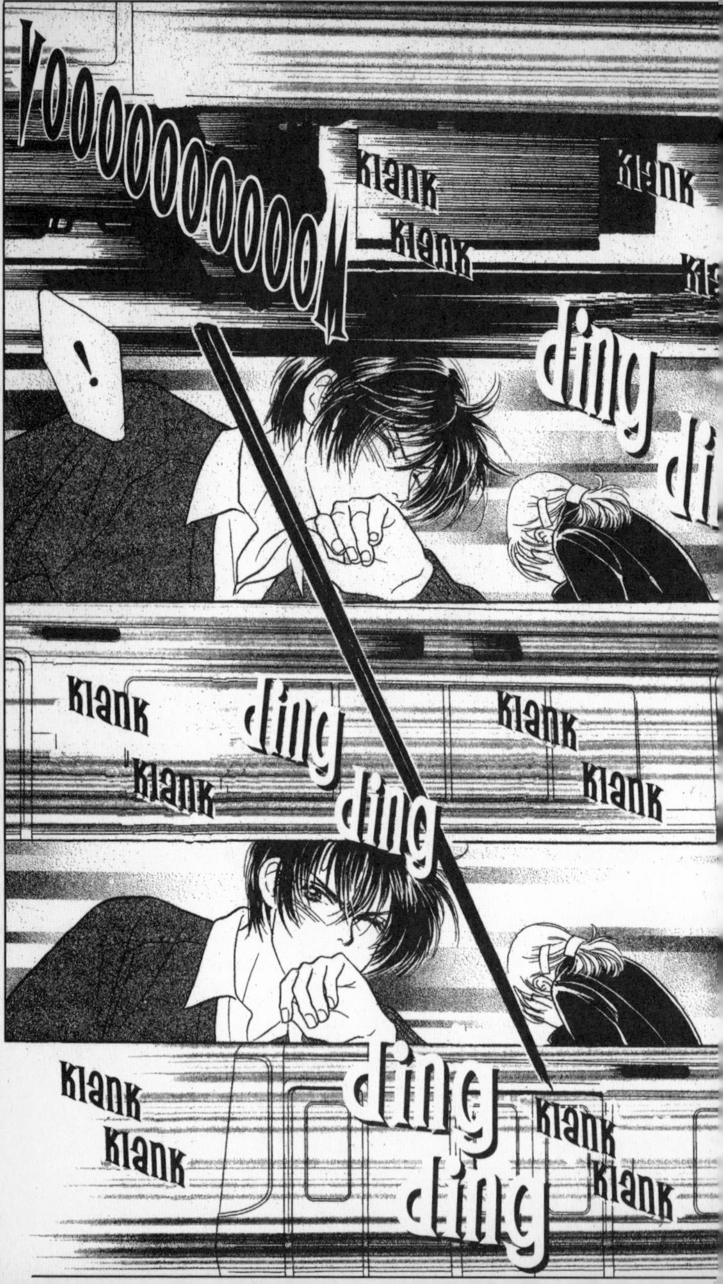

YOOOOOOOOOOM
KLANK
KLANK
KLANK
ding
!
KLANK
ding
KLANK
KLANK
KLANK
ding
KLANK
KLANK
ding
KLANK
KLANK
ding
ding

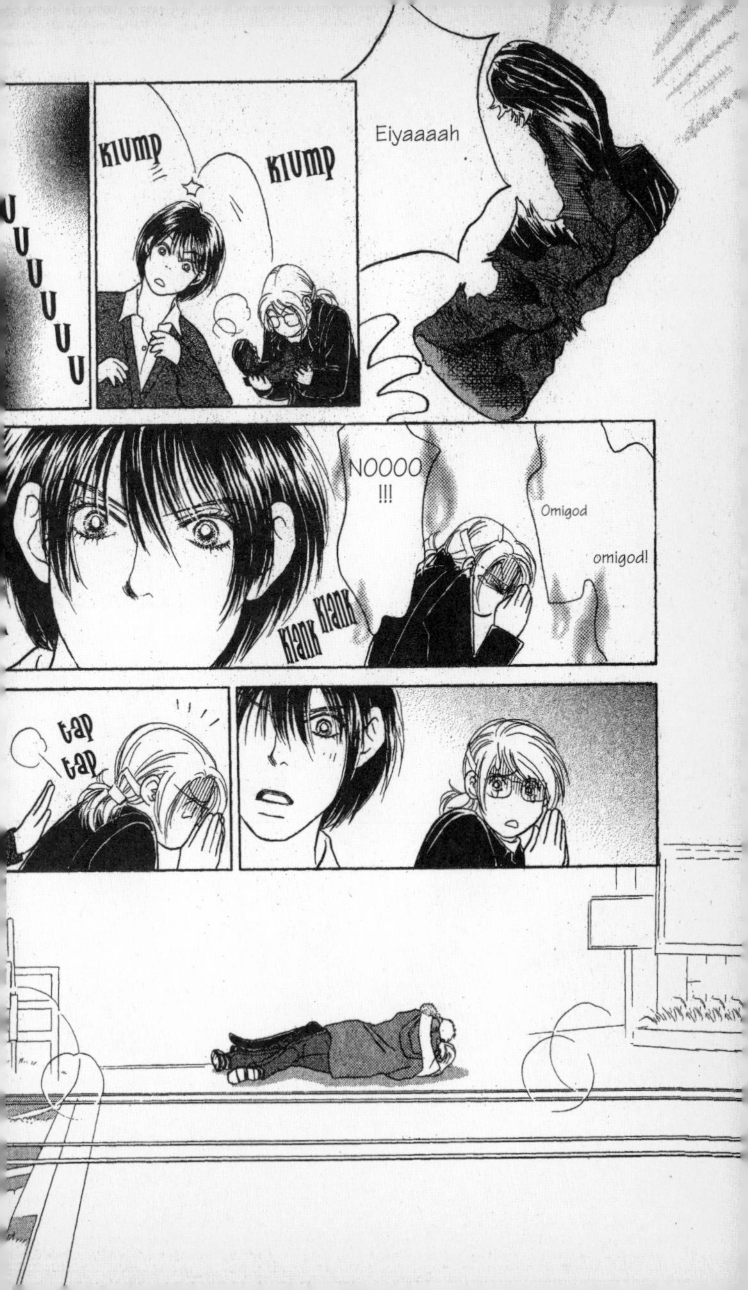
UUUUUUU
KLUMP
KLUMP
Eiyaaaah
NOOOO !!!
KLANK KLANK
Omigod
omigod!
tap tap

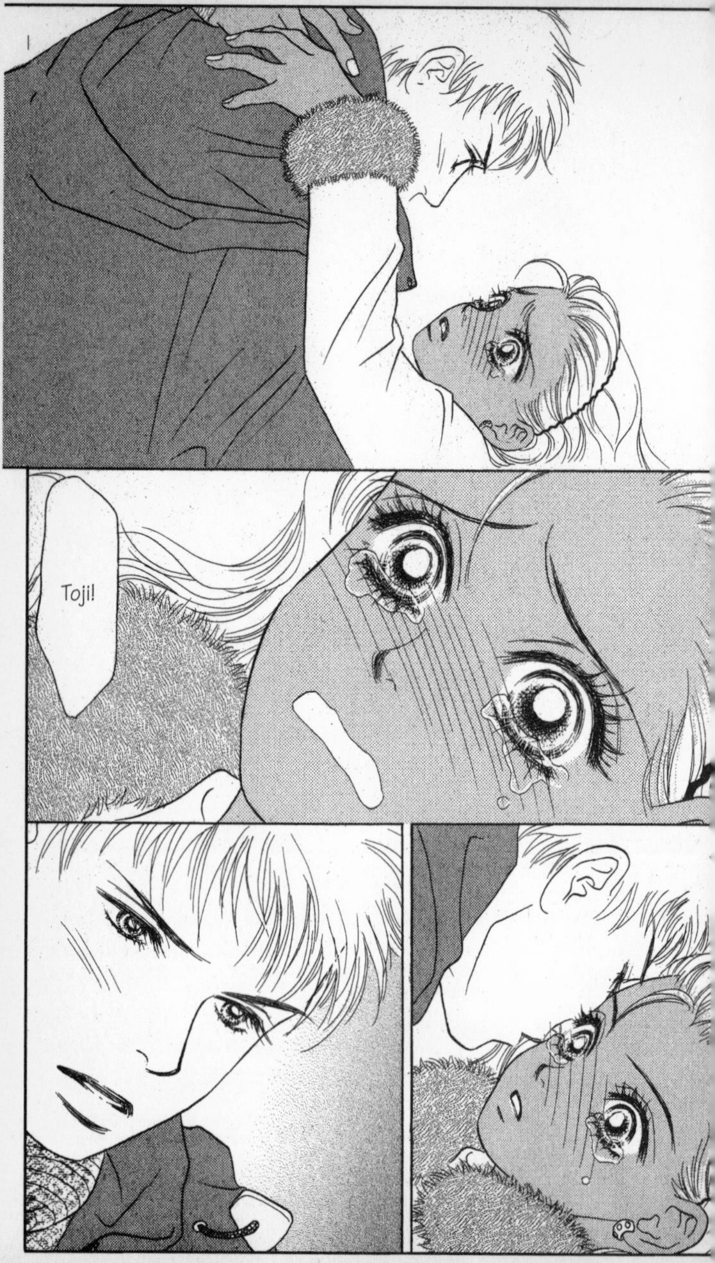
Toji!

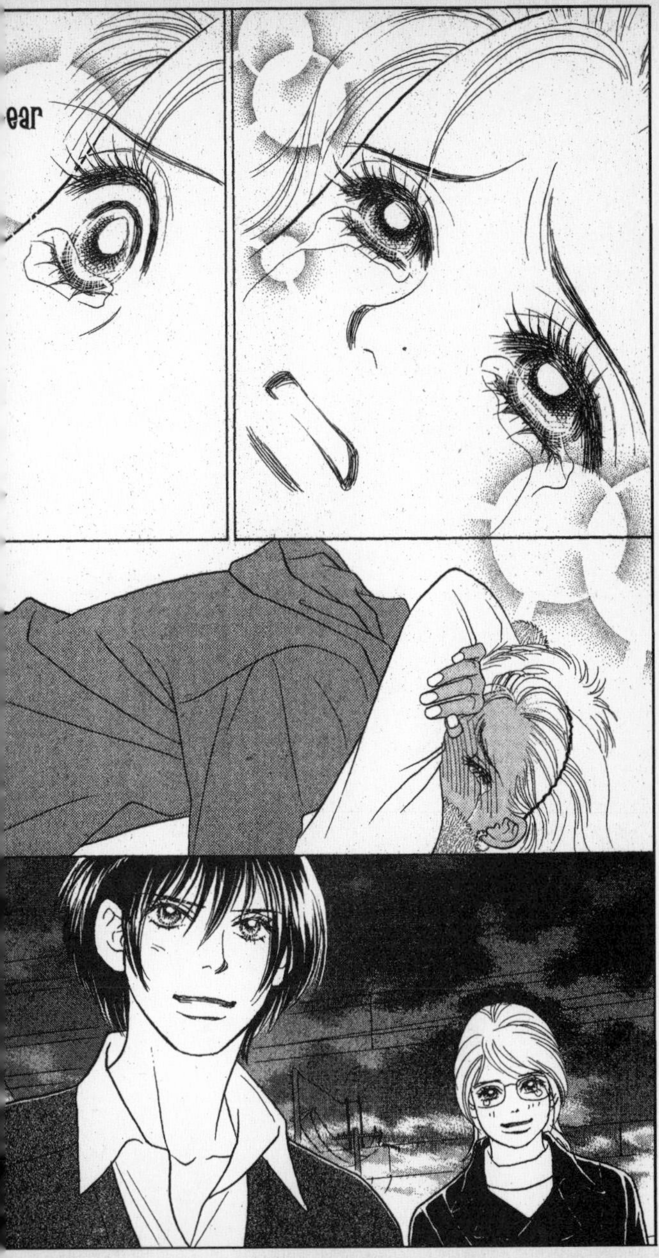

ear

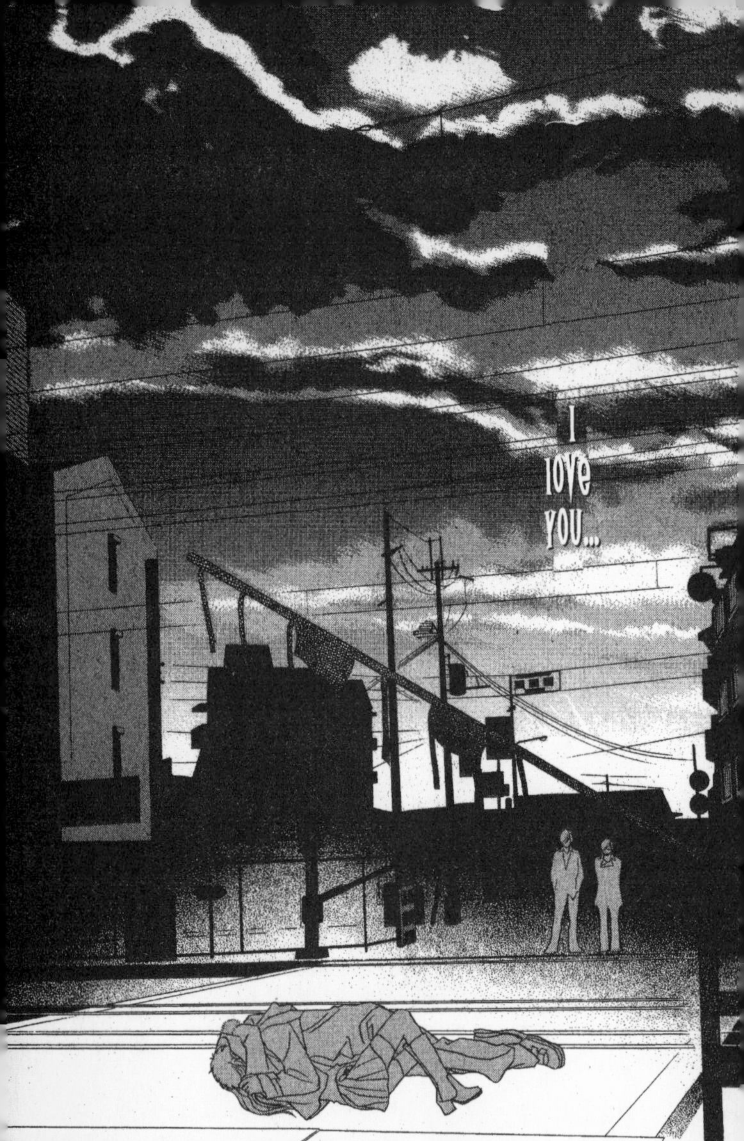
I love you...

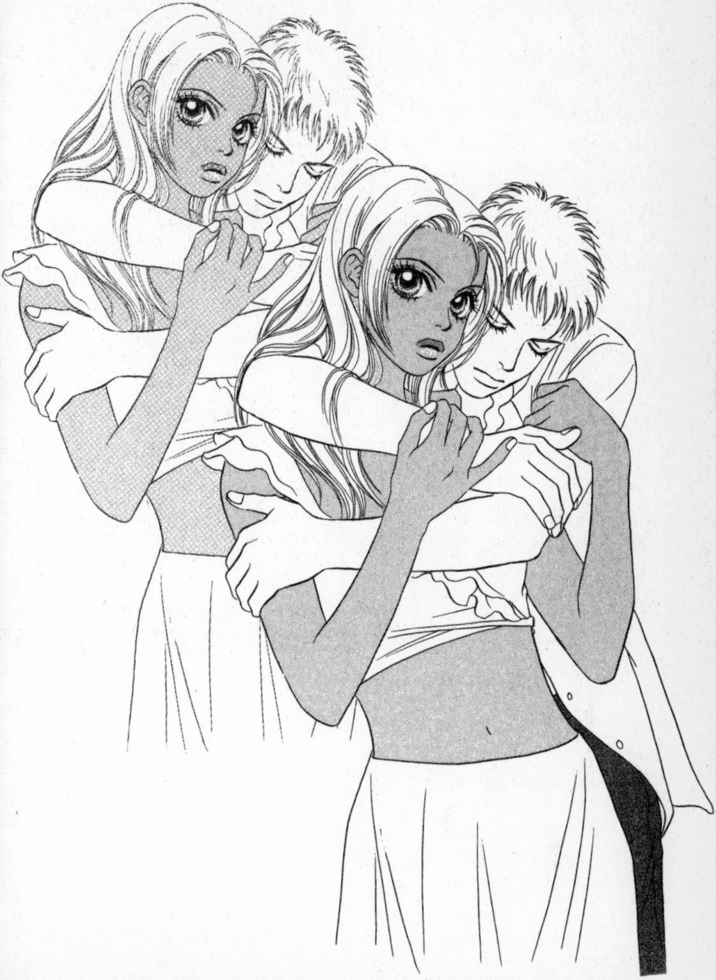

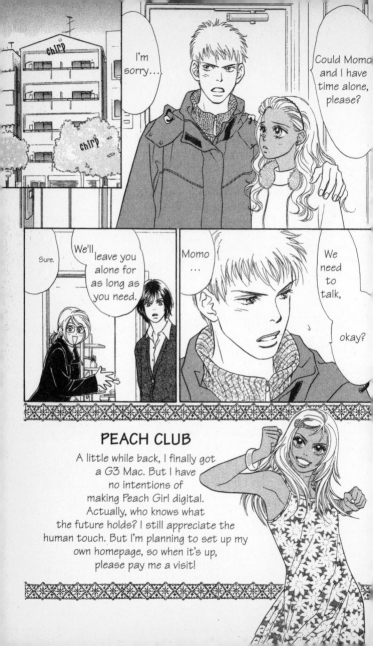

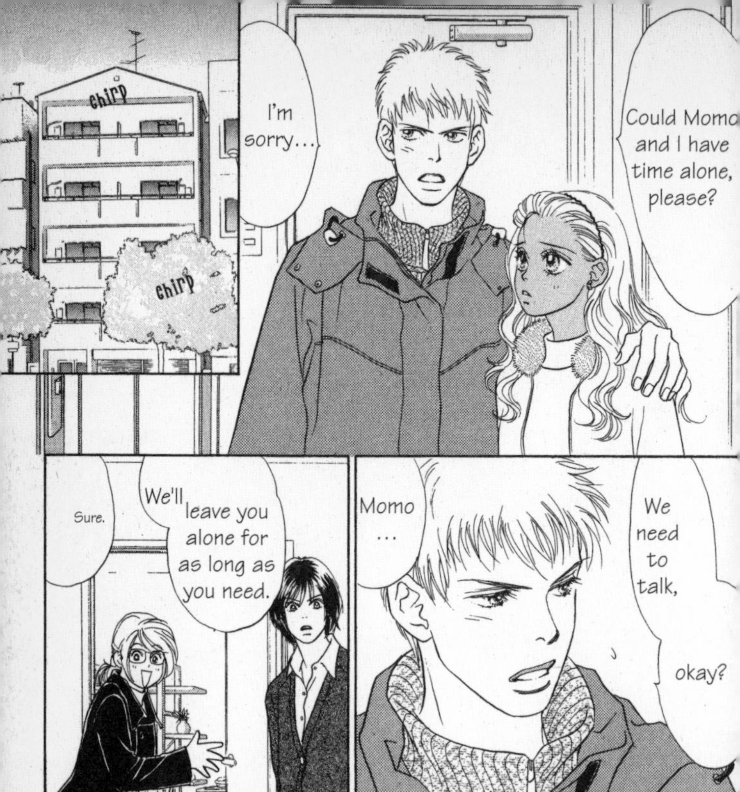
chirp
chirp
I'm sorry...
Could Momo and I have time alone, please?
Sure.
We'll leave you alone for as long as you need.
Momo...
We need to talk, okay?

PEACH CLUB

A little while back, I finally got a G3 Mac. But I have no intentions of making Peach Girl digital. Actually, who knows what the future holds? I still appreciate the human touch. But I'm planning to set up my own homepage, so when it's up, please pay me a visit!

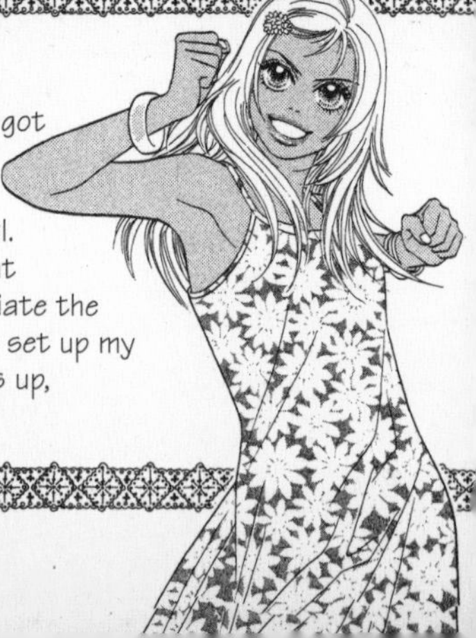

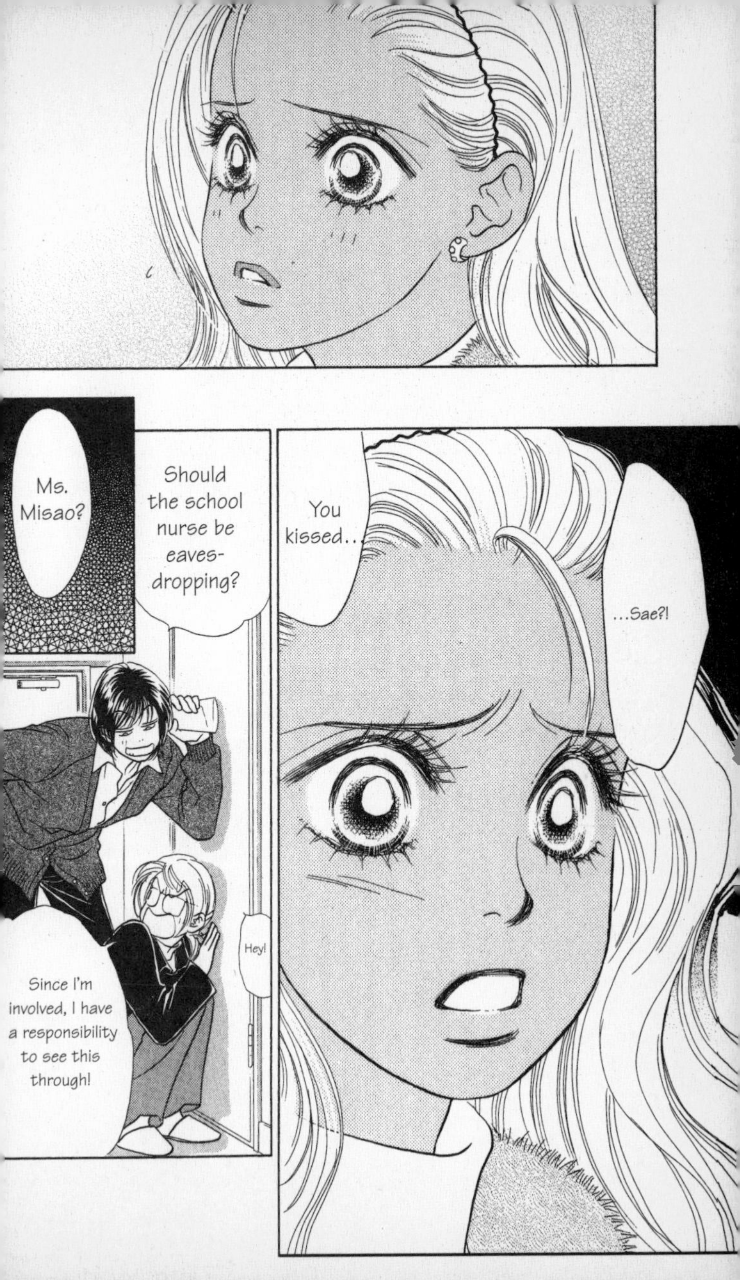

Ms. Misao?
Should the school nurse be eaves-dropping?
Hey!
Since I'm involved, I have a responsibility to see this through!
You kissed...
...Sae?!

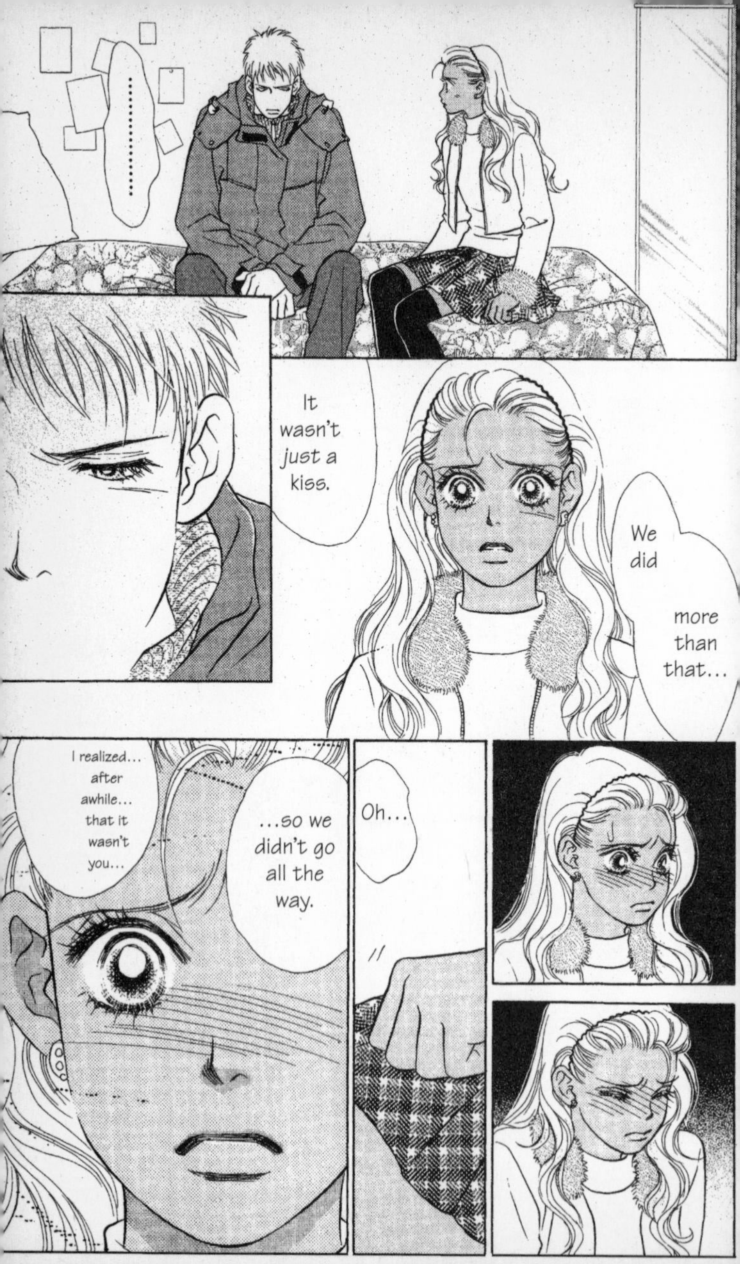
......
It wasn't just a kiss.
We did more than that...
I realized... after awhile... that it wasn't you...
...so we didn't go all the way.
Oh...

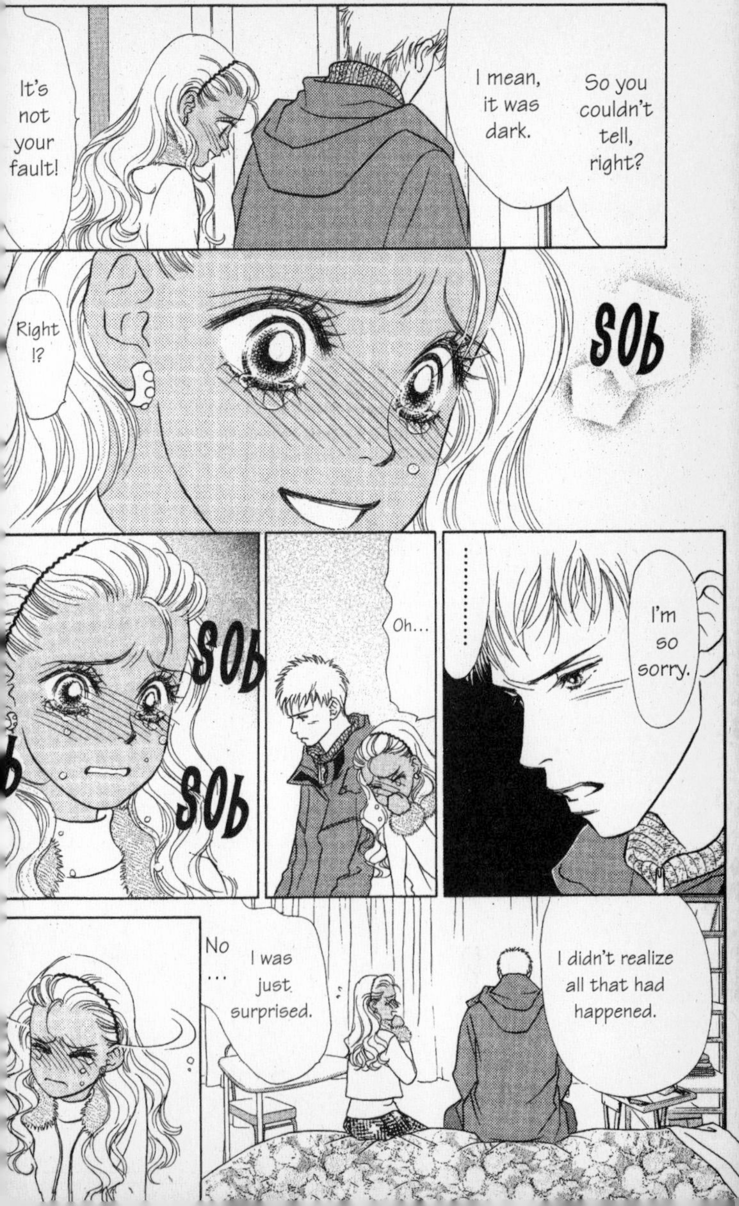
It's not your fault!
I mean, it was dark.
So you couldn't tell, right?
Right !?
SOB
SOB
SOB
Oh...
......
I'm so sorry.
No ...
I was just surprised.
I didn't realize all that had happened.

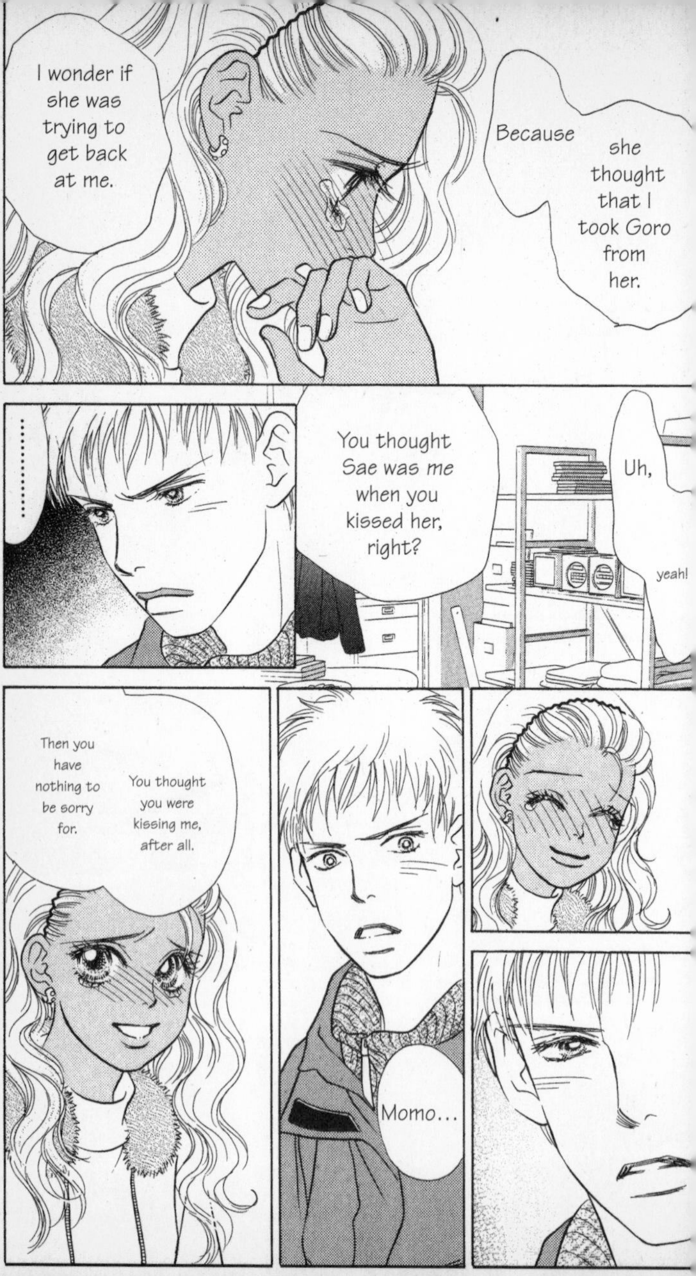
I wonder if she was trying to get back at me.
Because she thought that I took Goro from her.
....
You thought Sae was me when you kissed her, right?
Uh, yeah!
Then you have nothing to be sorry for.
You thought you were kissing me, after all.
Momo...

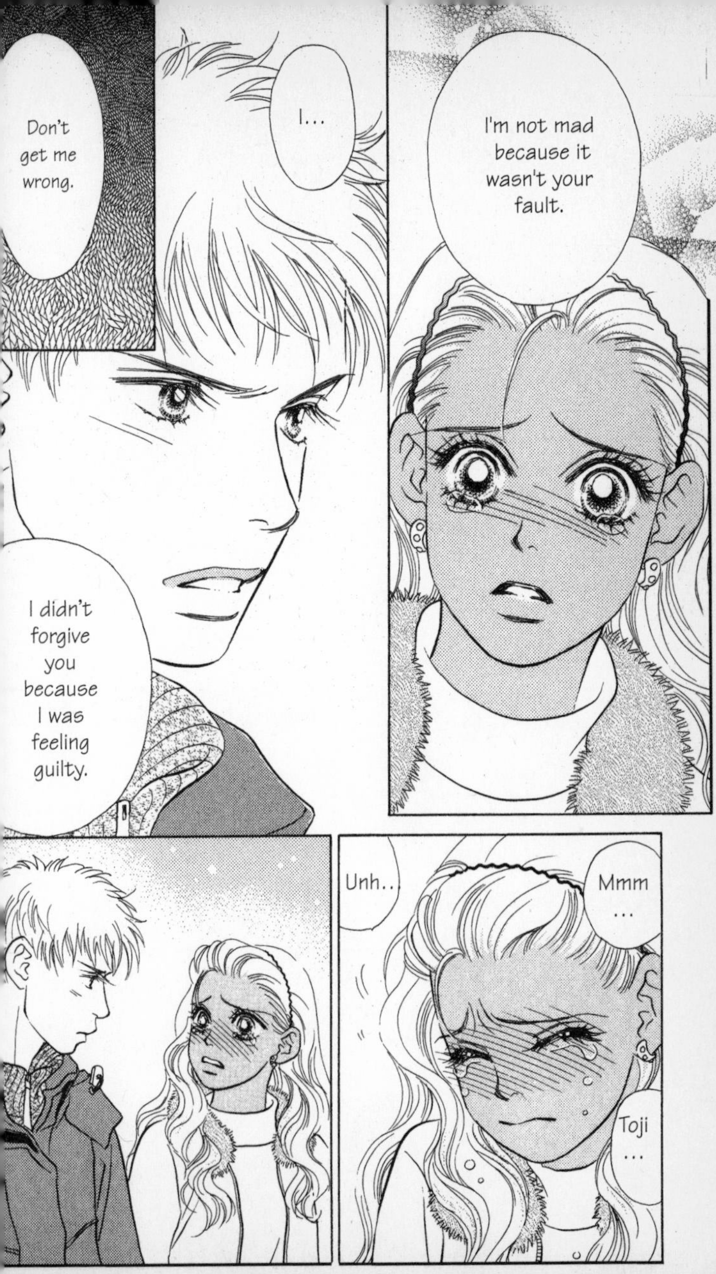
Don't get me wrong.
I...
I didn't forgive you because I was feeling guilty.
I'm not mad because it wasn't your fault.
Unh...
Mmm ...
Toji ...

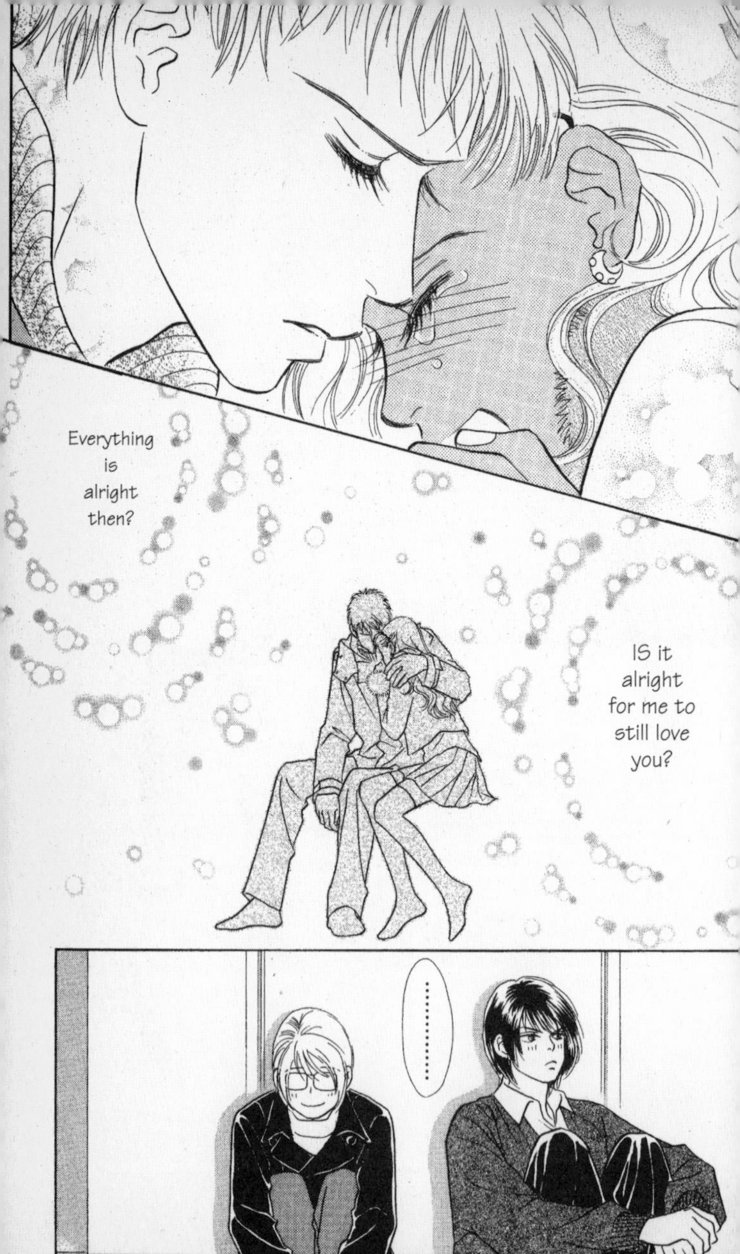
Everything is alright then?
IS it alright for me to still love you?
......

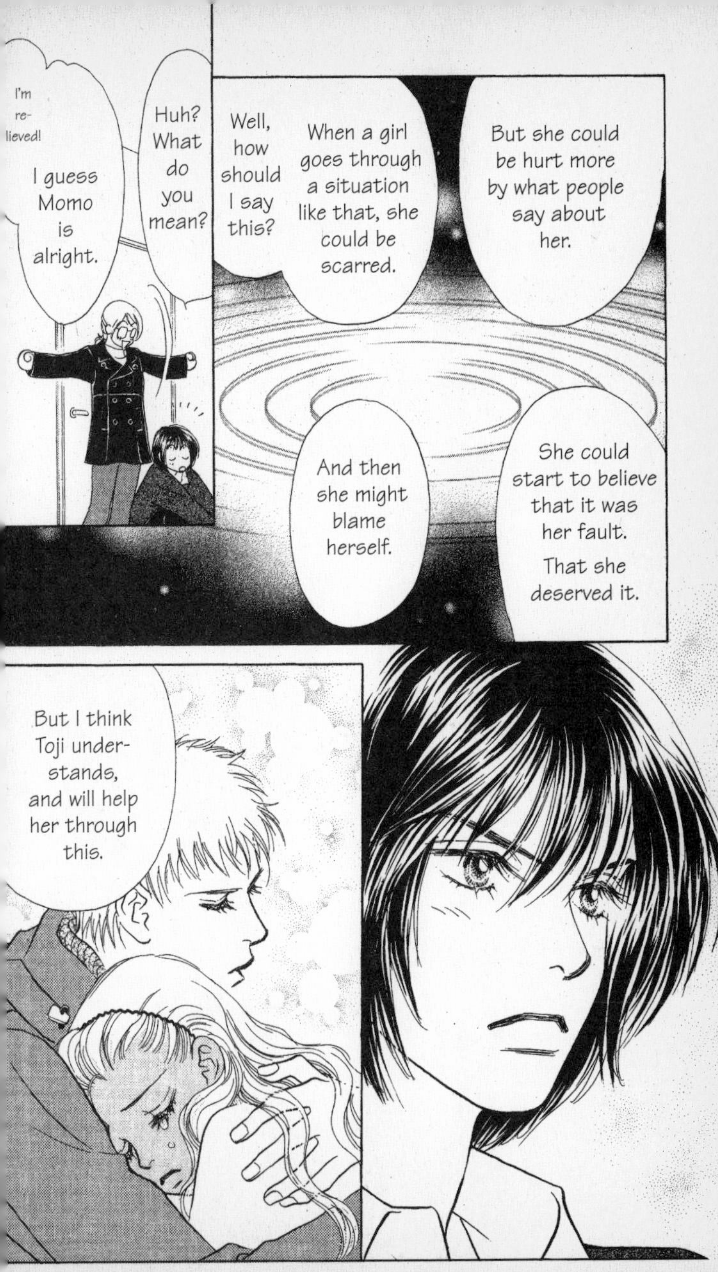

I guess Momo is alright.
I'm re-lieved!
Huh? What do you mean?
Well, how should I say this?
When a girl goes through a situation like that, she could be scarred.
But she could be hurt more by what people say about her.
And then she might blame herself.
She could start to believe that it was her fault.
That she deserved it.
But I think Toji under-stands, and will help her through this.

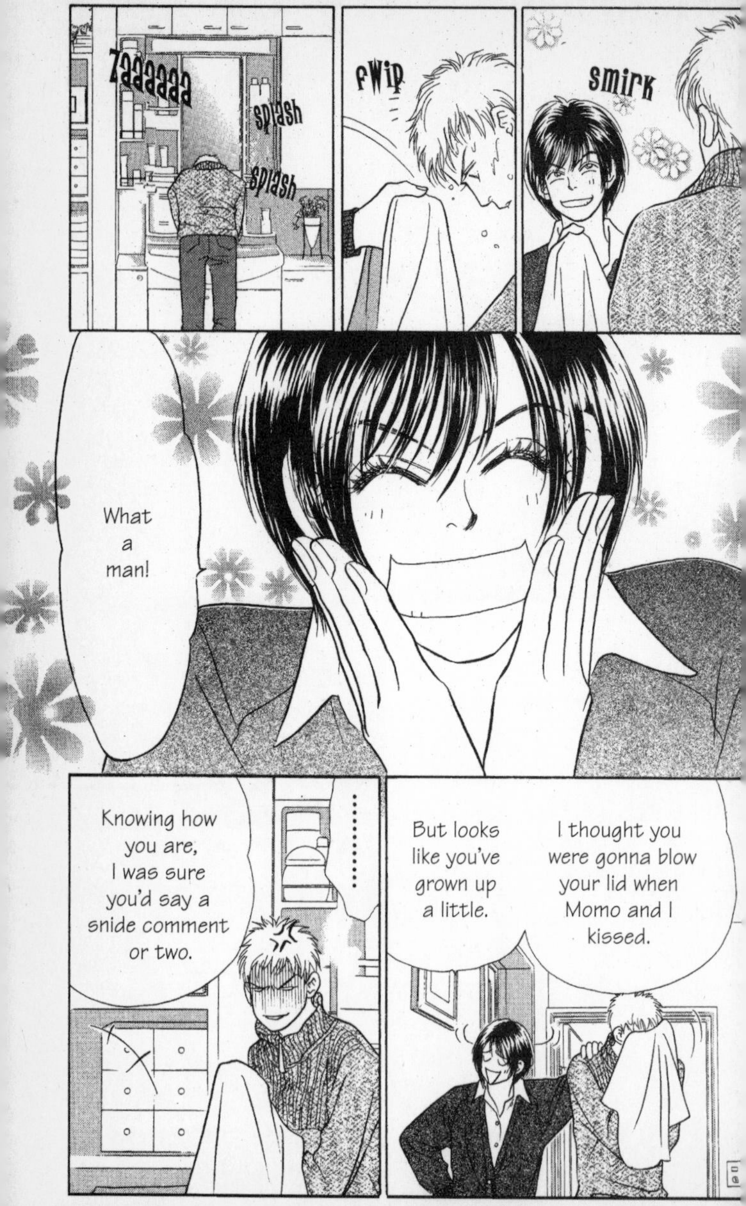
Zaaaaaa
splash
splash
fwip
smirk
What a man!
Knowing how you are, I was sure you'd say a snide comment or two.
....
But looks like you've grown up a little.
I thought you were gonna blow your lid when Momo and I kissed.

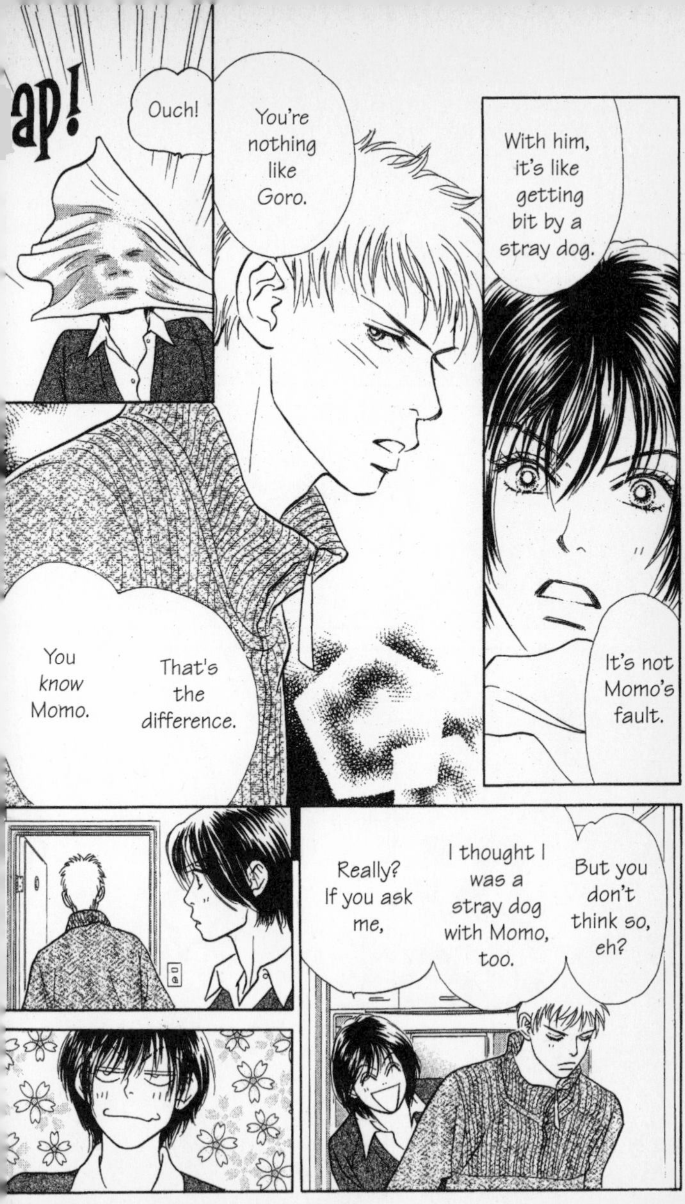
ap!
Ouch!
You're nothing like Goro.
With him, it's like getting bit by a stray dog.
You know Momo.
That's the difference.
It's not Momo's fault.
Really? If you ask me,
I thought I was a stray dog with Momo, too.
But you don't think so, eh?

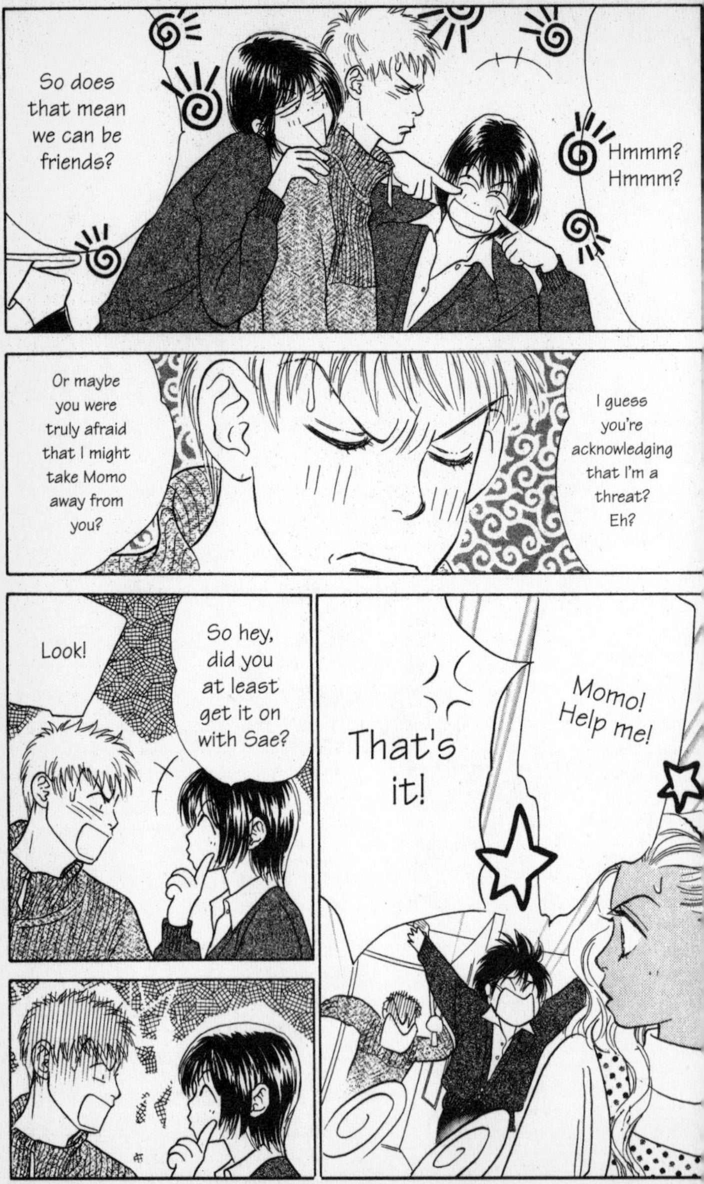
So does that mean we can be friends?
Hmmm? Hmmm?
Or maybe you were truly afraid that I might take Momo away from you?
I guess you're acknowledging that I'm a threat? Eh?
Look!
So hey, did you at least get it on with Sae?
That's it!
Momo! Help me!

Hey, don't get mad. It's your fault for mixing up the two.

Besides, how can you make that mistake even if it was dark? She's your girlfriend.

I thought it was Momo! Sae was wearing the same perfume!

Perfume?

!

You mean the perfume you gave me for my birthday?

. . .

That's not all.

She was wearing the same clothes, and had her hair done the same way.

That's why...

Come to think of it, she was wearing the exact same outfit.

That hair must

have been a wig.

She was copying me again?

What a freak!

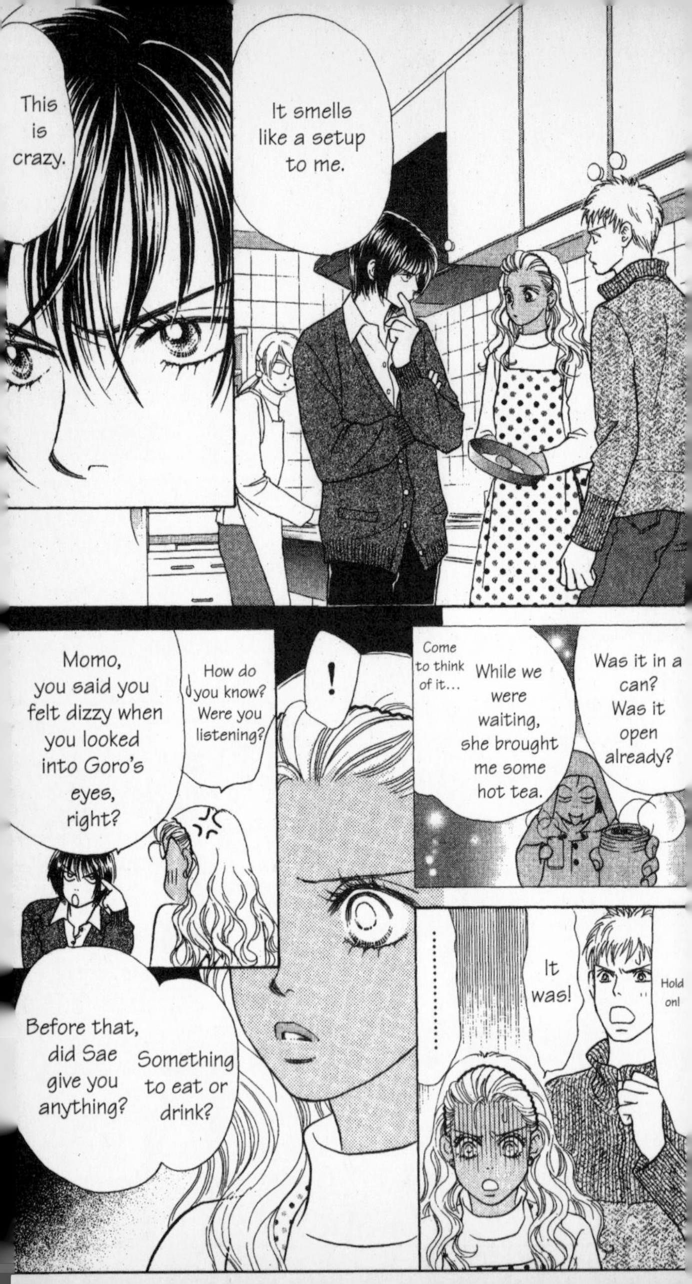
This is crazy.
It smells like a setup to me.
Momo, you said you felt dizzy when you looked into Goro's eyes, right?
How do you know? Were you listening?
!
Come to think of it...
While we were waiting, she brought me some hot tea.
Was it in a can? Was it open already?
Before that, did Sae give you anything?
Something to eat or drink?
....
It was!
Hold on!

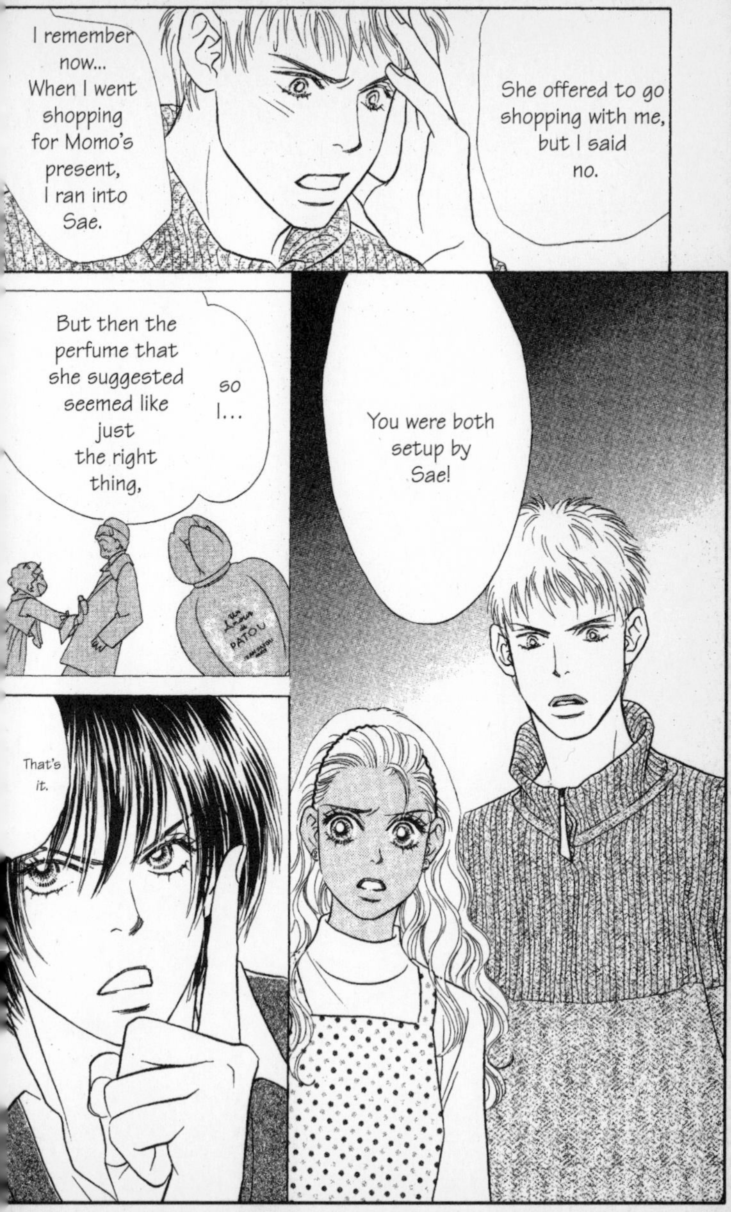
I remember now... When I went shopping for Momo's present, I ran into Sae.
She offered to go shopping with me, but I said no.
But then the perfume that she suggested seemed like just the right thing,
so I...
That's it.
You were both setup by Sae!

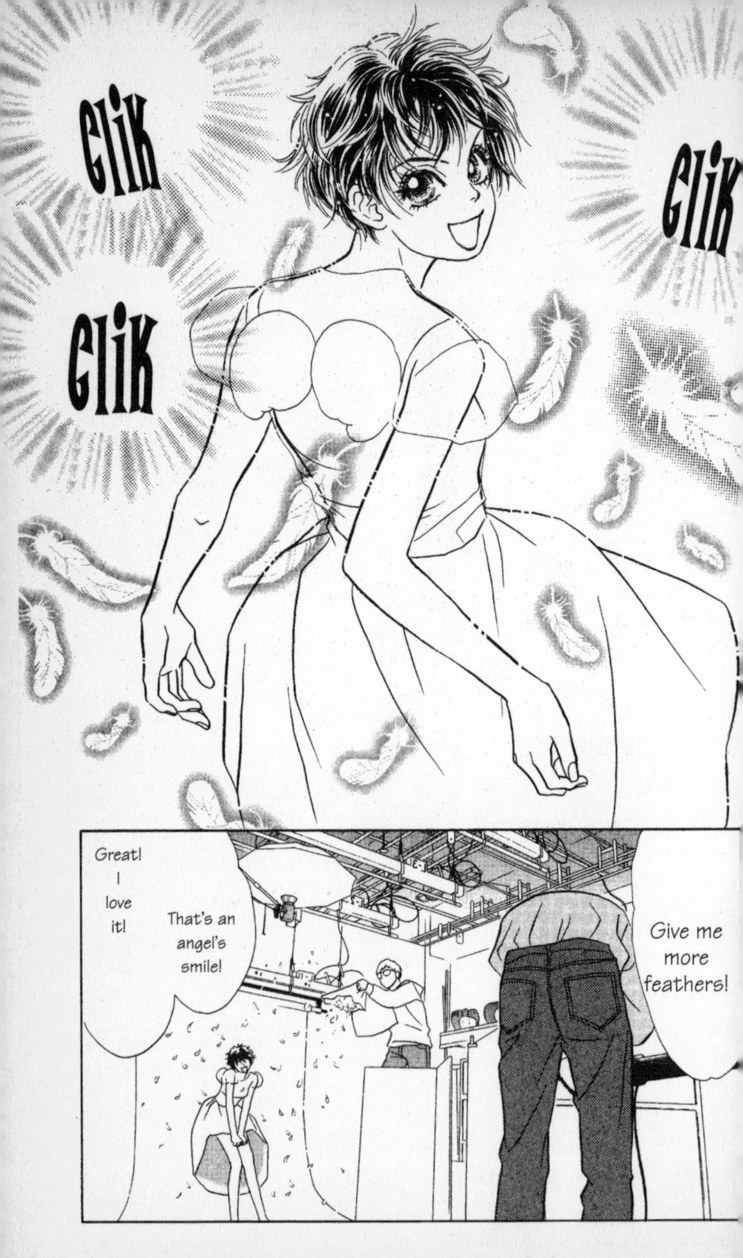
CliK
CliK
CliK
Give me more feathers!
That's an angel's smile!
Great! I love it!

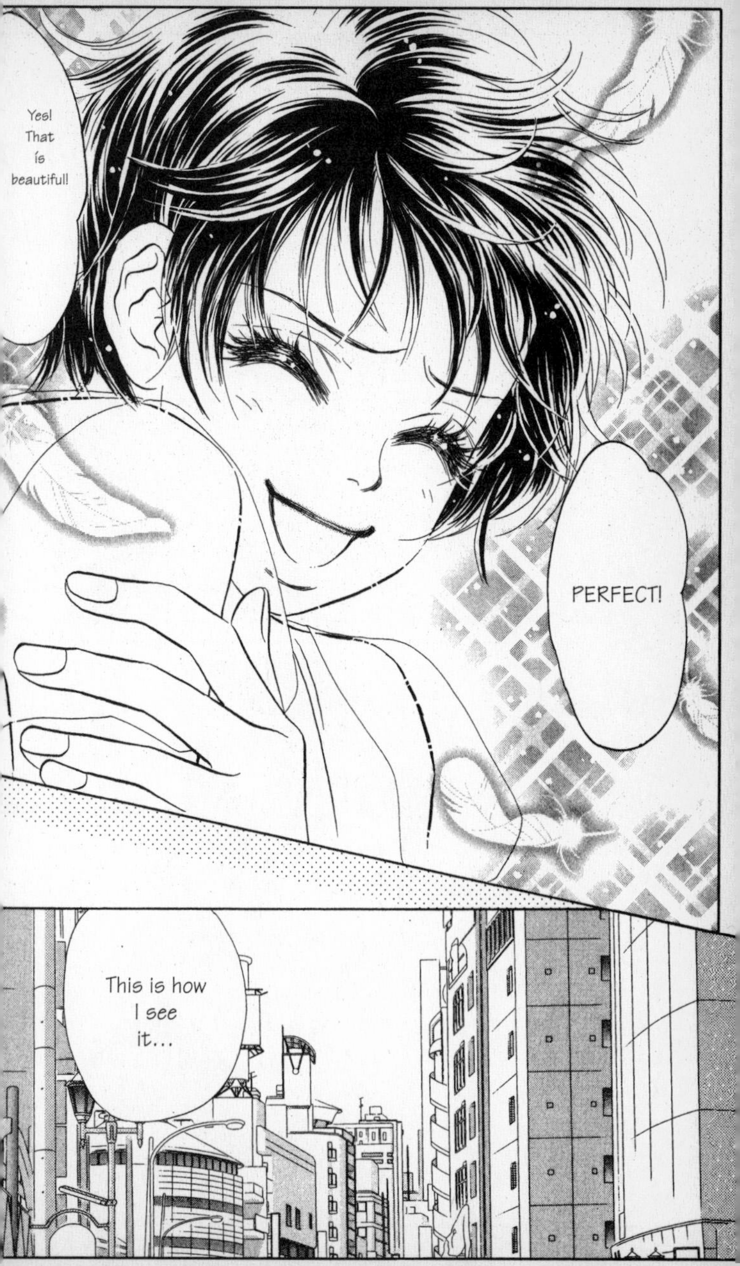
Yes! That is beautiful!
PERFECT!
This is how I see it...

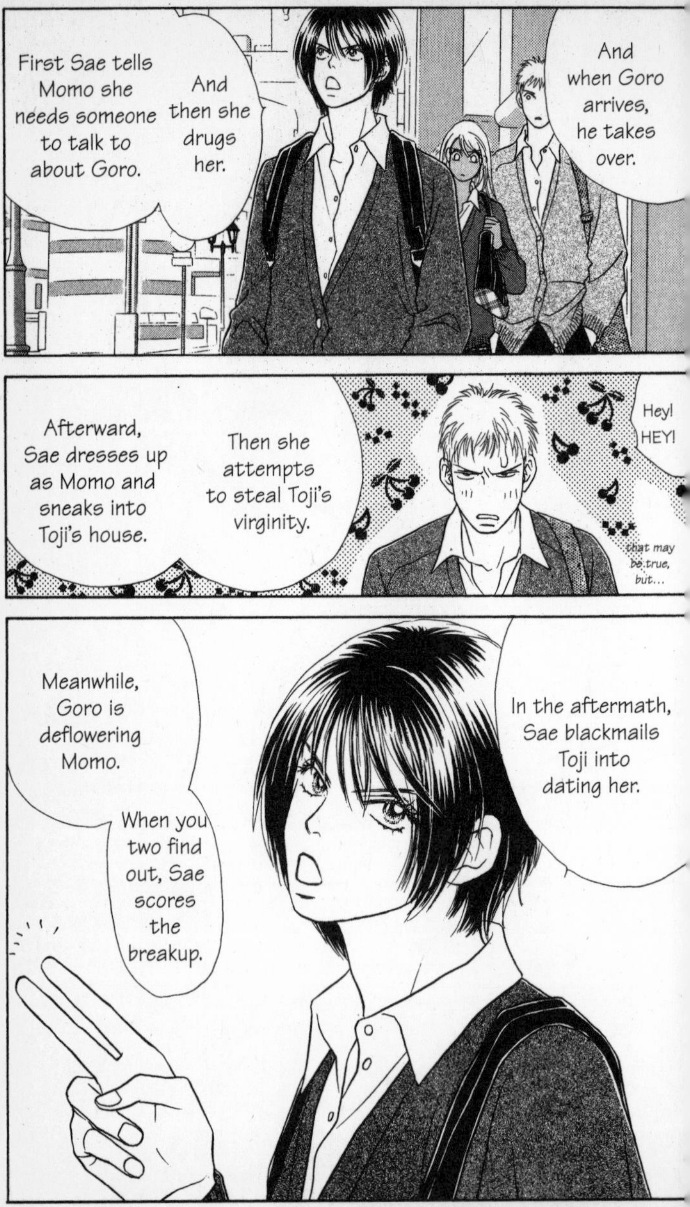
First Sae tells Momo she needs someone to talk to about Goro.
And then she drugs her.
And when Goro arrives, he takes over.
Afterward, Sae dresses up as Momo and sneaks into Toji's house.
Then she attempts to steal Toji's virginity.
Hey! HEY!
that may be true, but...
Meanwhile, Goro is deflowering Momo.
When you two find out, Sae scores the breakup.
In the aftermath, Sae blackmails Toji into dating her.

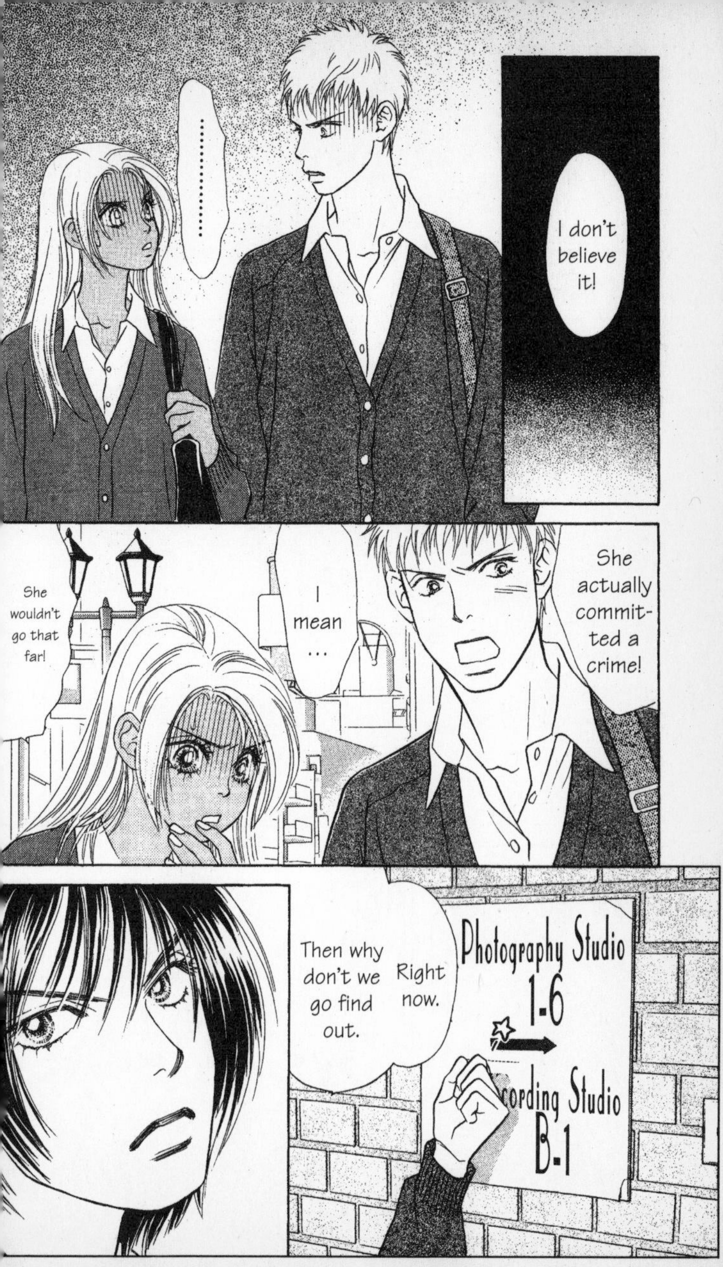
......
I don't believe it!
She wouldn't go that far!
I mean ...
She actually commit-ted a crime!
Then why don't we go find out.
Right now.
Photography Studio 1-6
cording Studio B-1

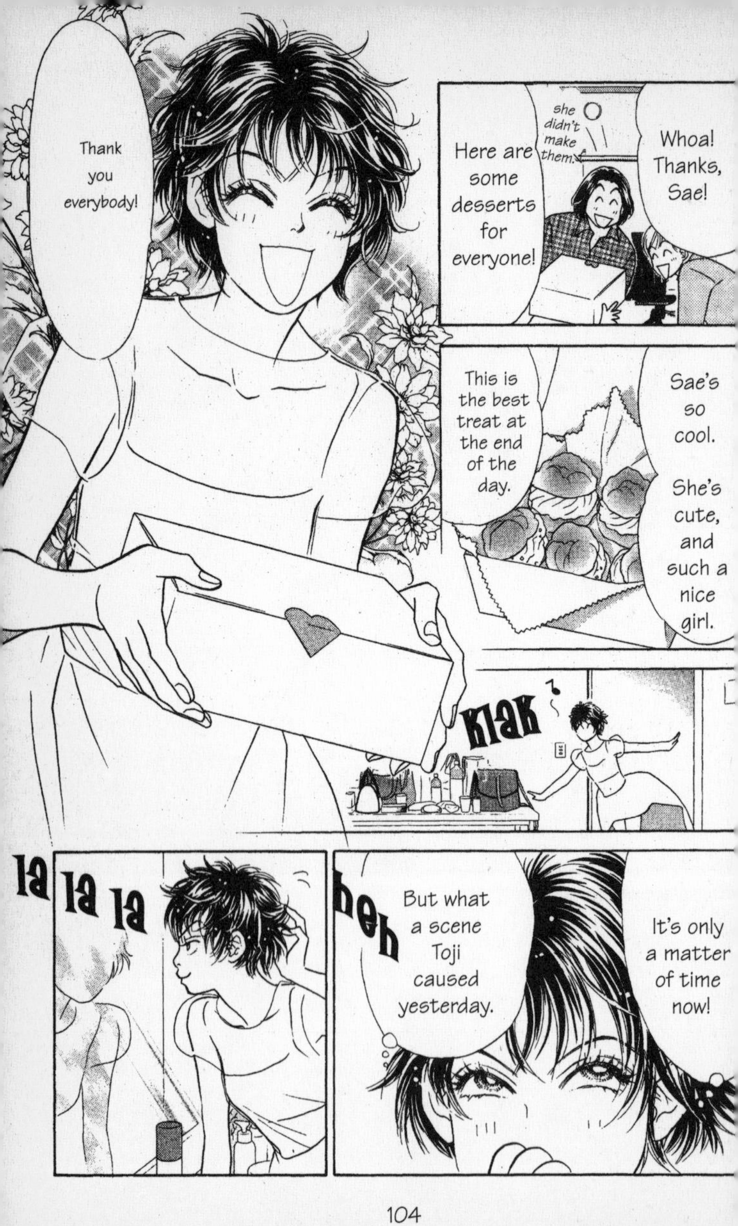

Thank you everybody!
Here are some desserts for everyone!
she didn't make them.
Whoa! Thanks, Sae!
This is the best treat at the end of the day.
Sae's so cool.
She's cute, and such a nice girl.
KLAK
la la la
heh
But what a scene Toji caused yesterday.
It's only a matter of time now!

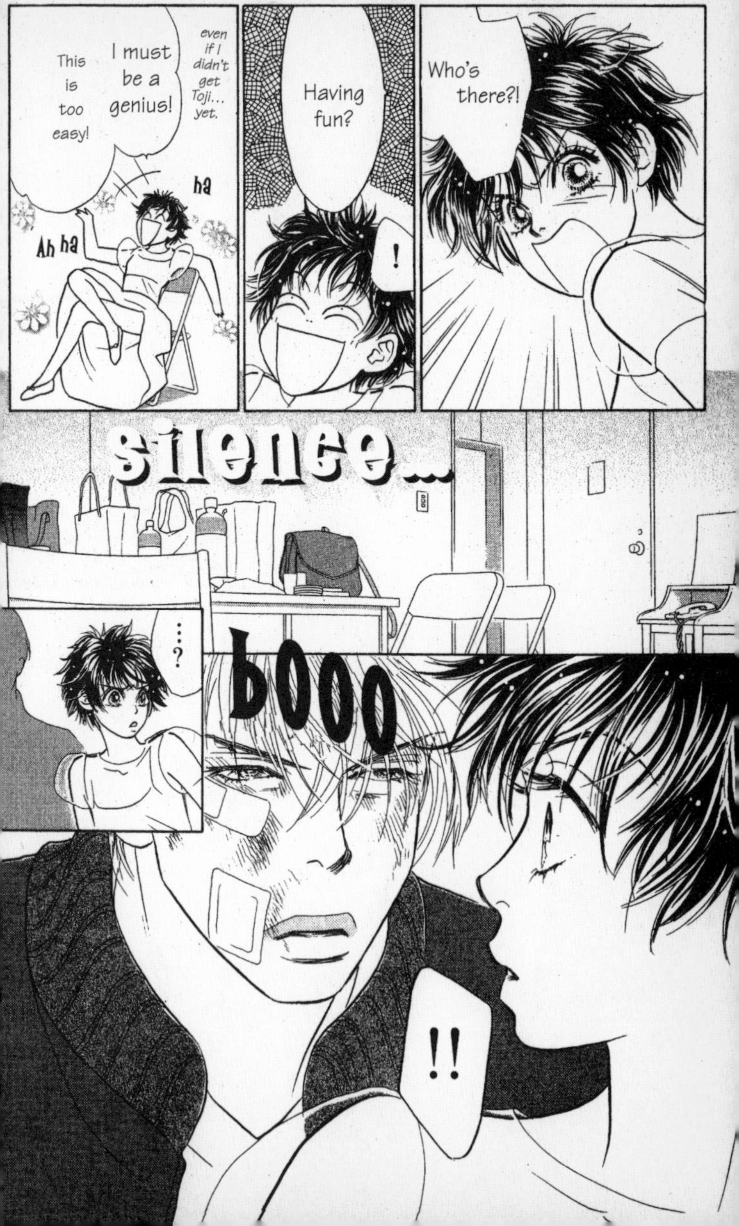
This is too easy!
I must be a genius!
even if I didn't get Toji... yet.
Ah ha
ha
Having fun?
!
Who's there?!
silence...
...?
booo
!!

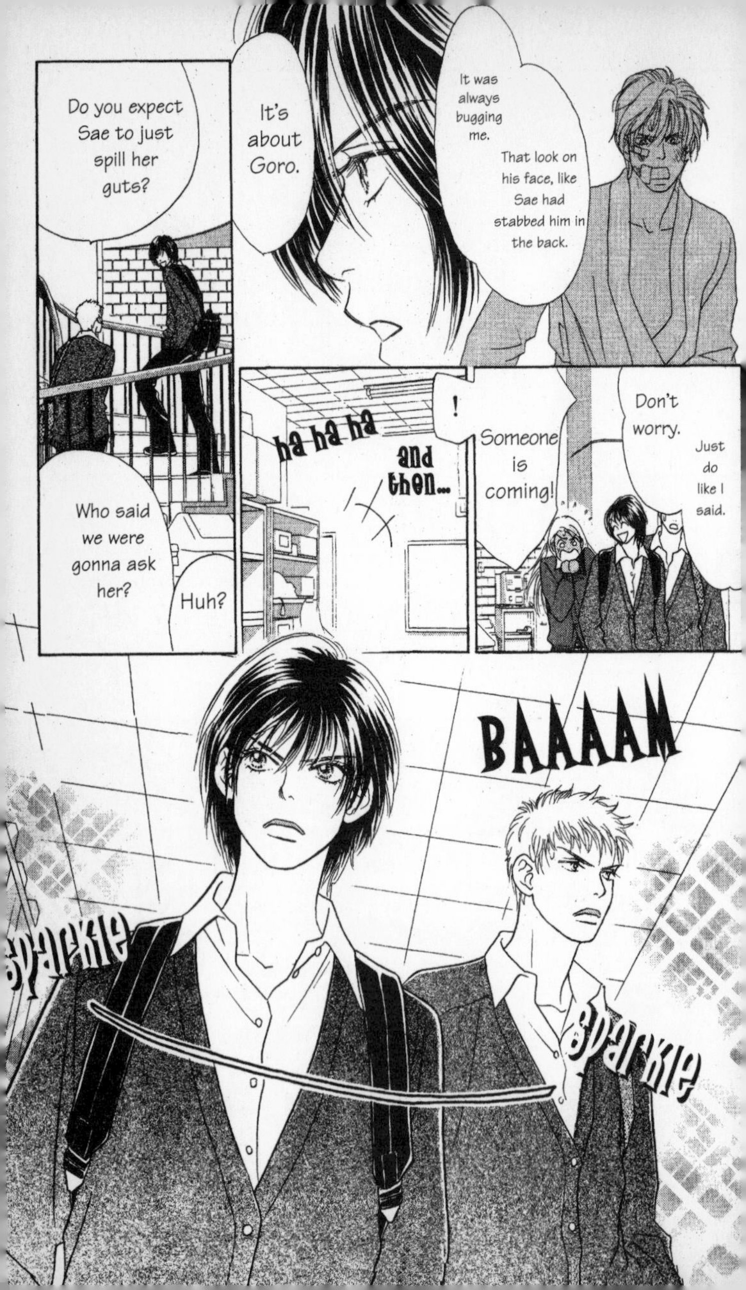
Do you expect Sae to just spill her guts?
Who said we were gonna ask her?
Huh?
It's about Goro.
It was always bugging me.
That look on his face, like Sae had stabbed him in the back.
ha ha ha
and then...
!
Someone is coming!
Don't worry.
Just do like I said.
BAAAAM
sparkle
sparkle

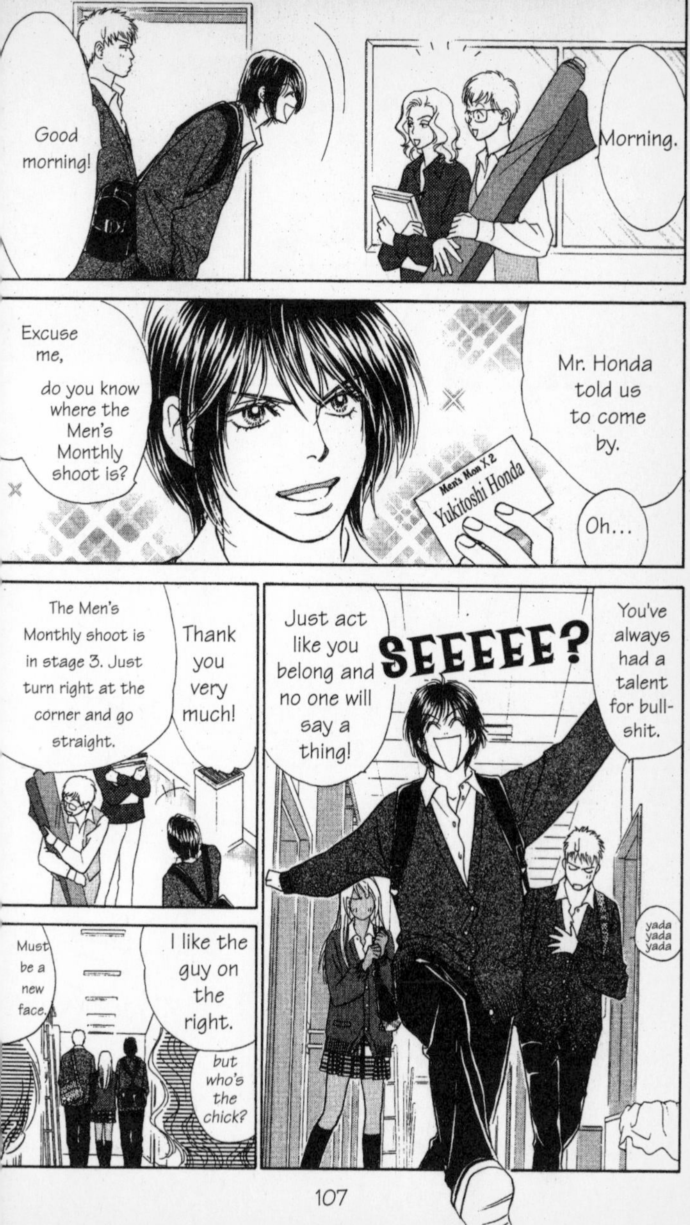
Good morning!
Morning.
Excuse me,
do you know where the Men's Monthly shoot is?
Mr. Honda told us to come by.
Men's Mon X 2
Yukitoshi Honda
Oh...
The Men's Monthly shoot is in stage 3. Just turn right at the corner and go straight.
Thank you very much!
Just act like you belong and no one will say a thing!
SEEEEEE?
You've always had a talent for bull-shit.
yada yada yada
Must be a new face.
I like the guy on the right.
but who's the chick?

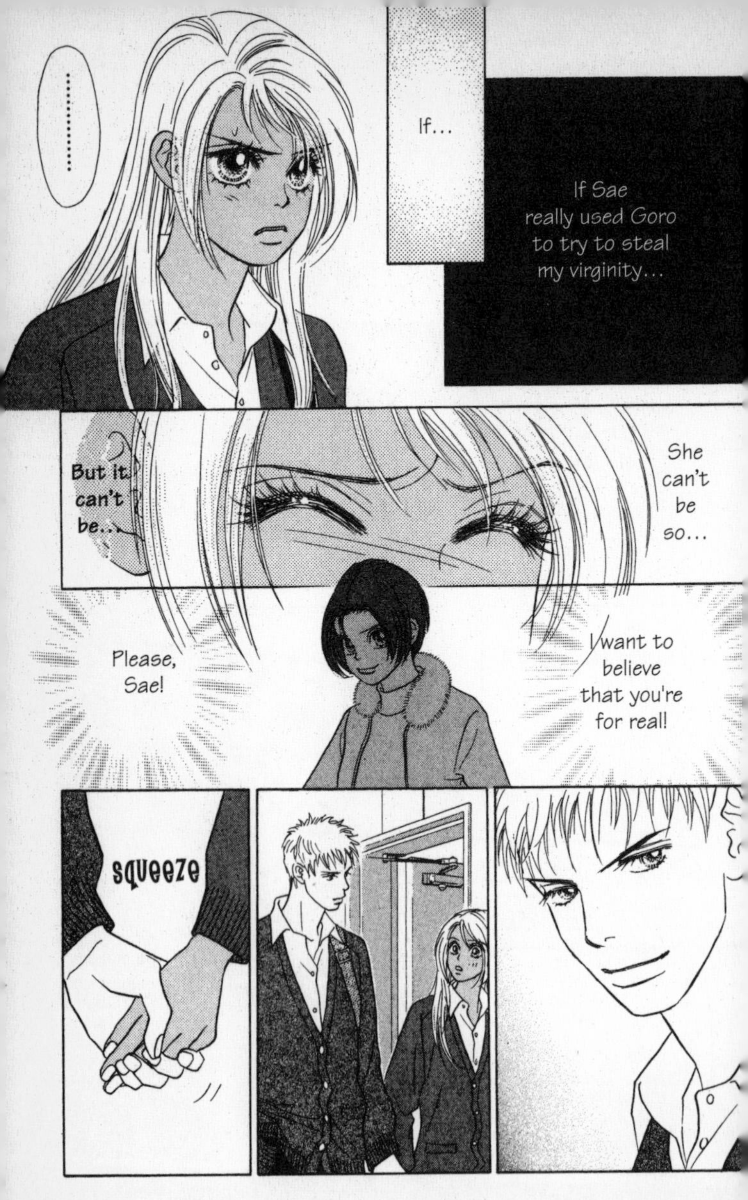

……
If…
If Sae really used Goro to try to steal my virginity…
But it can't be…
She can't be so…
Please, Sae!
I want to believe that you're for real!
squeeze

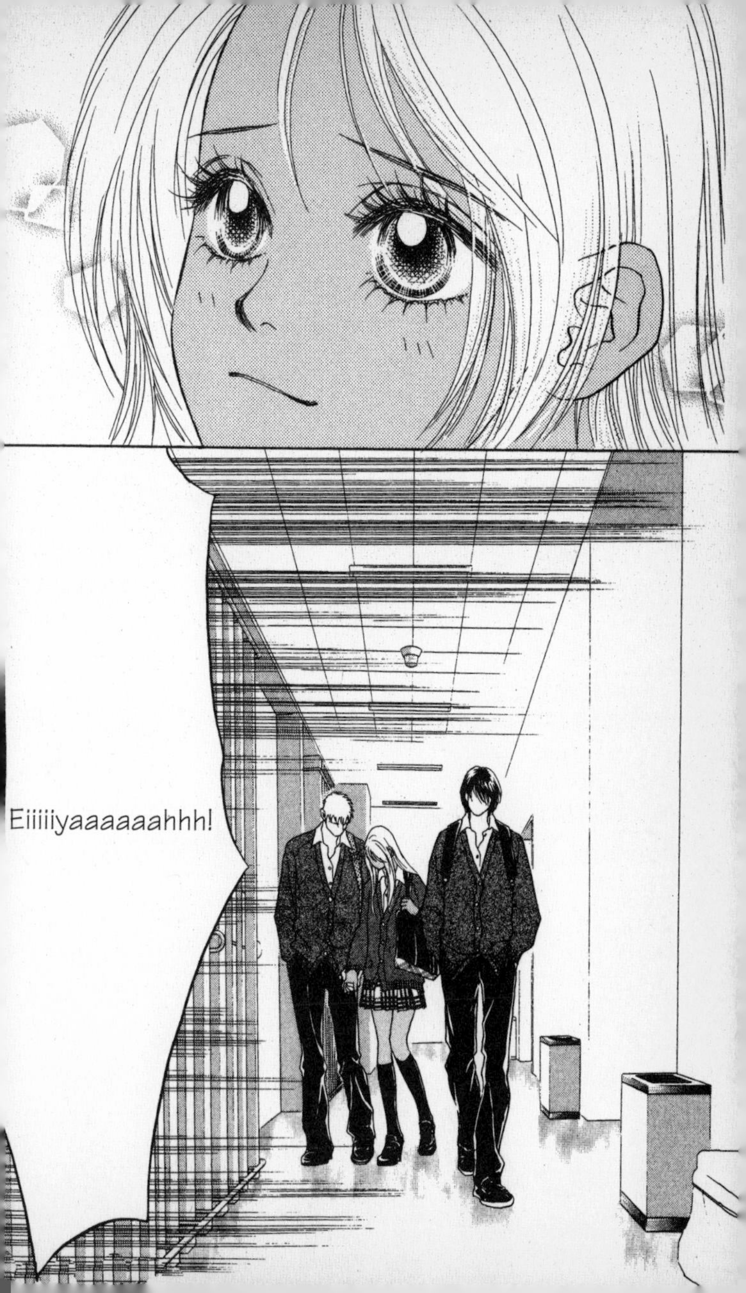
Eiiiiiyaaaaaaahhh!

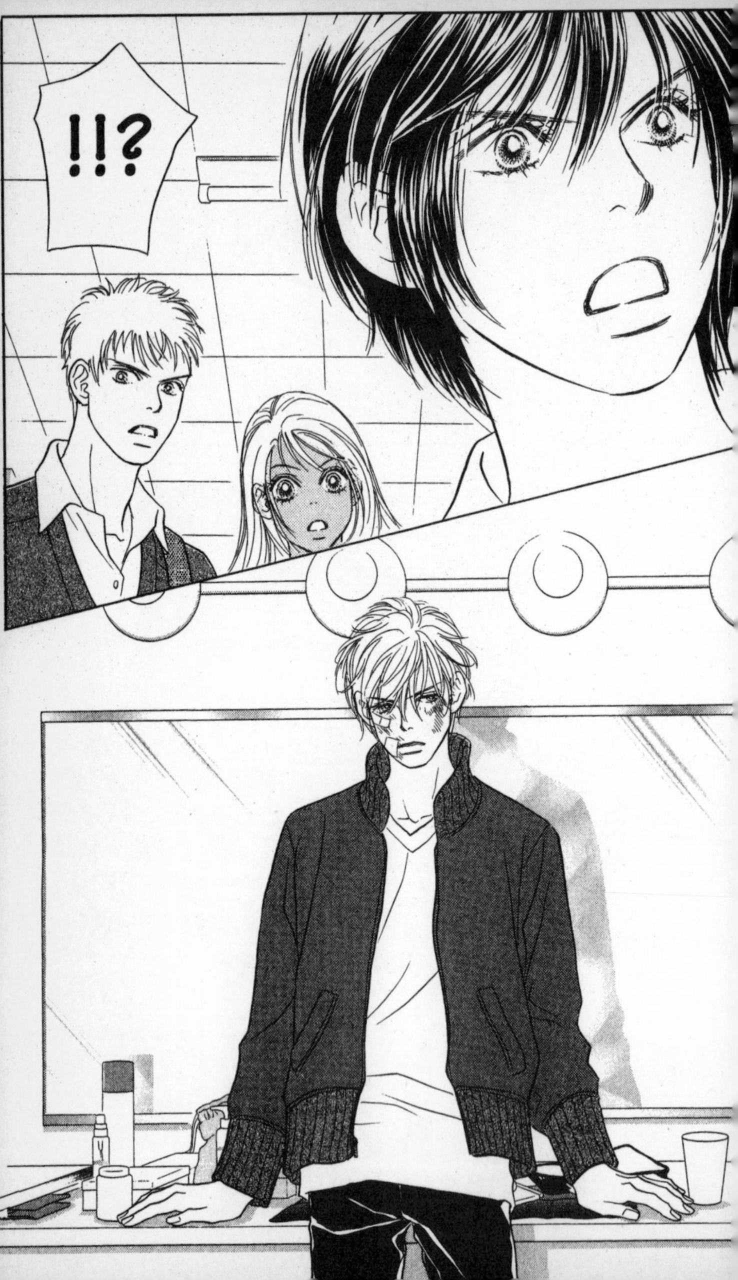
!!?

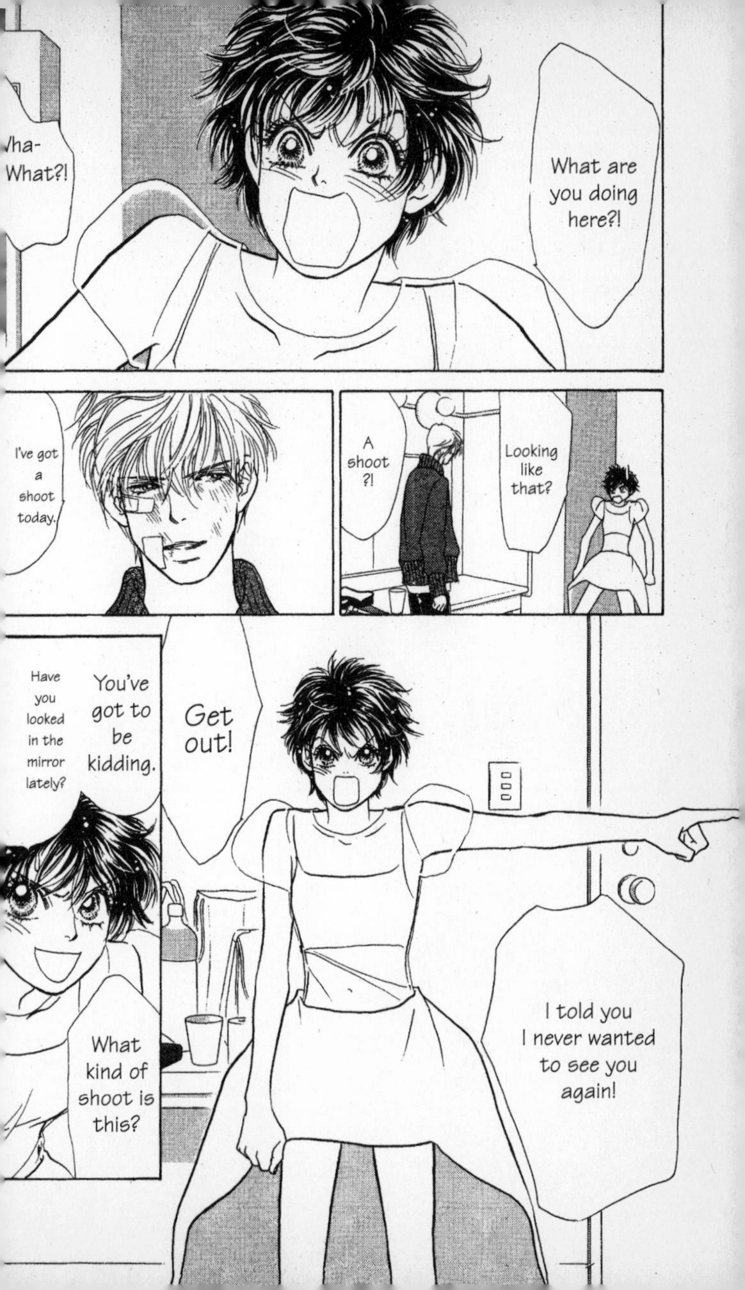

ha- What?!
What are you doing here?!
I've got a shoot today.
A shoot ?!
Looking like that?
Have you looked in the mirror lately?
You've got to be kidding.
What kind of shoot is this?
Get out!
I told you I never wanted to see you again!

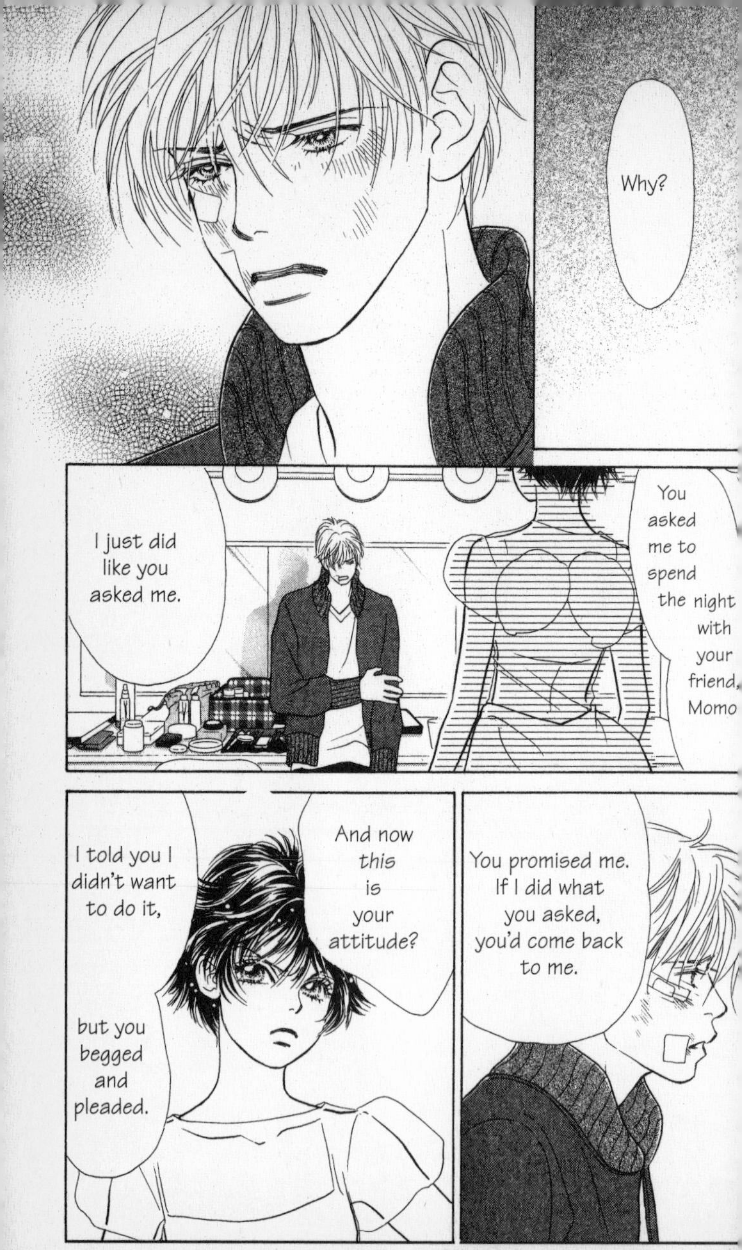
Why?
I just did like you asked me.
You asked me to spend the night with your friend, Momo
I told you I didn't want to do it,
but you begged and pleaded.
And now this is your attitude?
You promised me. If I did what you asked, you'd come back to me.

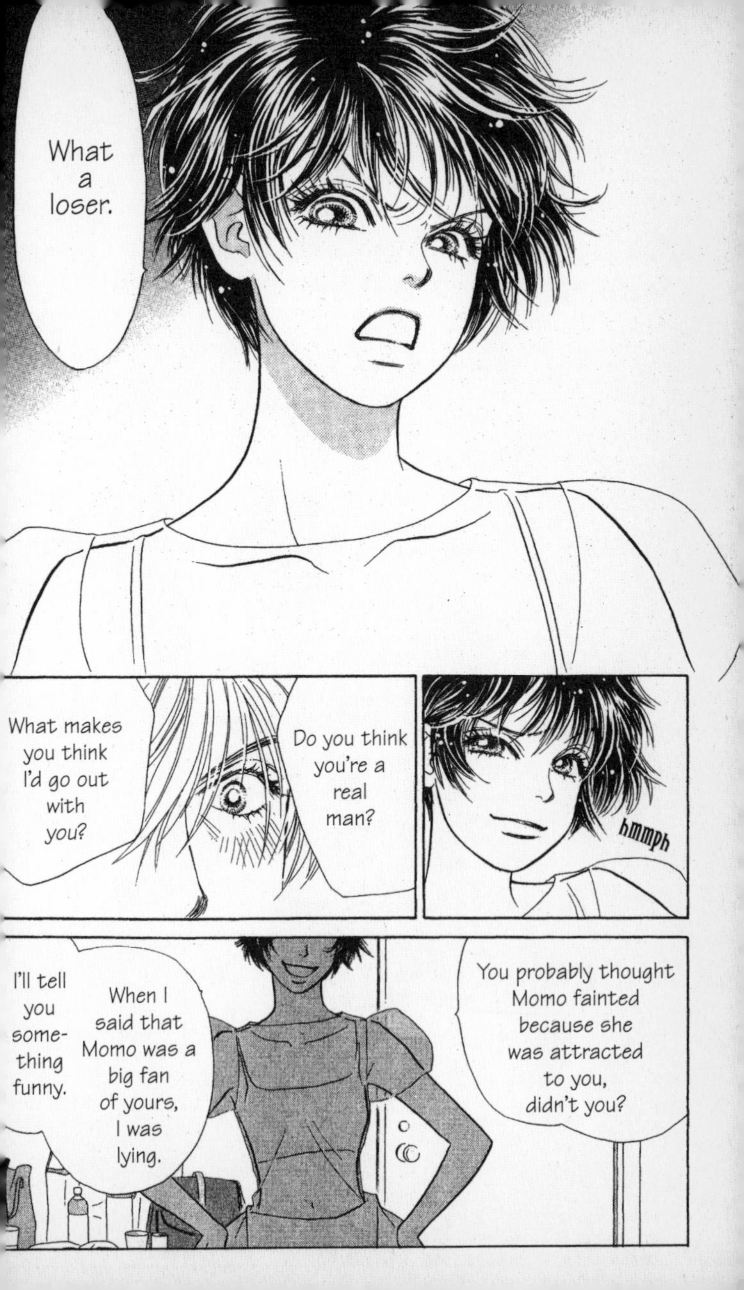
What a loser.
What makes you think I'd go out with you?
Do you think you're a real man?
hmmph
I'll tell you some-thing funny.
When I said that Momo was a big fan of yours, I was lying.
You probably thought Momo fainted because she was attracted to you, didn't you?

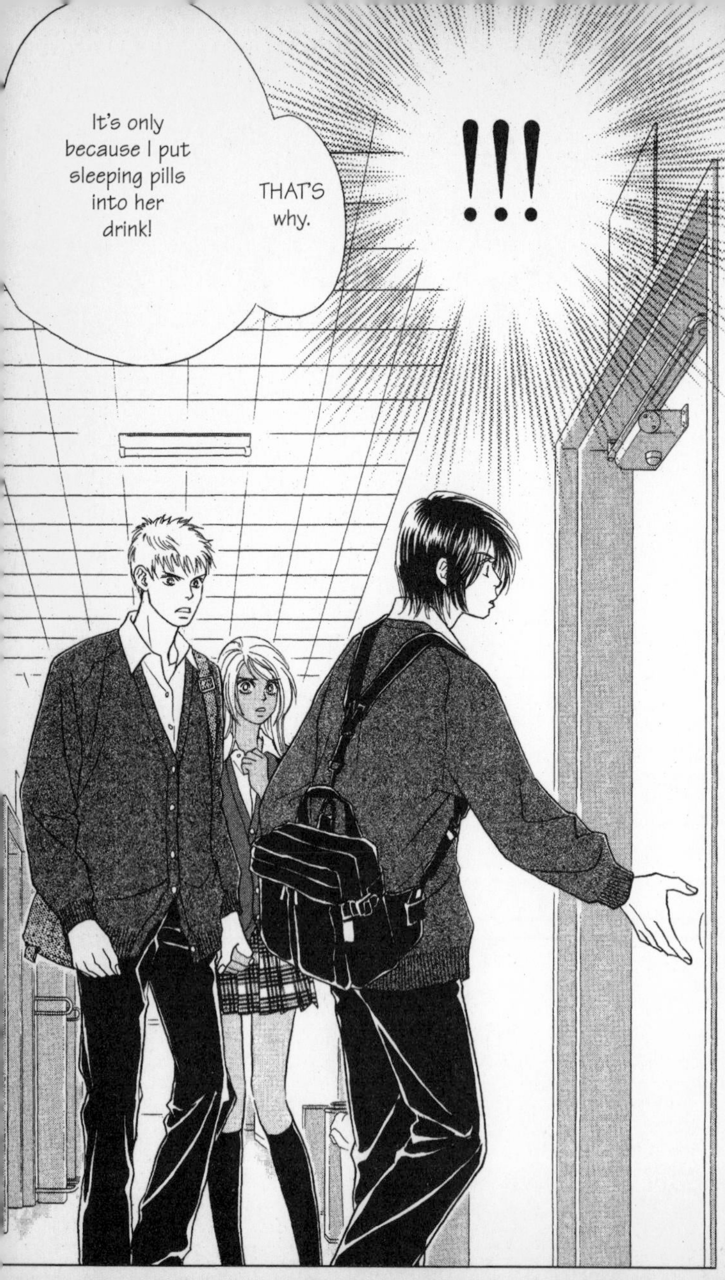
It's only because I put sleeping pills into her drink!
THAT'S why.
!!!

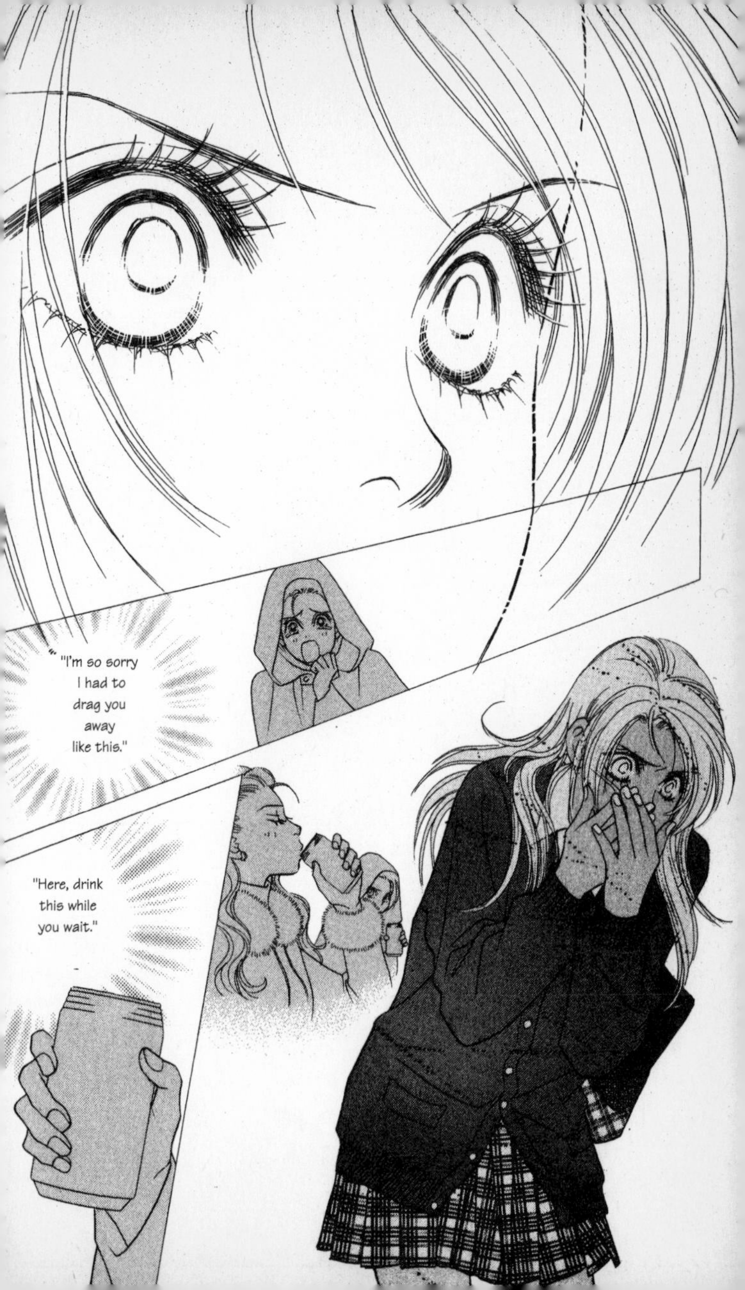
"I'm so sorry I had to drag you away like this."
"Here, drink this while you wait."

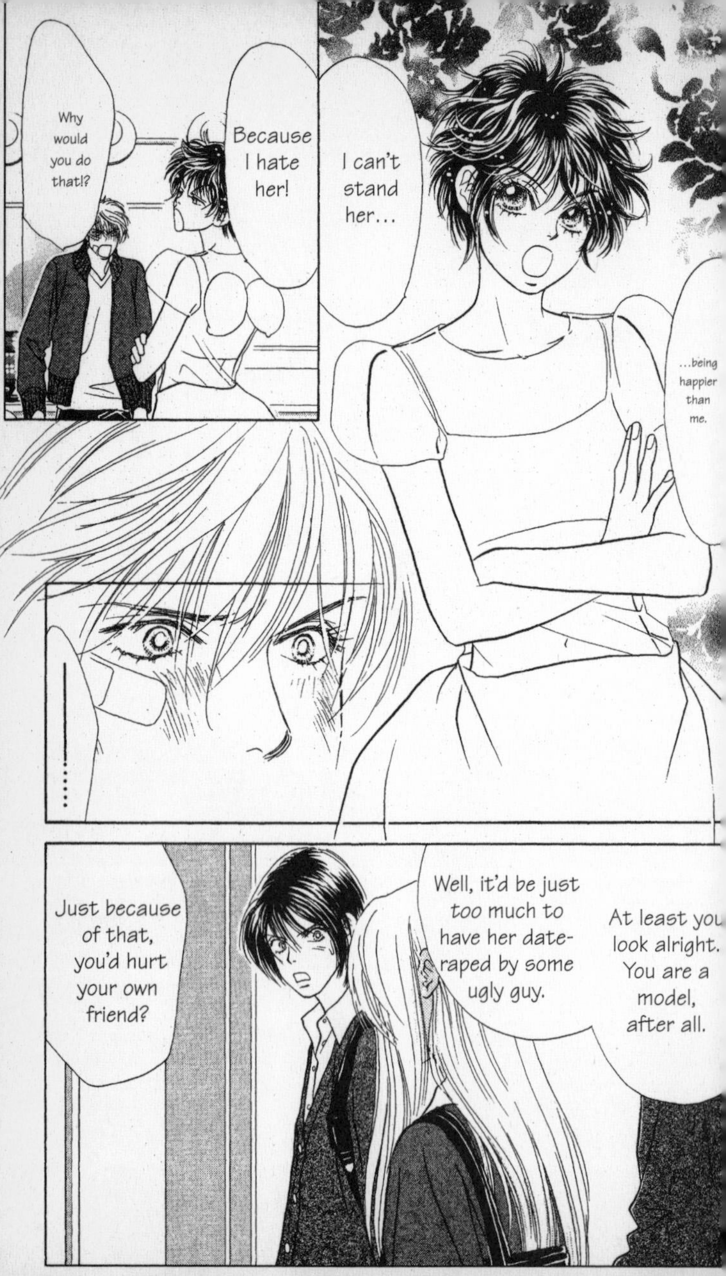
Why would you do that!?
Because I hate her!
I can't stand her...
...being happier than me.
......
Just because of that, you'd hurt your own friend?
Well, it'd be just too much to have her date-raped by some ugly guy.
At least you look alright. You are a model, after all.

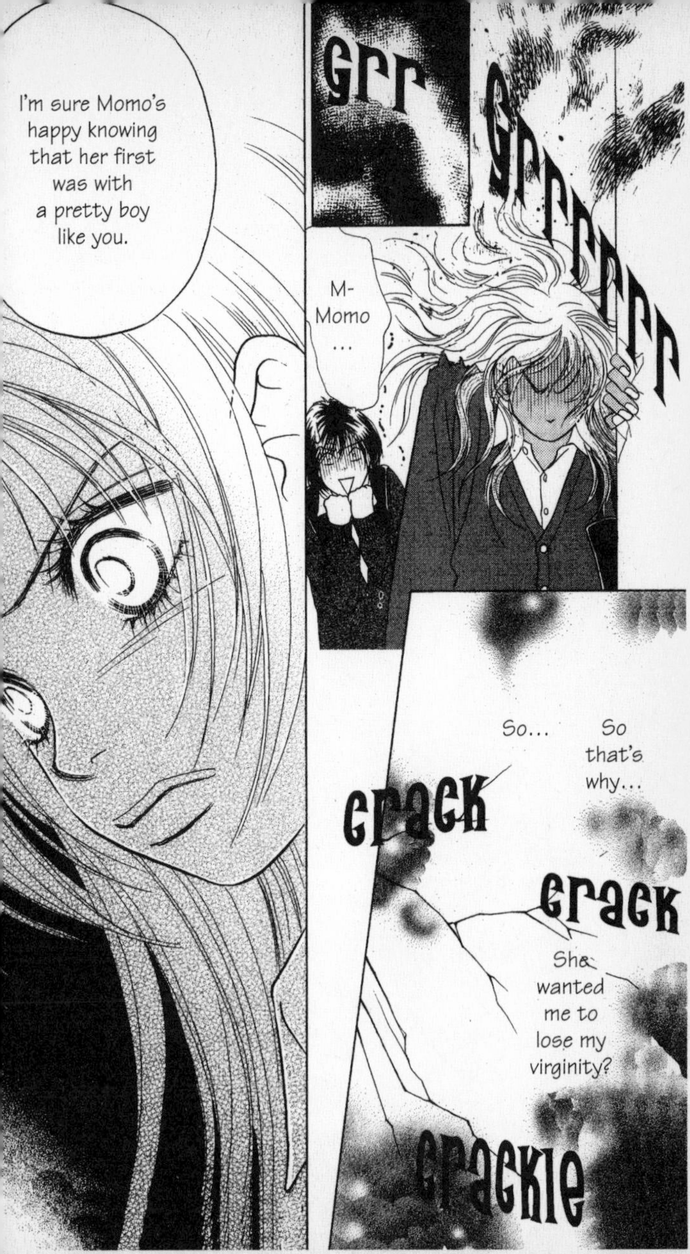
I'm sure Momo's happy knowing that her first was with a pretty boy like you.
Grr
Grrrrrrr
M-Momo ...
Crack
So... So that's why...
Crack
She wanted me to lose my virginity?
Crackle

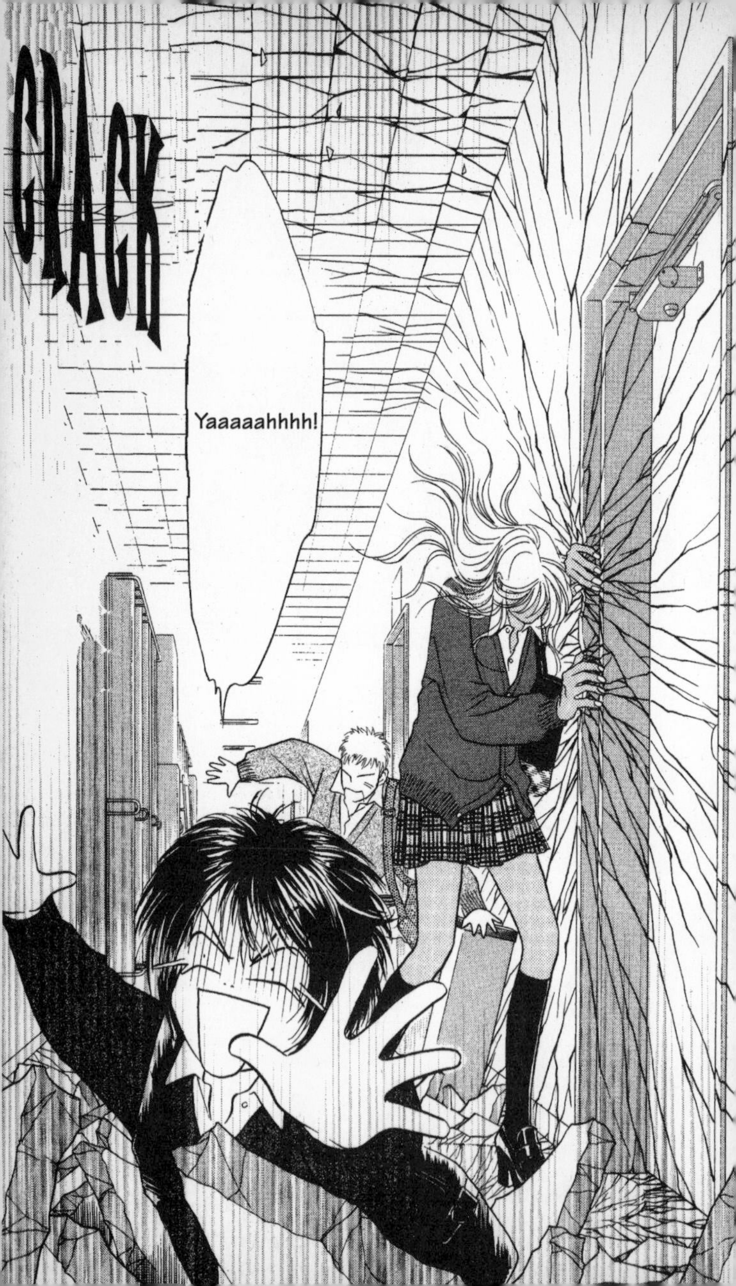
CRACK
Yaaaaahhhh!

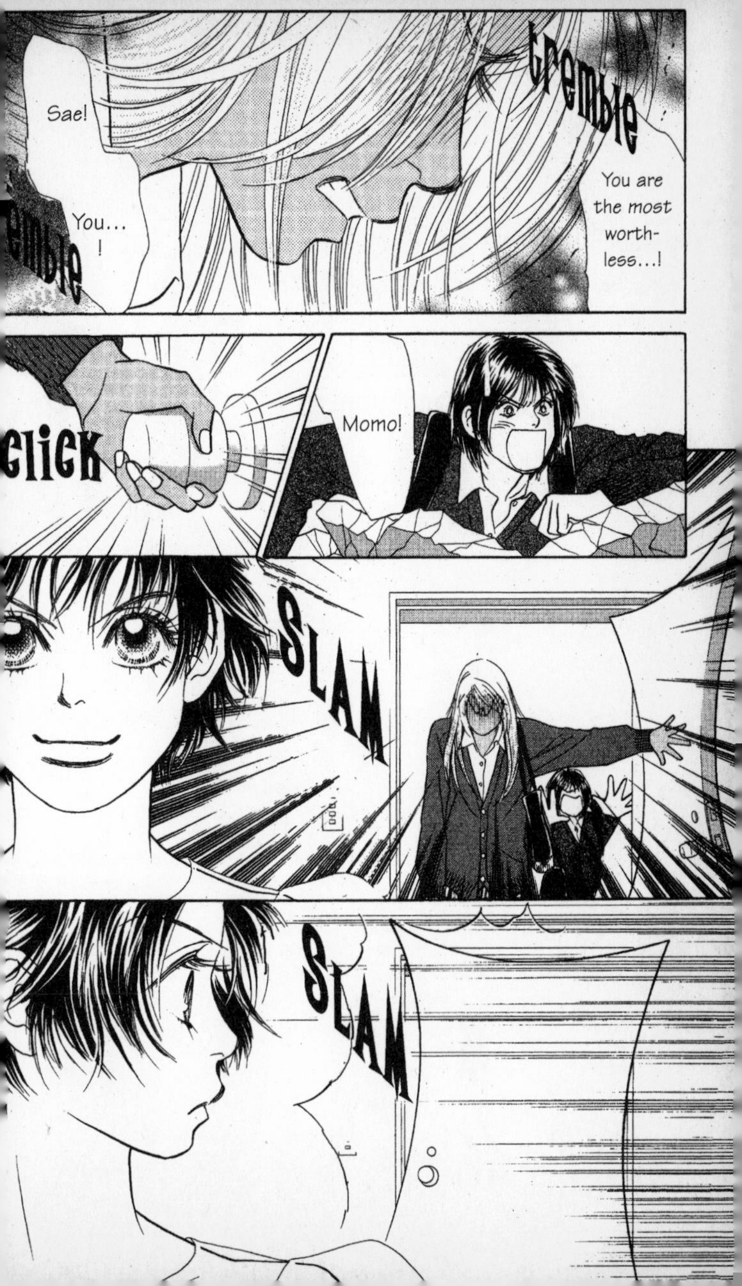

Sae!
You… !
tremble
tremble
You are the most worth-less…!
CLICK
Momo!
SLAM
SLAM

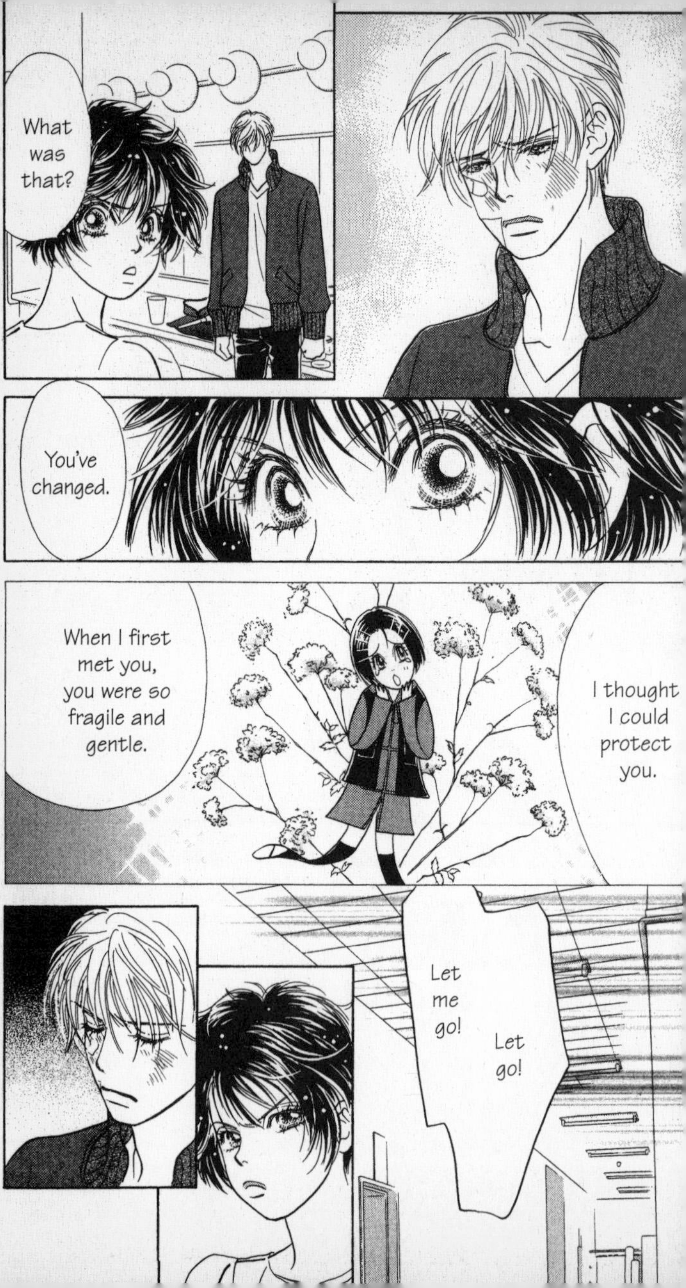
What was that?
You've changed.
When I first met you, you were so fragile and gentle.
I thought I could protect you.
Let me go!
Let go!

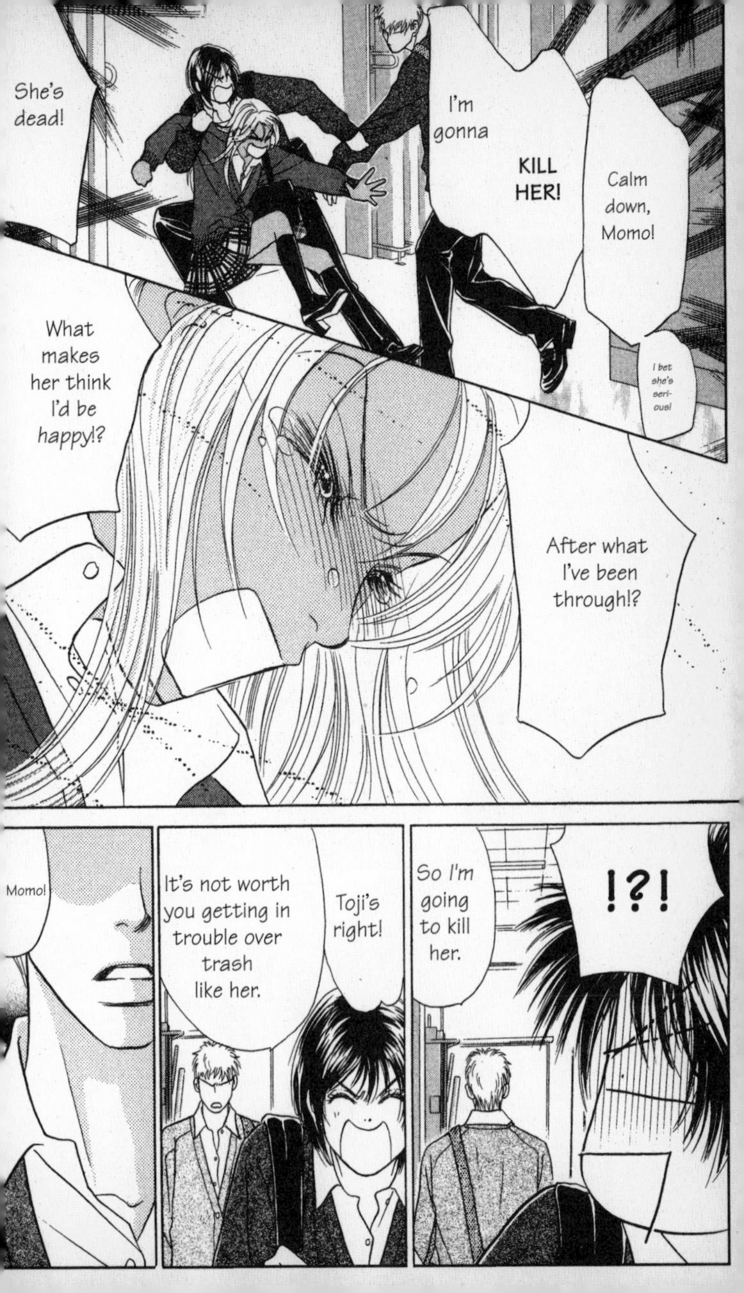
She's dead!
I'm gonna KILL HER!
Calm down, Momo!
I bet she's seri-ous!
What makes her think I'd be happy!?
After what I've been through!?
Momo!
It's not worth you getting in trouble over trash like her.
Toji's right!
So I'm going to kill her.
!?!

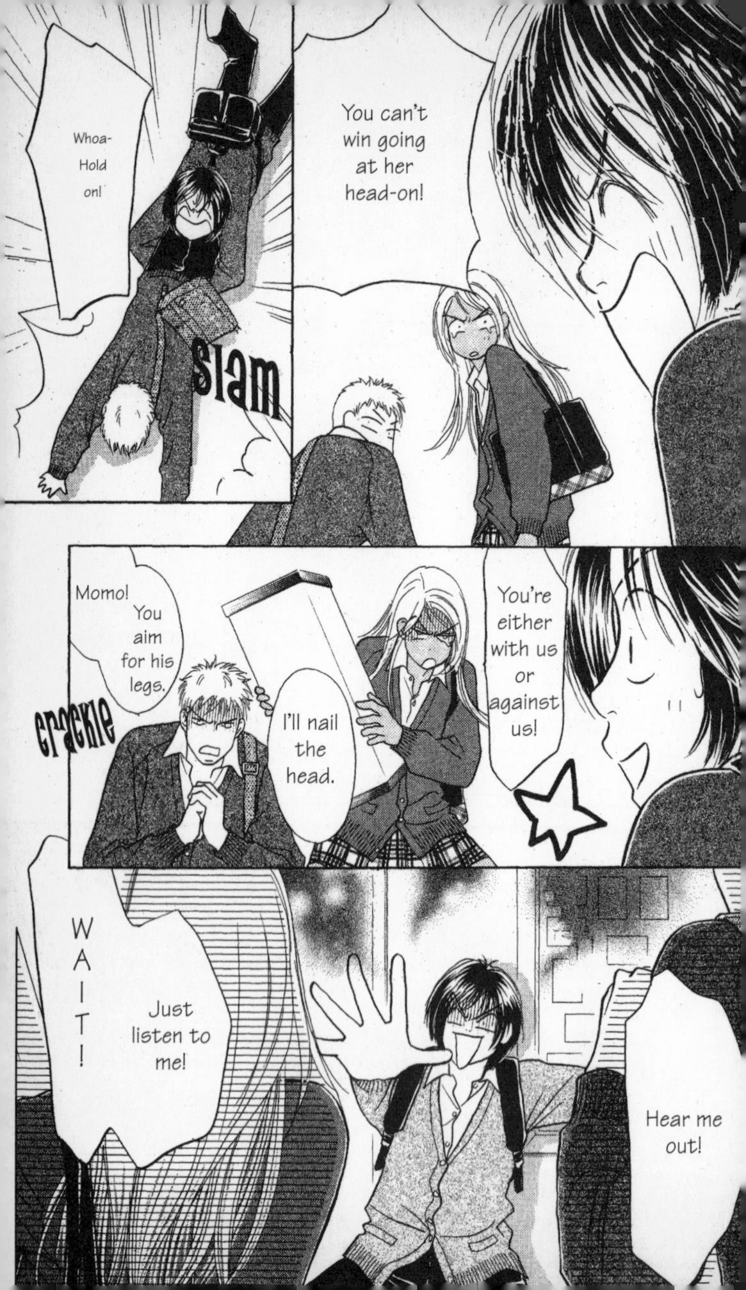

Whoa- Hold on!
slam
You can't win going at her head-on!
Momo! You aim for his legs.
crackle
I'll nail the head.
You're either with us or against us!
WAIT!
Just listen to me!
Hear me out!

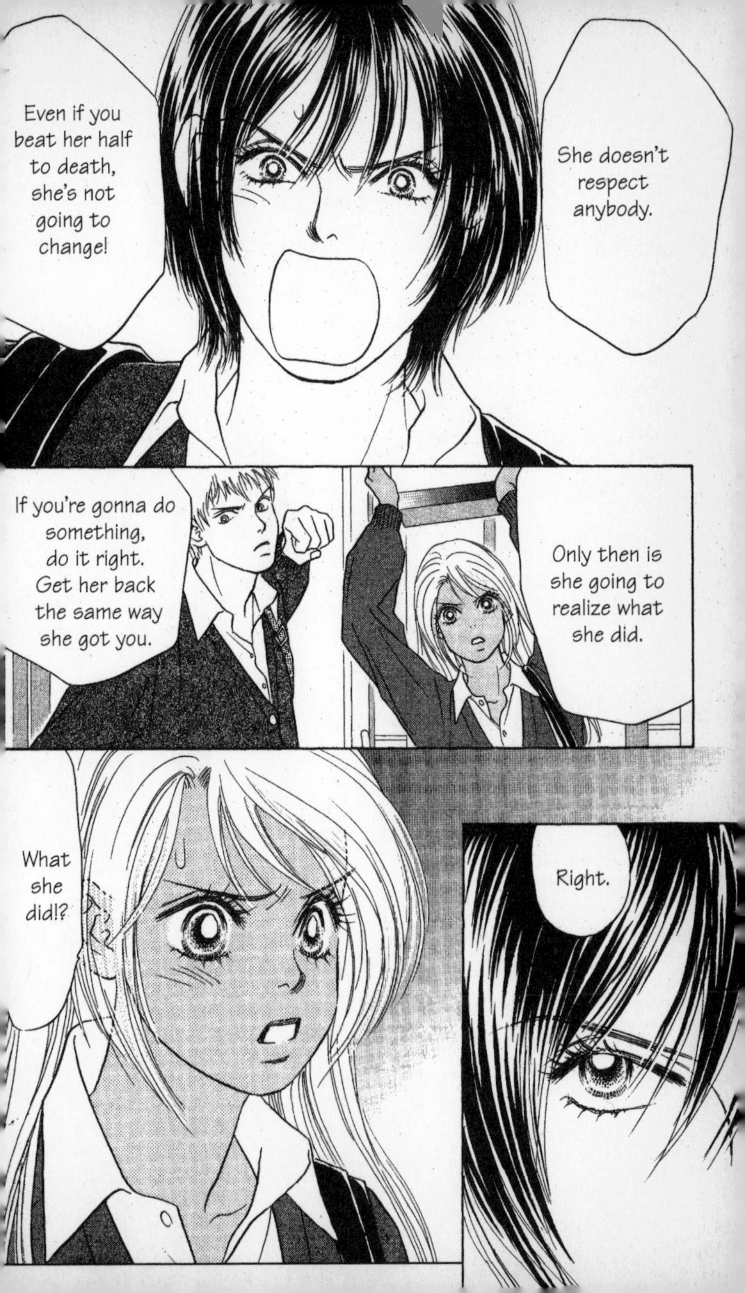
Even if you beat her half to death, she's not going to change!
She doesn't respect anybody.
If you're gonna do something, do it right. Get her back the same way she got you.
Only then is she going to realize what she did.
What she did!?
Right.

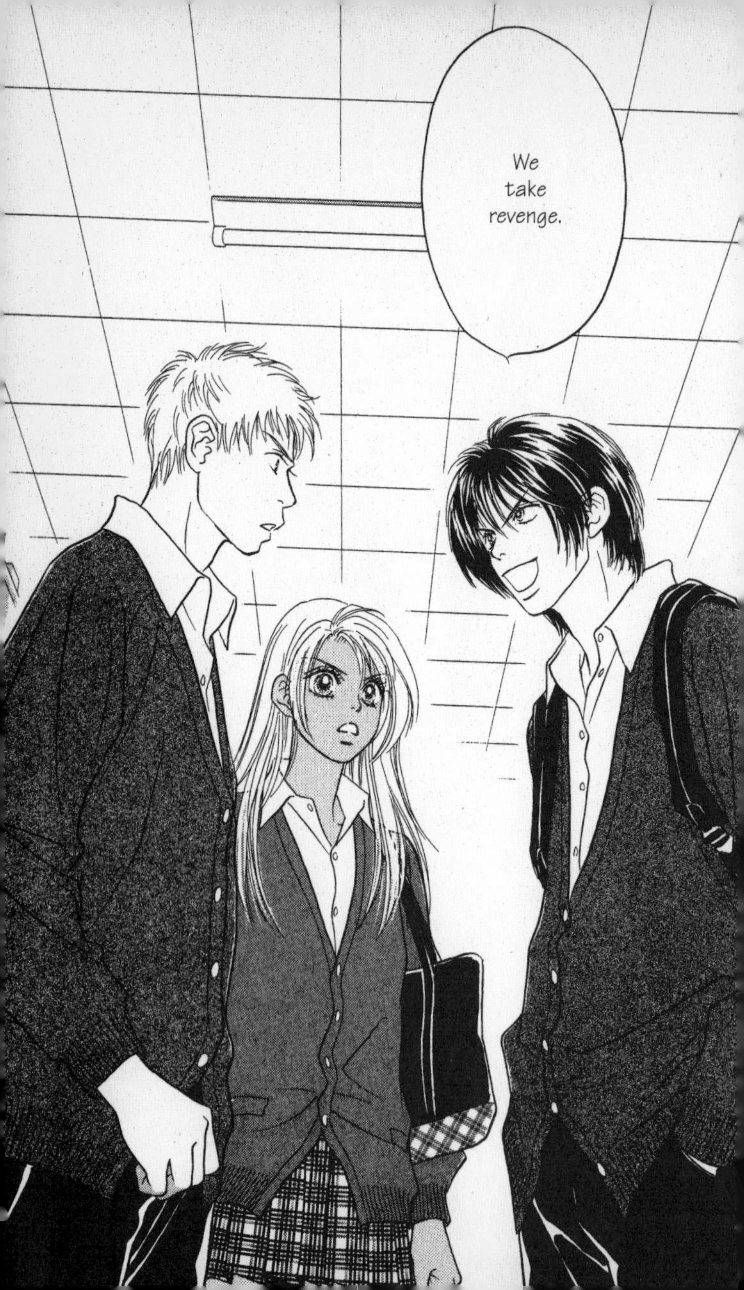
We take revenge.

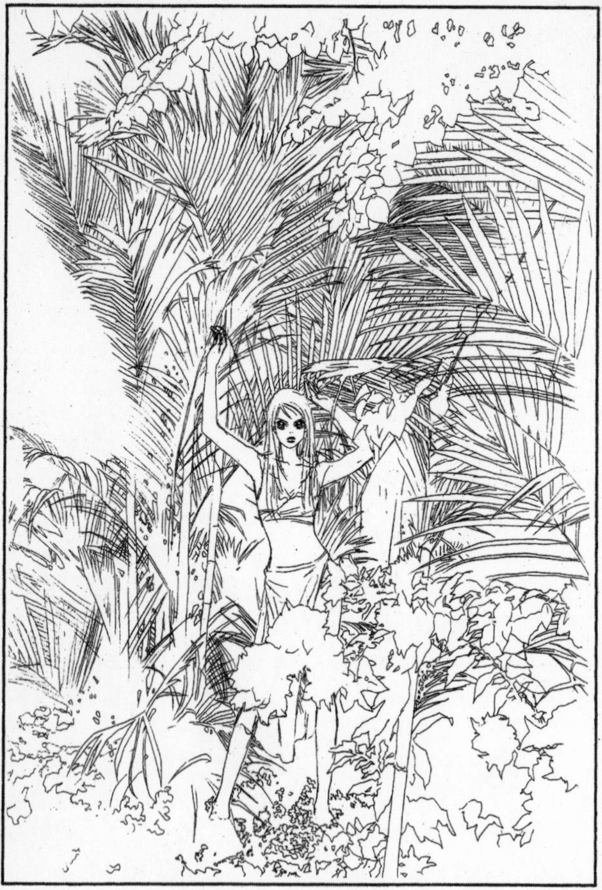

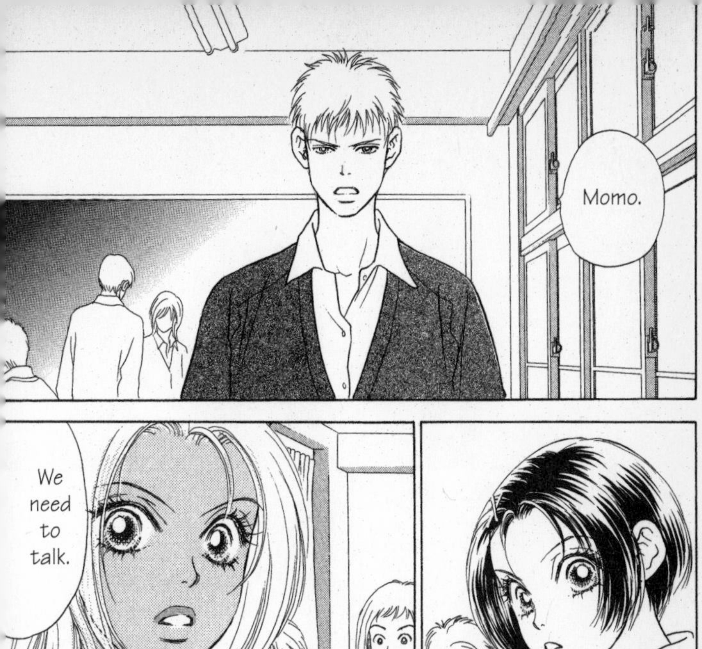
Momo.
We need to talk.

PEACH CLUB

I'd better start off by saying that there are some spoilers in this section. So if you don't want to find out, please stop reading right now.

This time, I think I ventured into some perverse territory. My friends asked me what I was using as research material. Hey, it's not like I'm a closet freak or anything! Well, maybe I sneaked a peek at some American underwear catalogs?! But that's all! The perv in this Book 6 will appear in Book 7, too! At least, he ends up being a crucial character, so I can't help it! Hey, don't look at me like that! Kiley's about to come into his own in upcoming episodes. And I promise to come clean regarding the mystery of Kiley. I'm still the same person, so don't give up on me...and stay tuned!

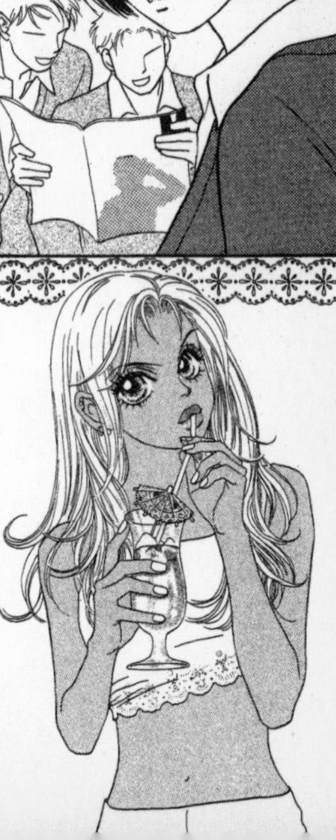

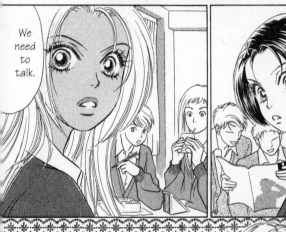

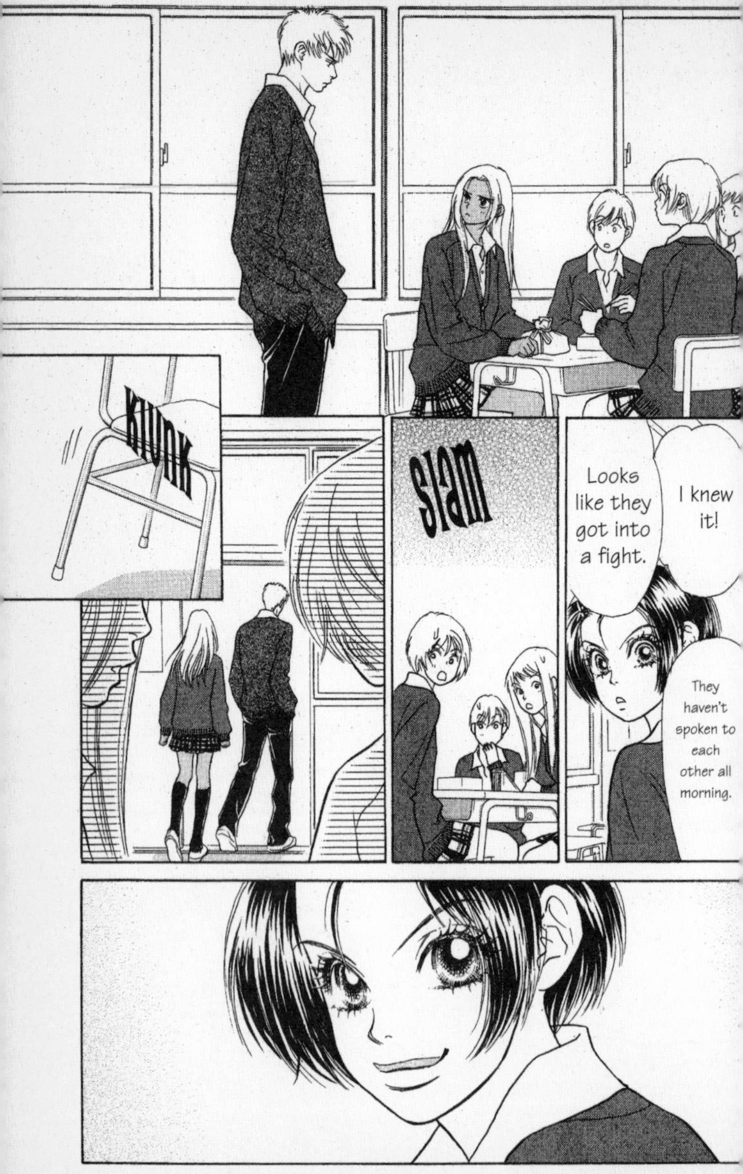
KLUNK
SLAM
Looks like they got into a fight.
I knew it!
They haven't spoken to each other all morning.

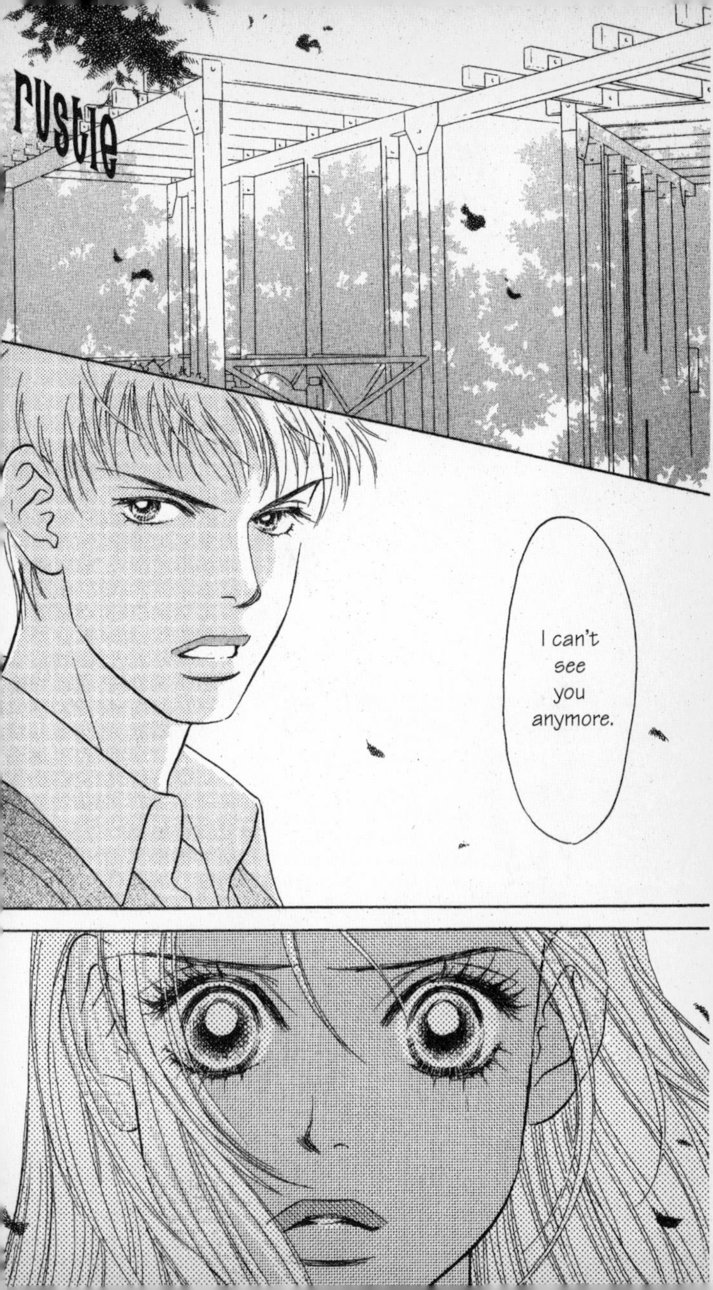
rustle
I can't see you anymore.

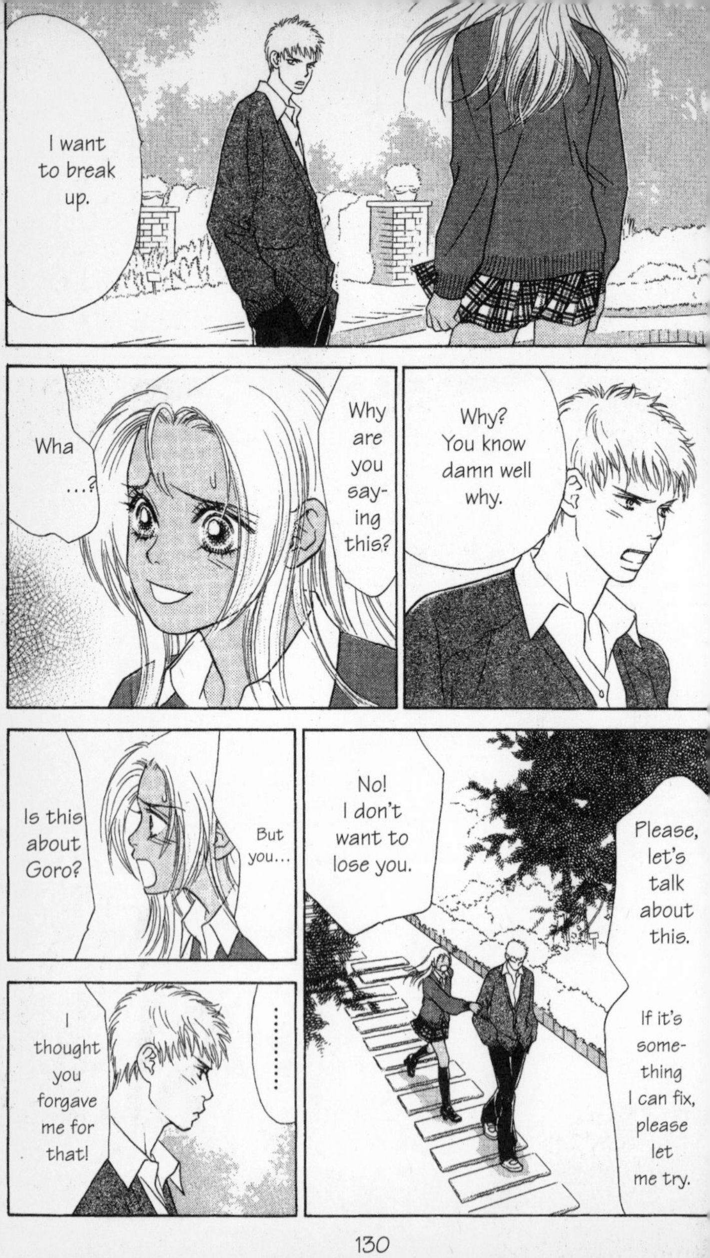
I want to break up.
Wha ...?
Why are you say-ing this?
Why? You know damn well why.
Is this about Goro?
But you...
I thought you forgave me for that!
......
No! I don't want to lose you.
Please, let's talk about this.
If it's some-thing I can fix, please let me try.

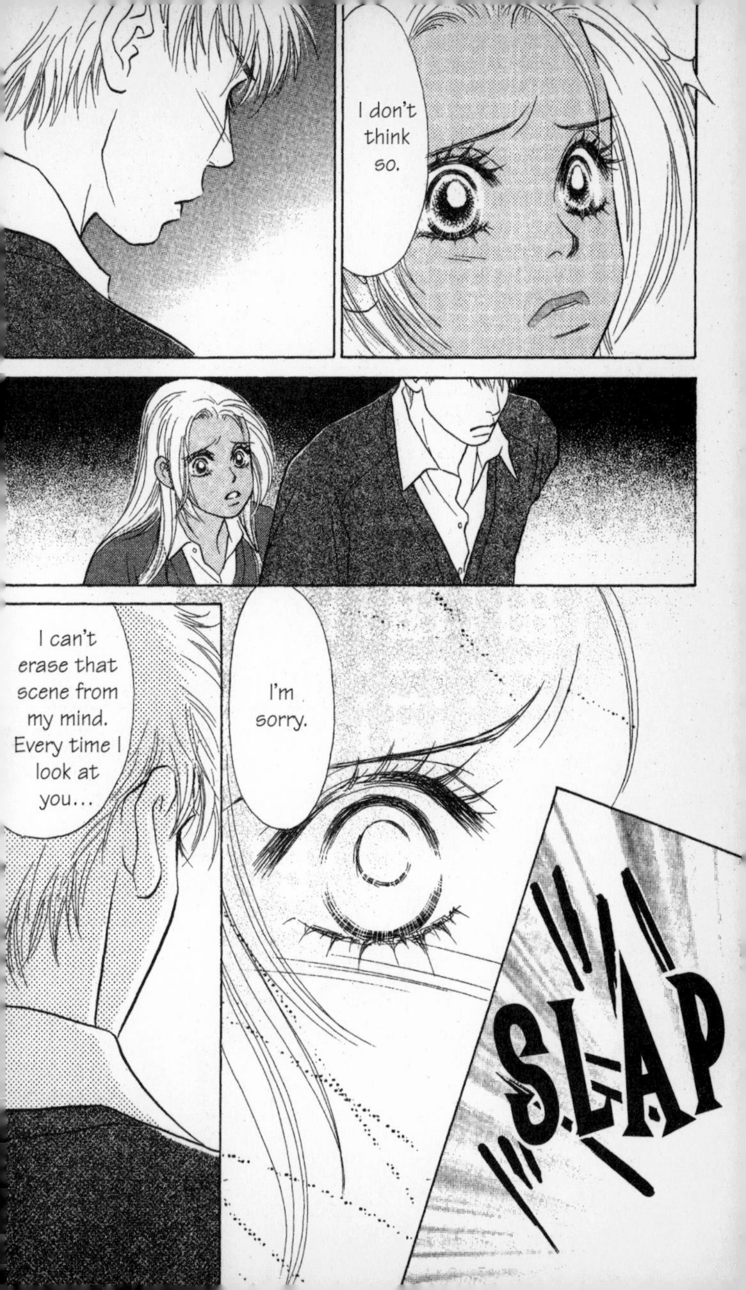
I don't think so.
I can't erase that scene from my mind. Every time I look at you…
I'm sorry.
SLAP

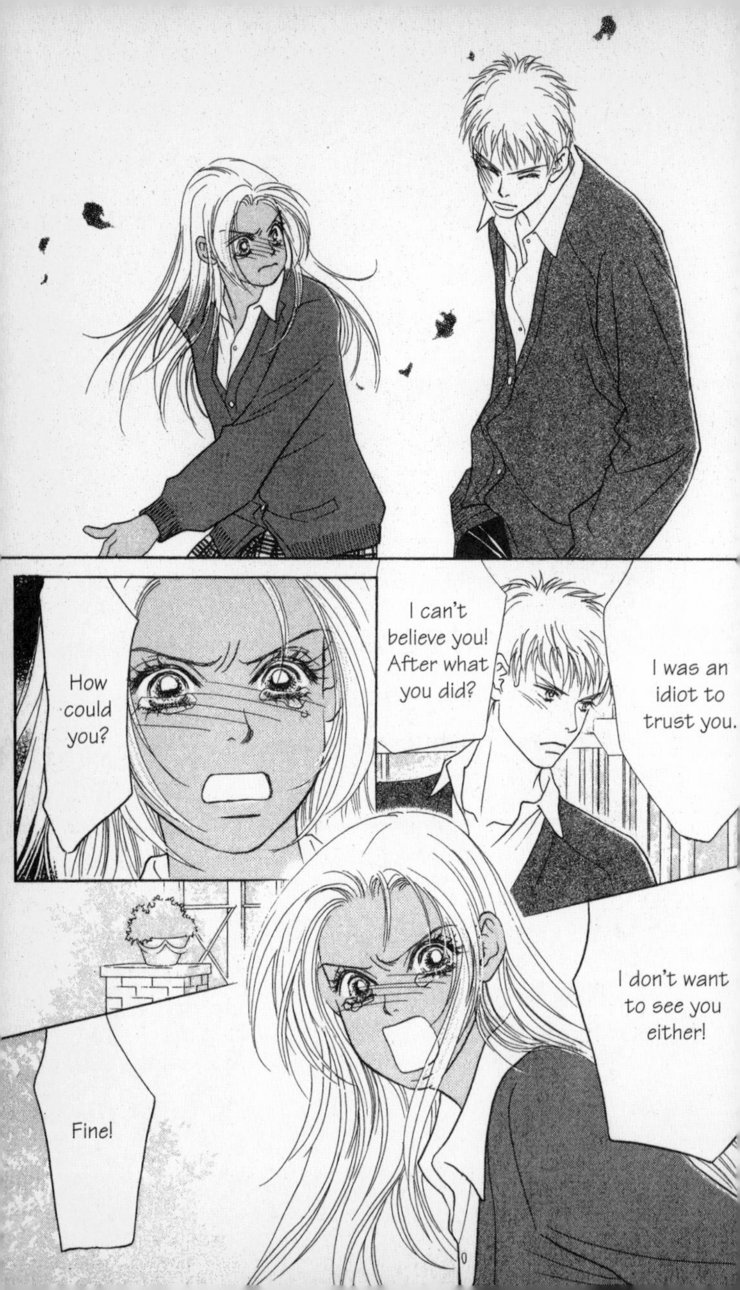
How could you?
I can't believe you! After what you did?
I was an idiot to trust you.
Fine!
I don't want to see you either!

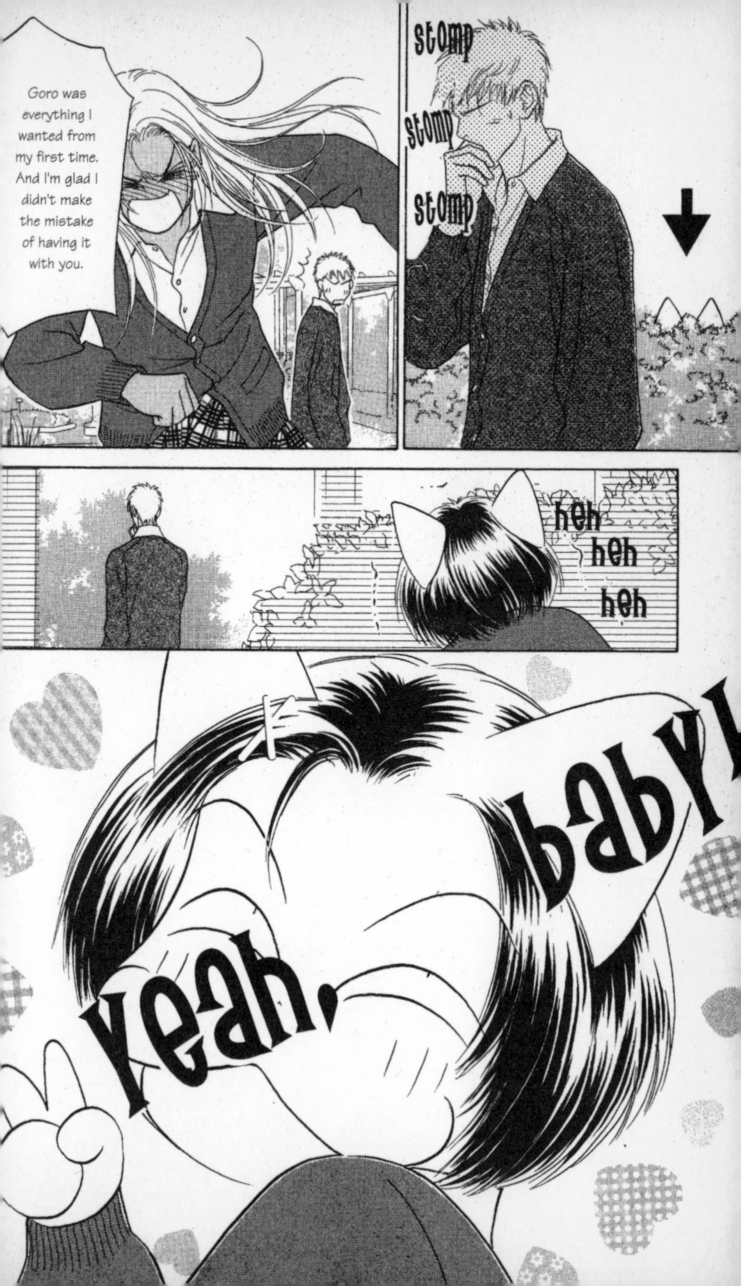

Goro was everything I wanted from my first time. And I'm glad I didn't make the mistake of having it with you.
stomp
stomp
stomp
heh
heh
heh
Yeah, baby!

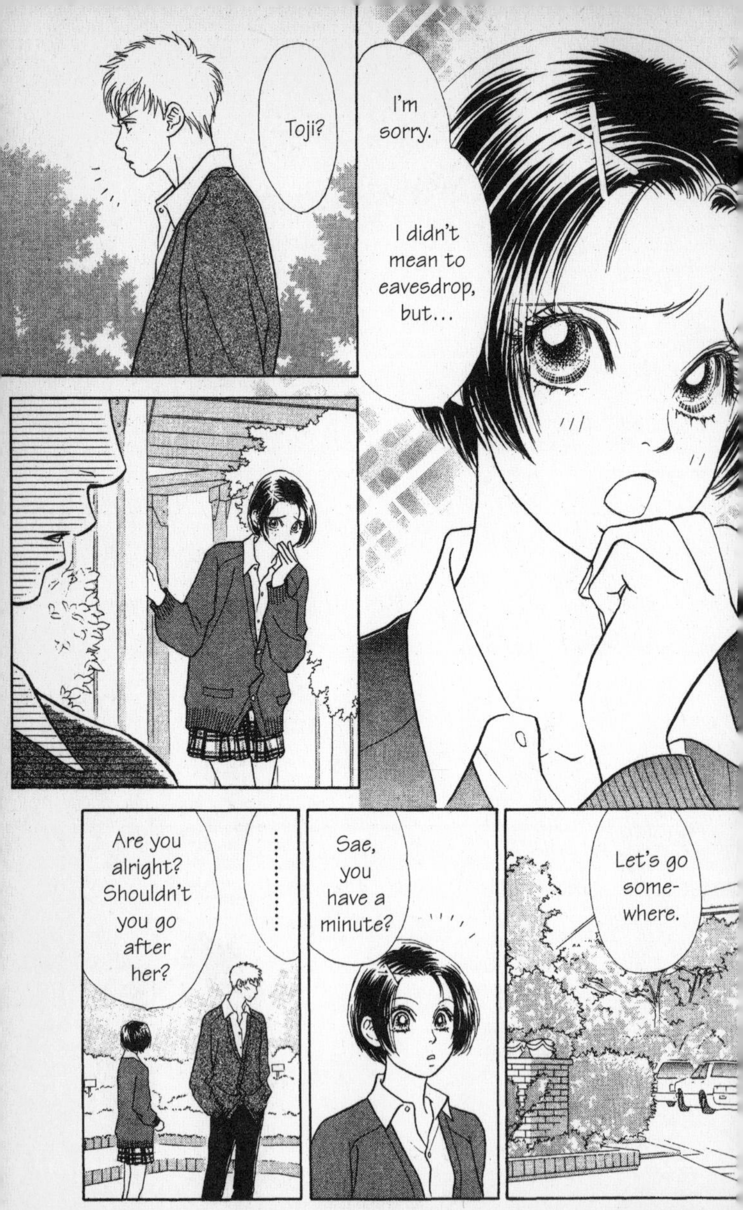
Toji?
I'm sorry.
I didn't mean to eavesdrop, but...
Are you alright? Shouldn't you go after her?
....
Sae, you have a minute?
Let's go some-where.

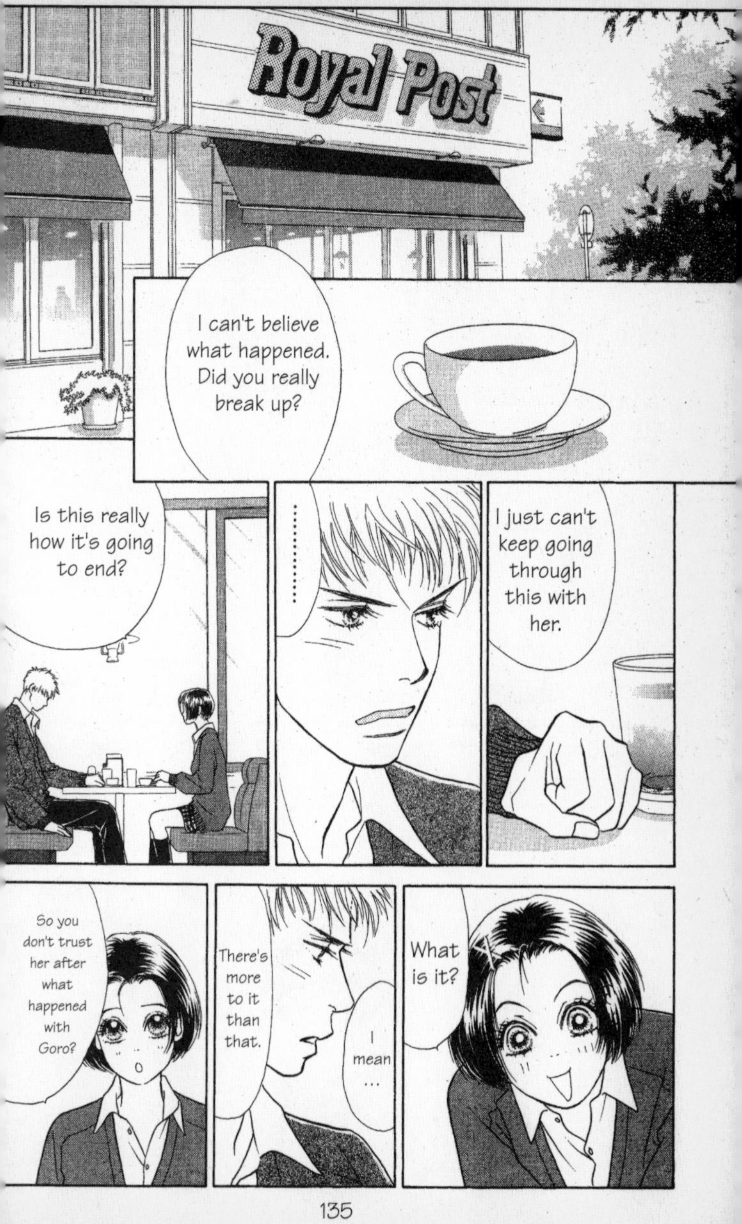
Royal Post
I can't believe what happened. Did you really break up?
Is this really how it's going to end?
....
I just can't keep going through this with her.
So you don't trust her after what happened with Goro?
There's more to it than that.
I mean ...
What is it?

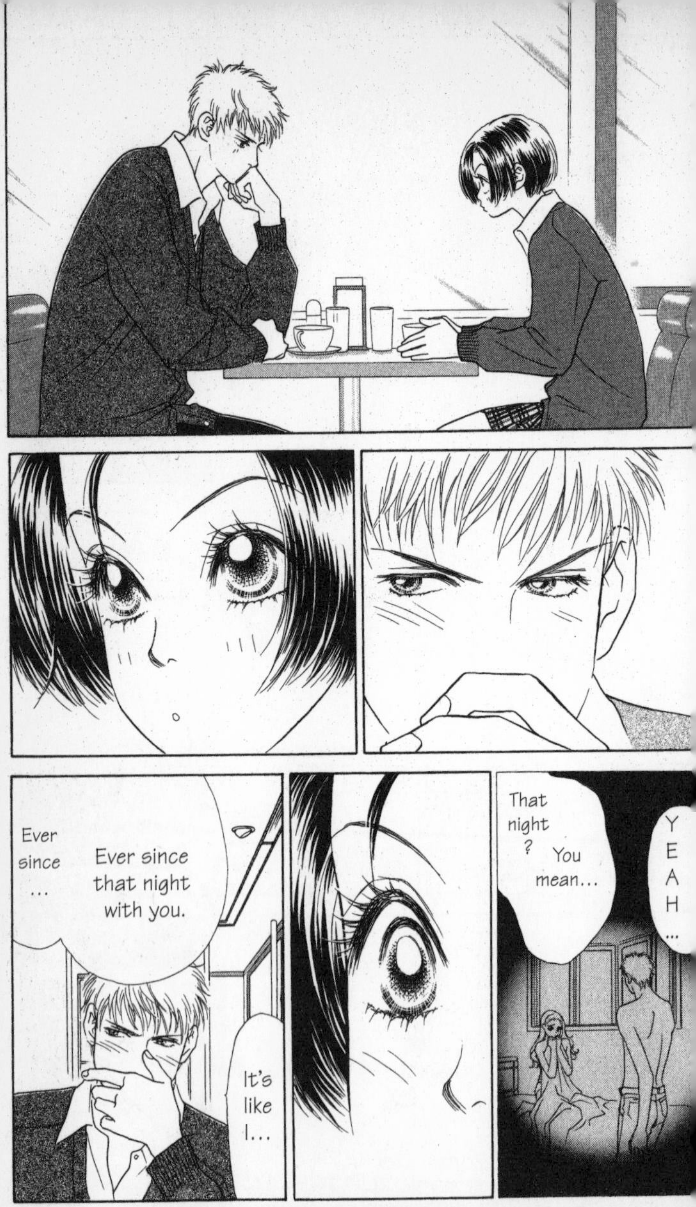
Ever since...
Ever since that night with you.
It's like I...
That night? You mean...
YEAH...

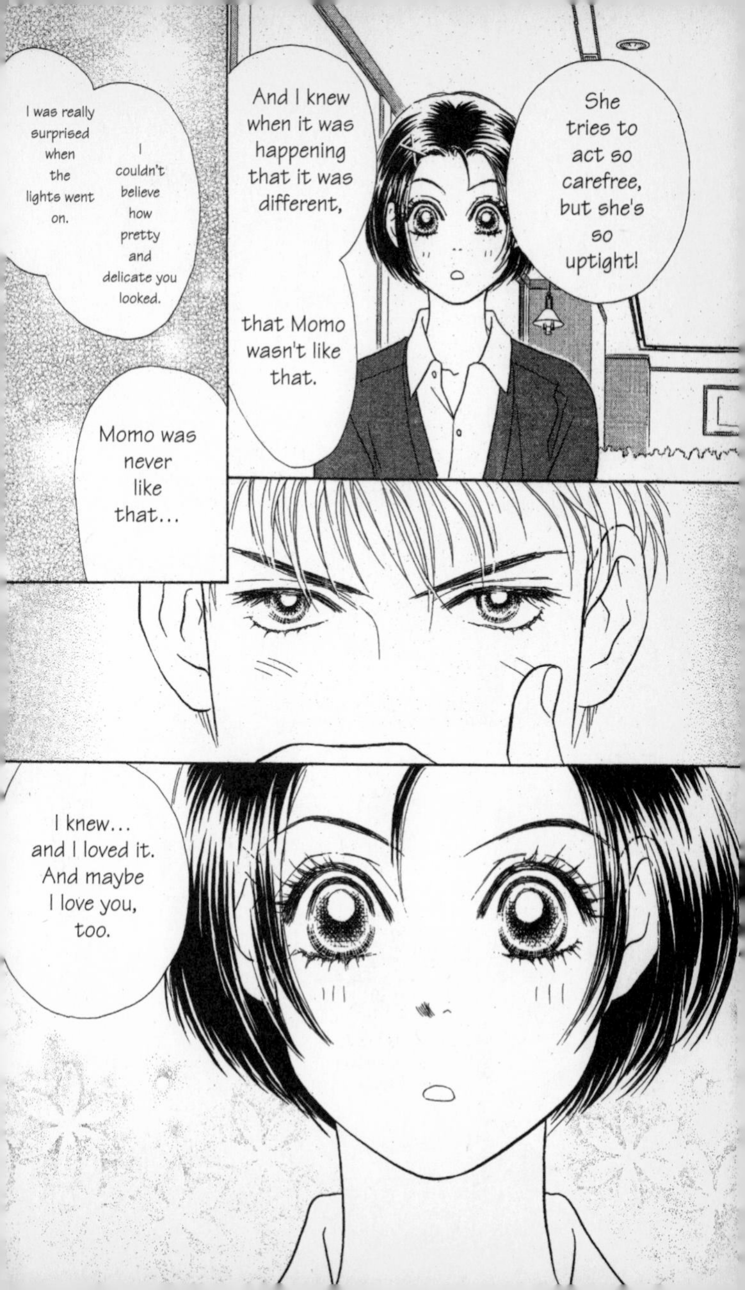
I was really surprised when the lights went on.
I couldn't believe how pretty and delicate you looked.
Momo was never like that...
And I knew when it was happening that it was different,
that Momo wasn't like that.
She tries to act so carefree, but she's so uptight!
I knew... and I loved it. And maybe I love you, too.

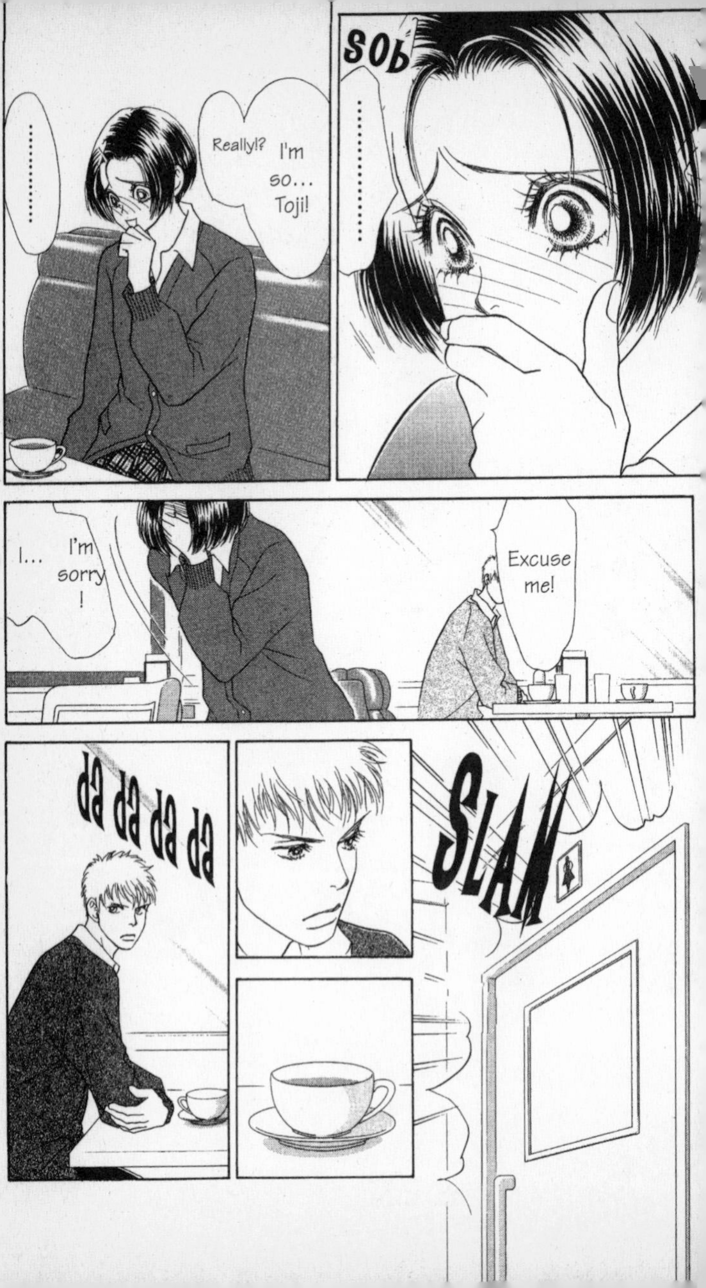
......
Really!? I'm so... Toji!
SOB
......
I... I'm sorry!
Excuse me!
da da da da
SLAM

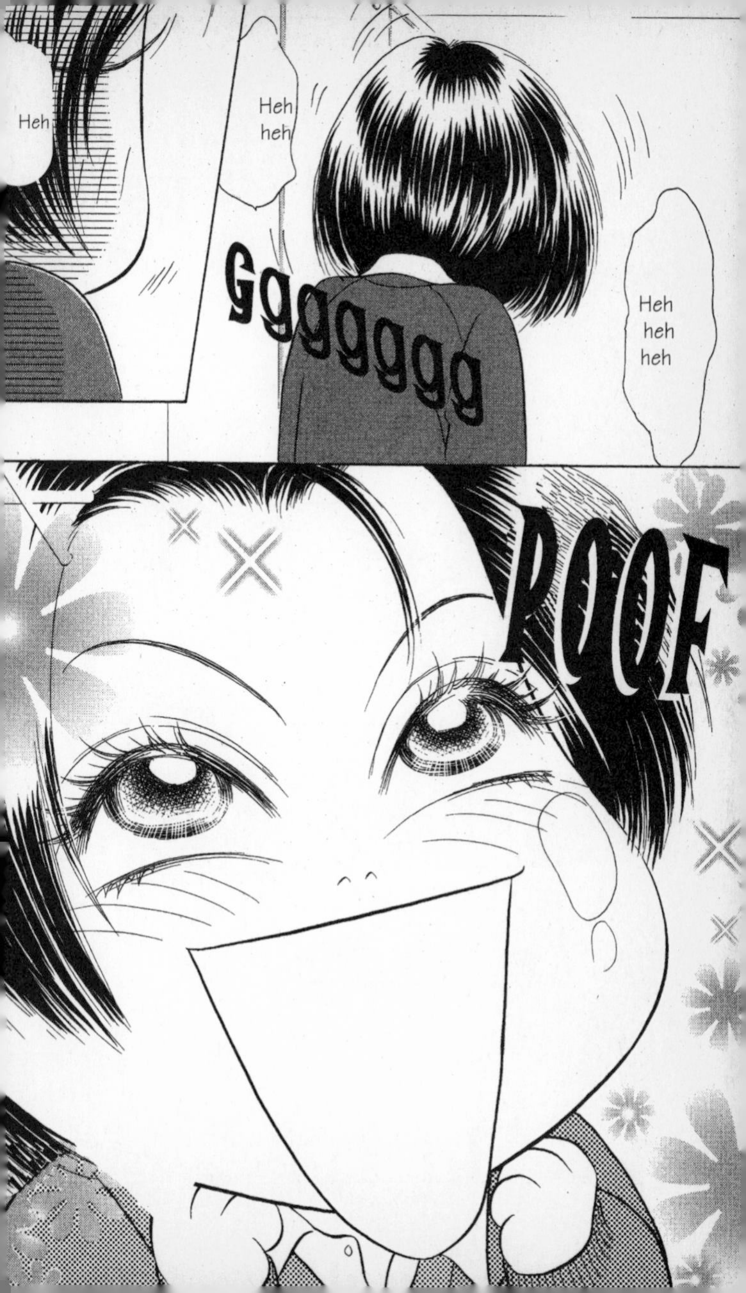

Heh
Heh heh
Gggggggg
Heh heh heh
POOF

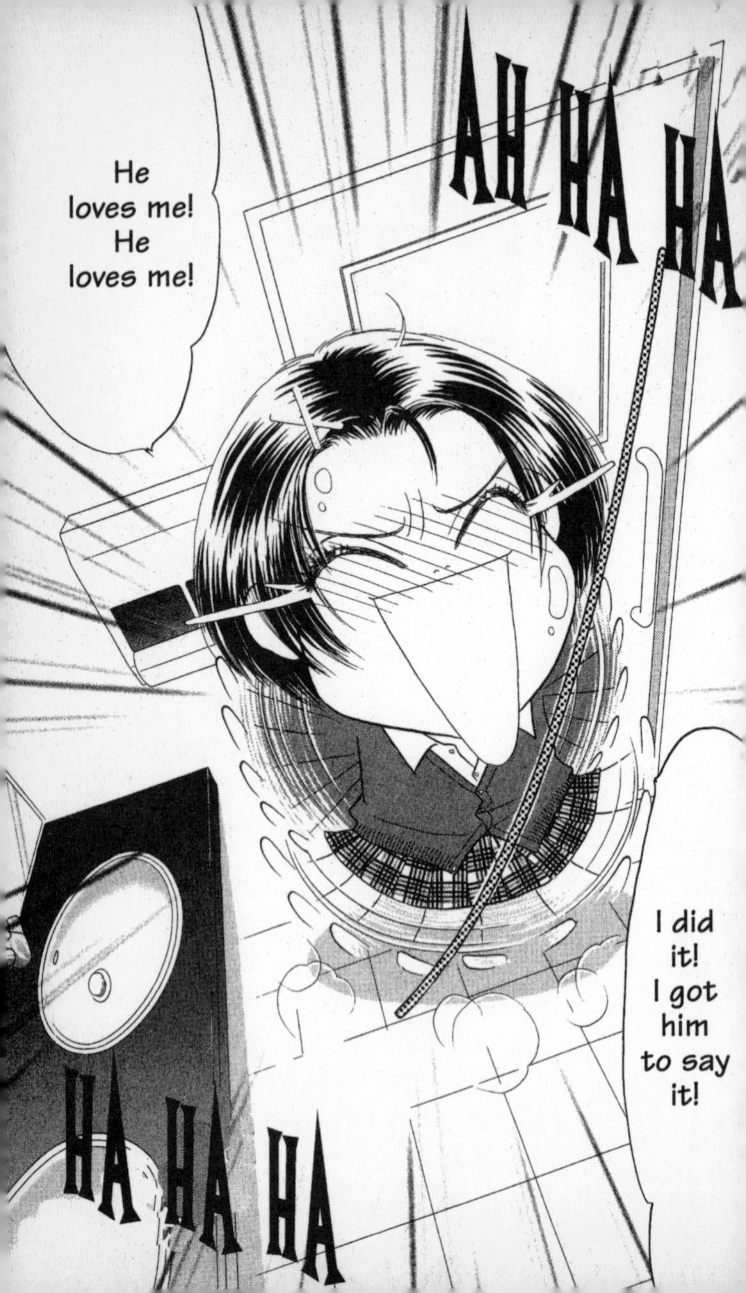
He loves me! He loves me!
AH HA HA HA
I did it! I got him to say it!
HA HA HA HA

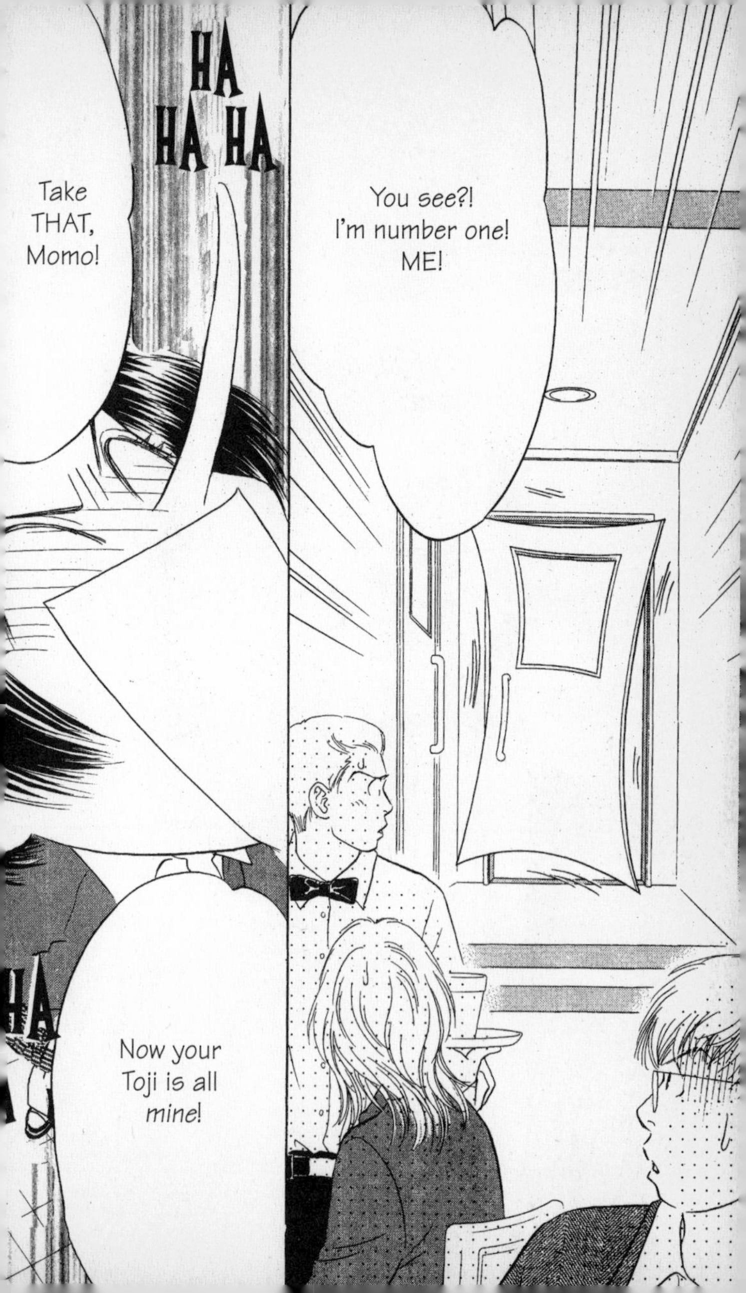
HA
HA HA
Take THAT, Momo!
HA
Now your Toji is all mine!
You see?! I'm number one! ME!

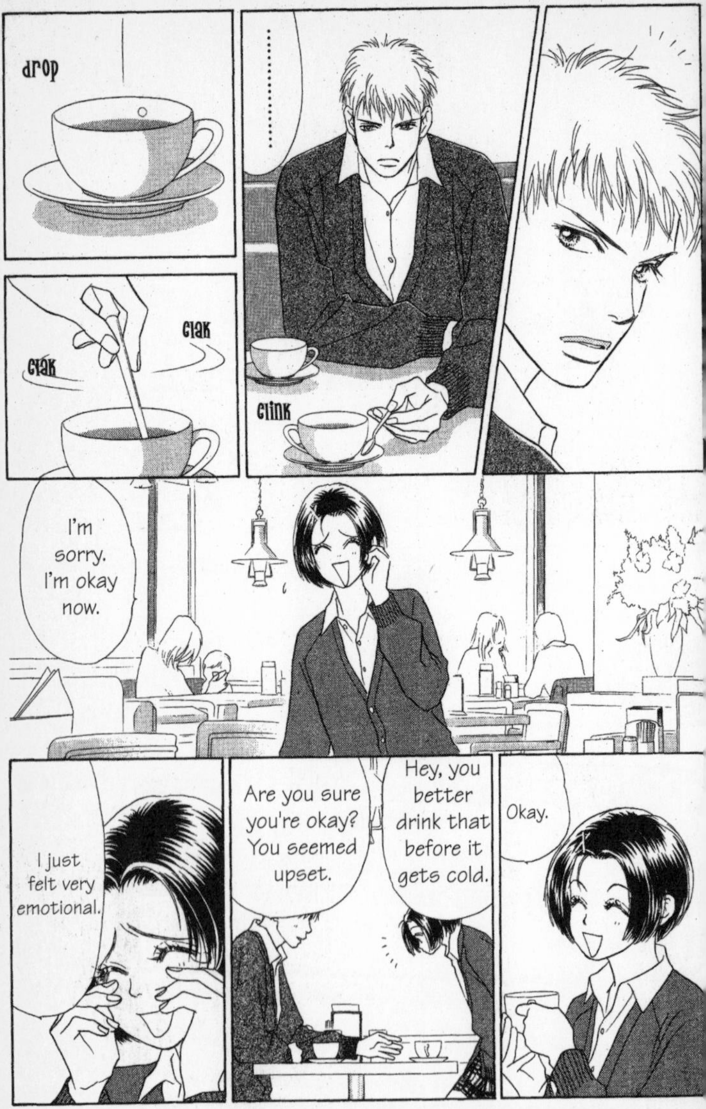
drop
......
Clak
Clak
Clink
I'm sorry. I'm okay now.
I just felt very emotional.
Are you sure you're okay? You seemed upset.
Hey, you better drink that before it gets cold.
Okay.

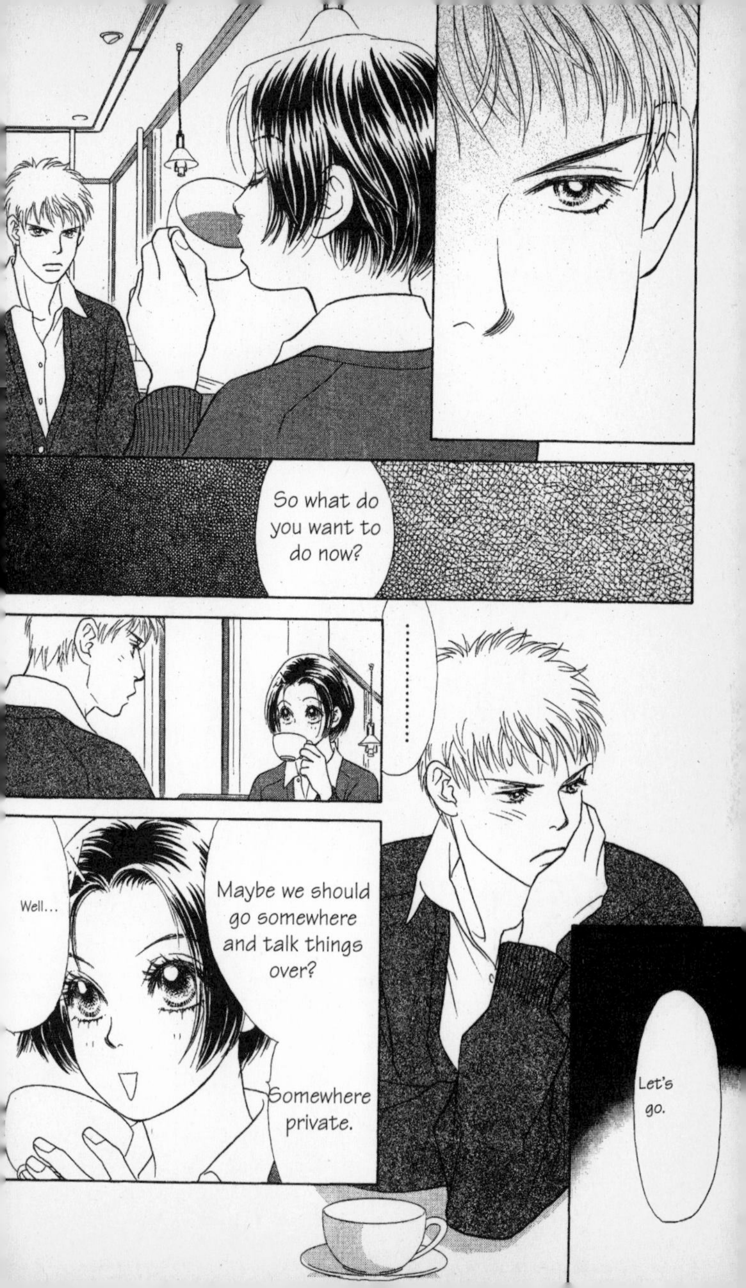
So what do you want to do now?
......
Well...
Maybe we should go somewhere and talk things over?
Somewhere private.
Let's go.

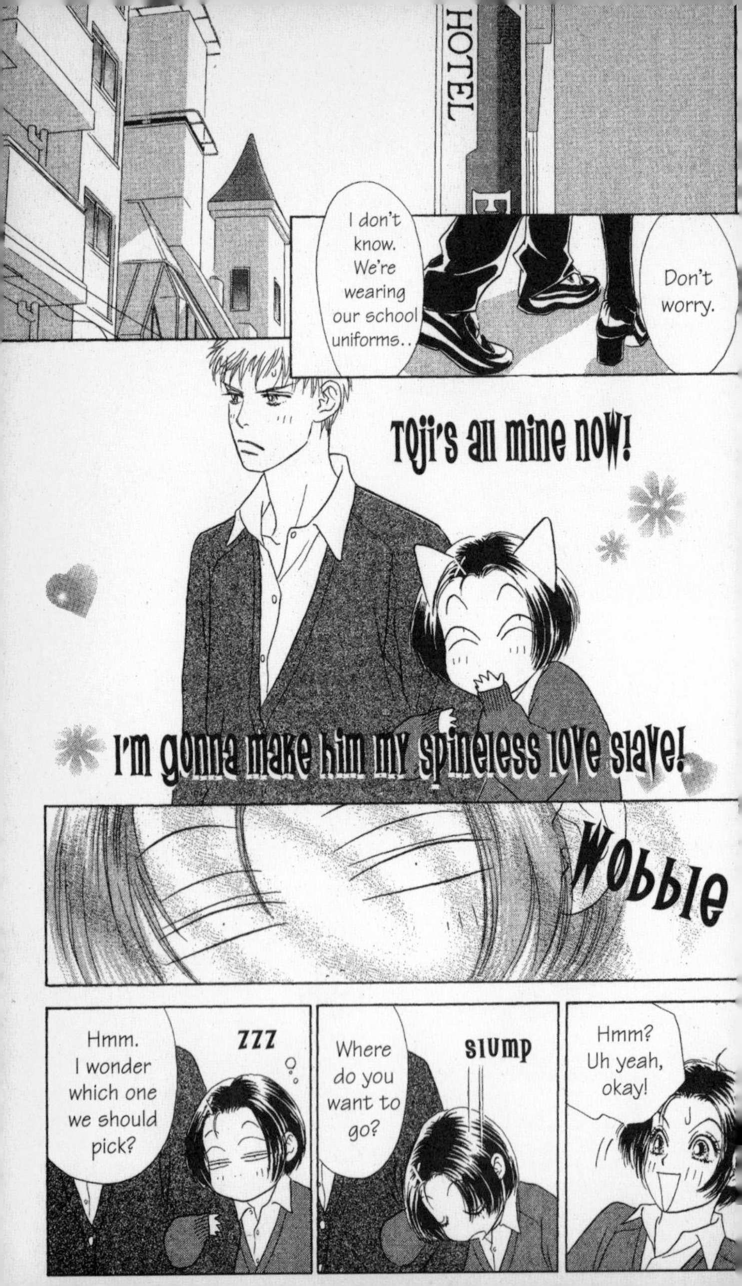
HOTEL
I don't know. We're wearing our school uniforms..
Don't worry.
TOJI'S ALL MINE NOW!
I'M GONNA MAKE HIM MY SPINELESS LOVE SLAVE!
WOBBLE
Hmm. I wonder which one we should pick?
ZZZ
Where do you want to go?
SLUMP
Hmm? Uh yeah, okay!

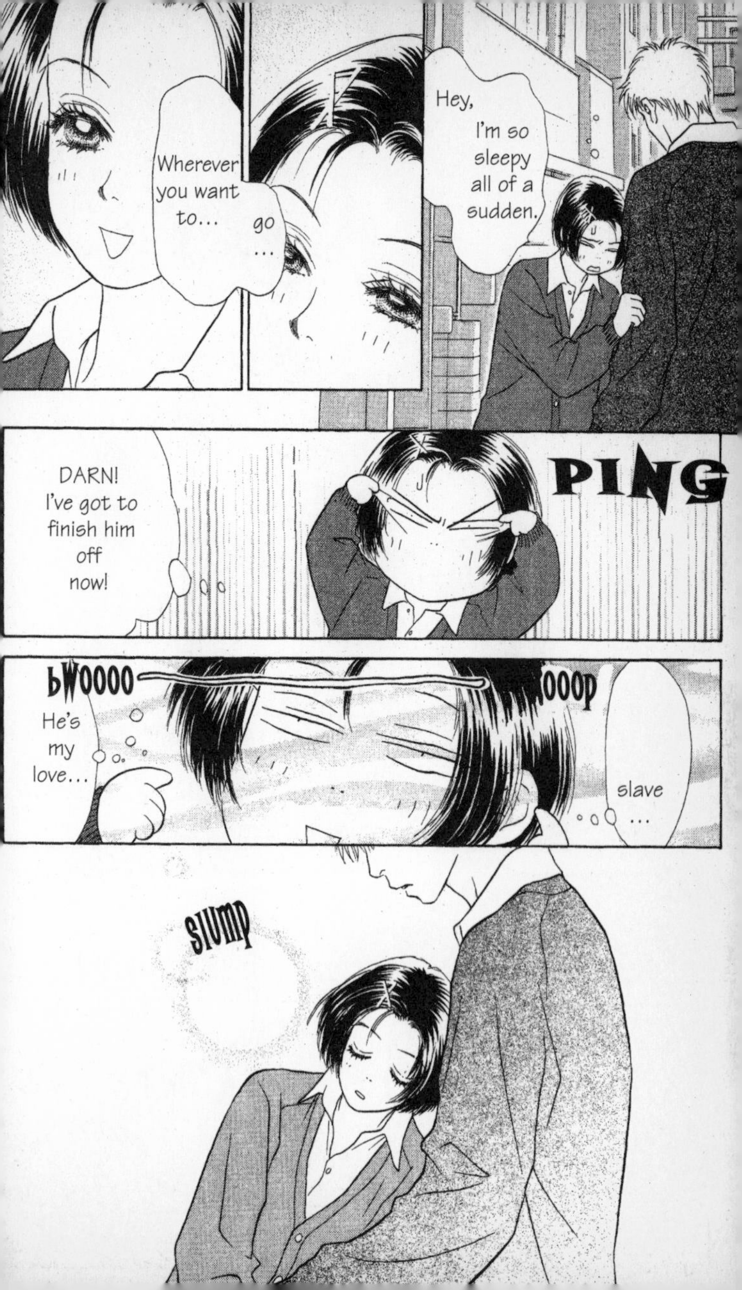

Wherever you want to...
go ...
Hey, I'm so sleepy all of a sudden.
DARN! I've got to finish him off now!
PING
bWOOOO
He's my love...
ooop
slave ...
SLUMP

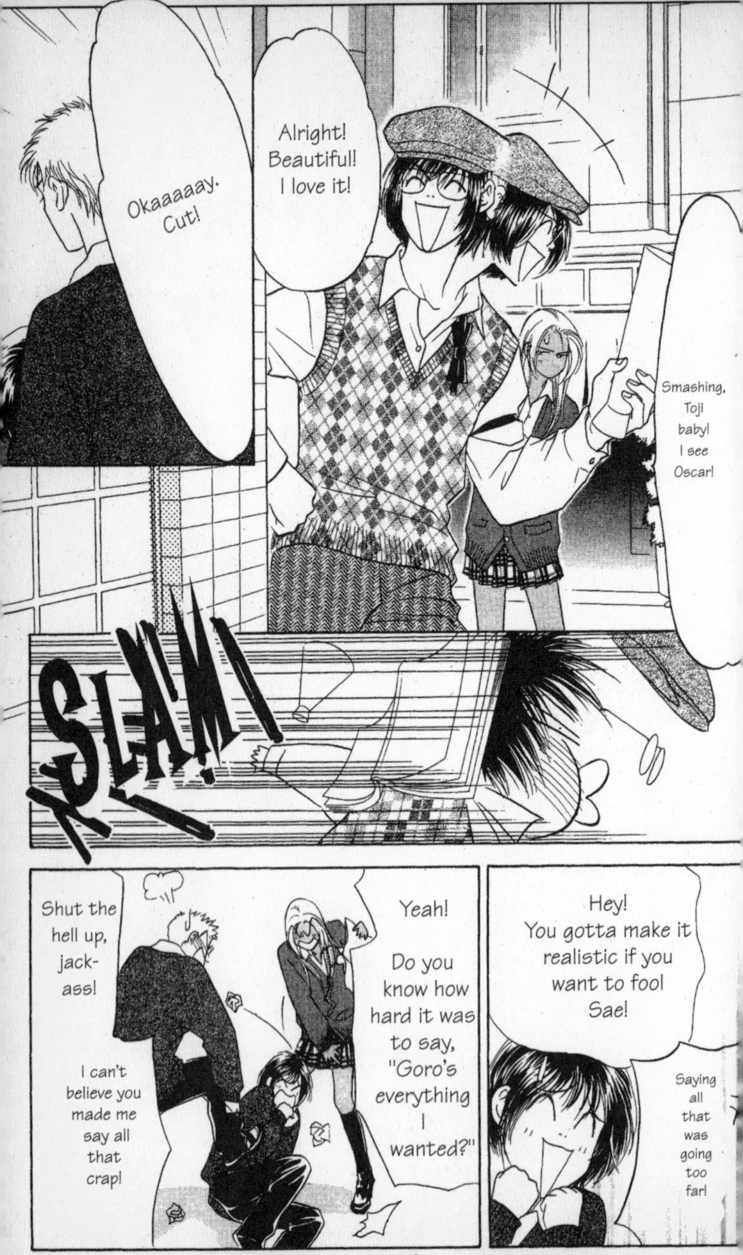
Okaaaaay. Cut!
Alright! Beautiful! I love it!
Smashing, Toji baby! I see Oscar!
SLAM!
Shut the hell up, jack-ass!
I can't believe you made me say all that crap!
Yeah! Do you know how hard it was to say, "Goro's everything I wanted?"
Hey! You gotta make it realistic if you want to fool Sae!
Saying all that was going too far!

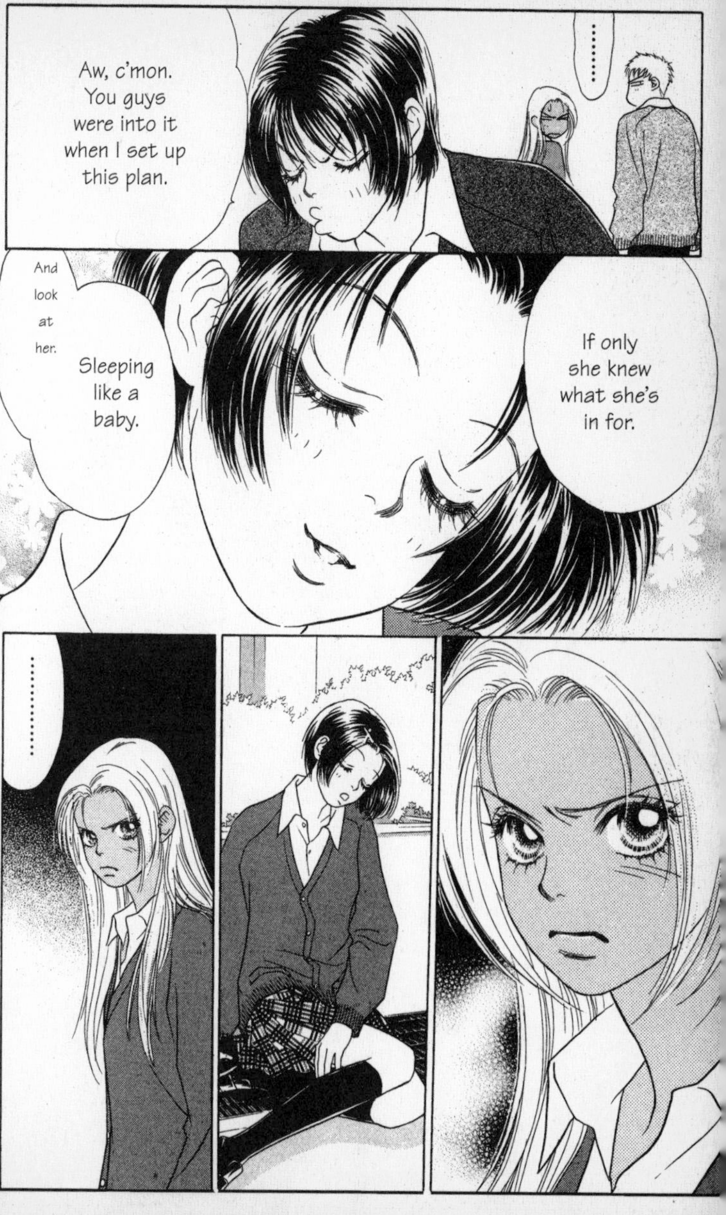
Aw, c'mon. You guys were into it when I set up this plan.
......
And look at her.
Sleeping like a baby.
If only she knew what she's in for.
....

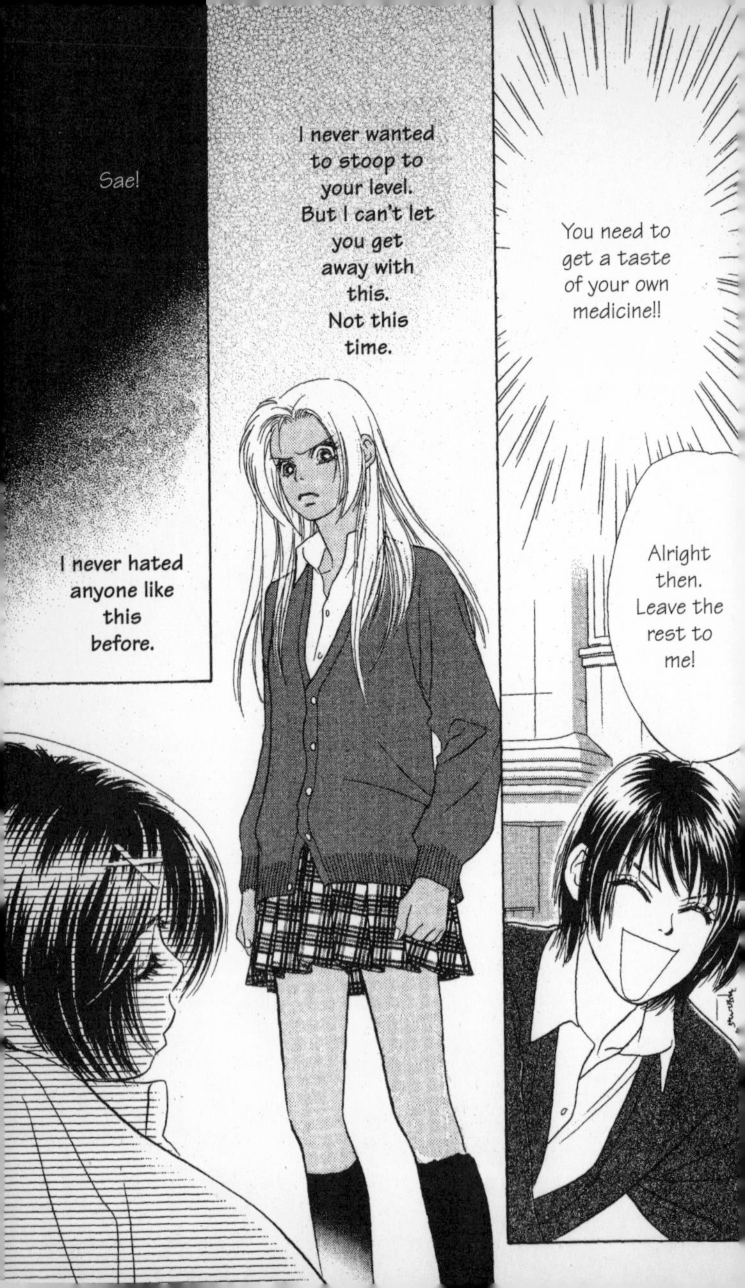
Sae!
I never hated anyone like this before.
I never wanted to stoop to your level. But I can't let you get away with this. Not this time.
You need to get a taste of your own medicine!!
Alright then. Leave the rest to me!

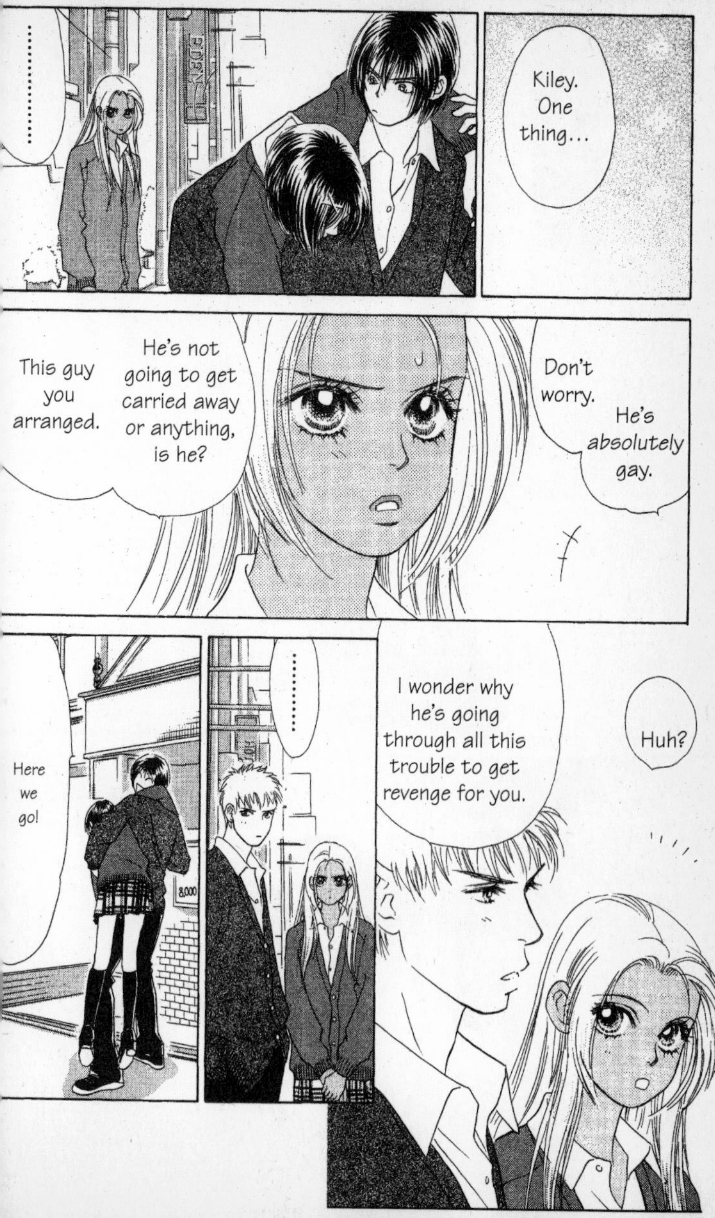

....
Kiley. One thing...
This guy you arranged.
He's not going to get carried away or anything, is he?
Don't worry.
He's absolutely gay.
Here we go!
....
I wonder why he's going through all this trouble to get revenge for you.
Huh?

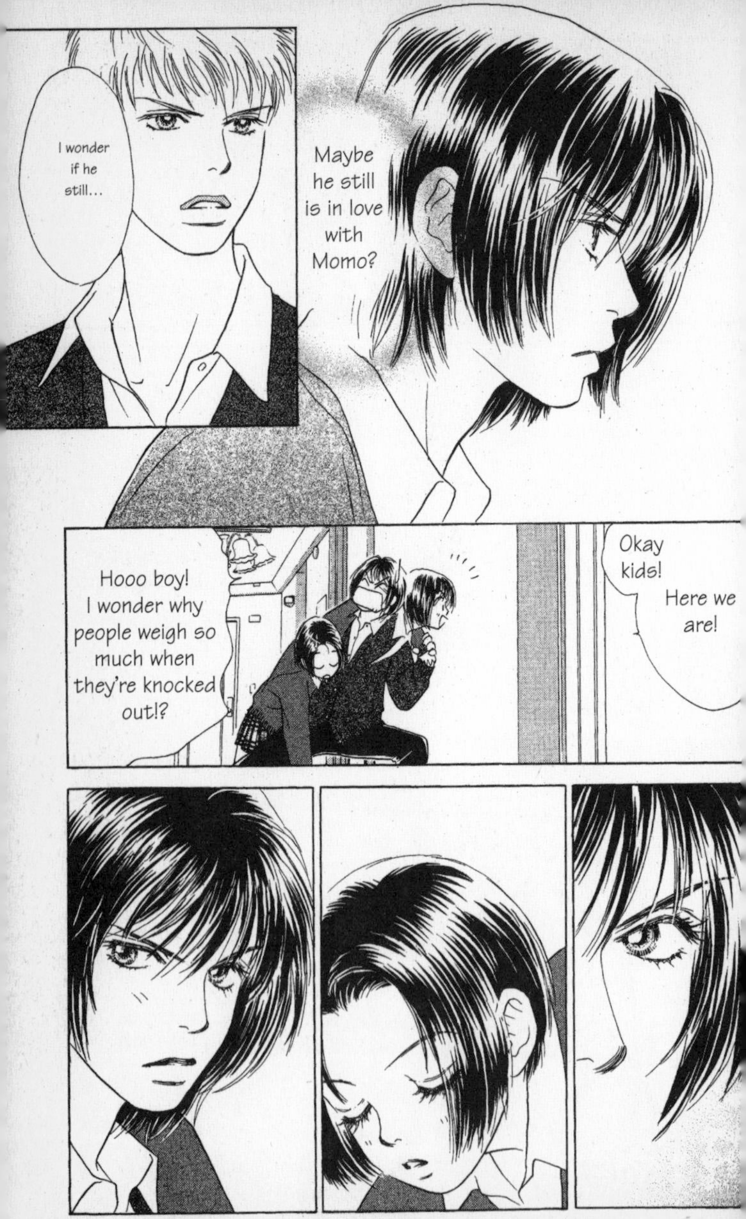
I wonder if he still...
Maybe he still is in love with Momo?
Hooo boy! I wonder why people weigh so much when they're knocked out!?
Okay kids! Here we are!

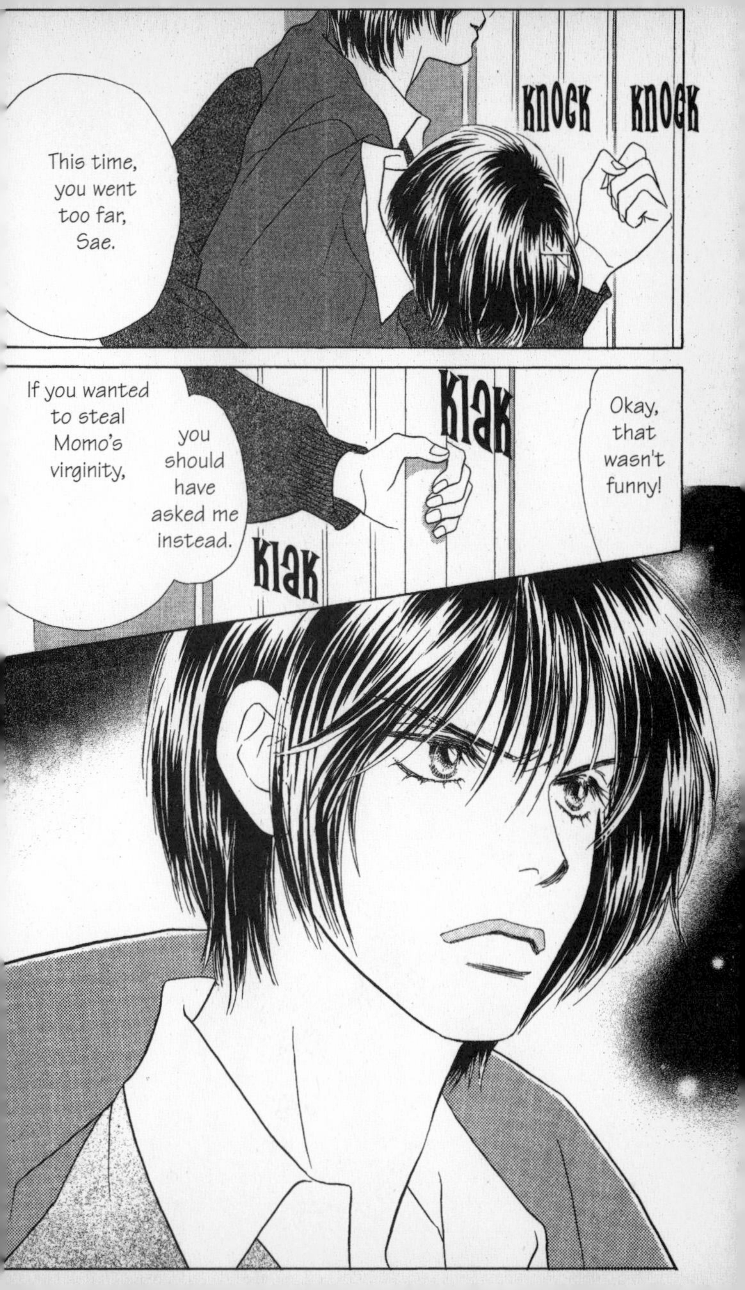
This time, you went too far, Sae.
KNOCK KNOCK
If you wanted to steal Momo's virginity,
you should have asked me instead.
KLAK
KLAK
Okay, that wasn't funny!

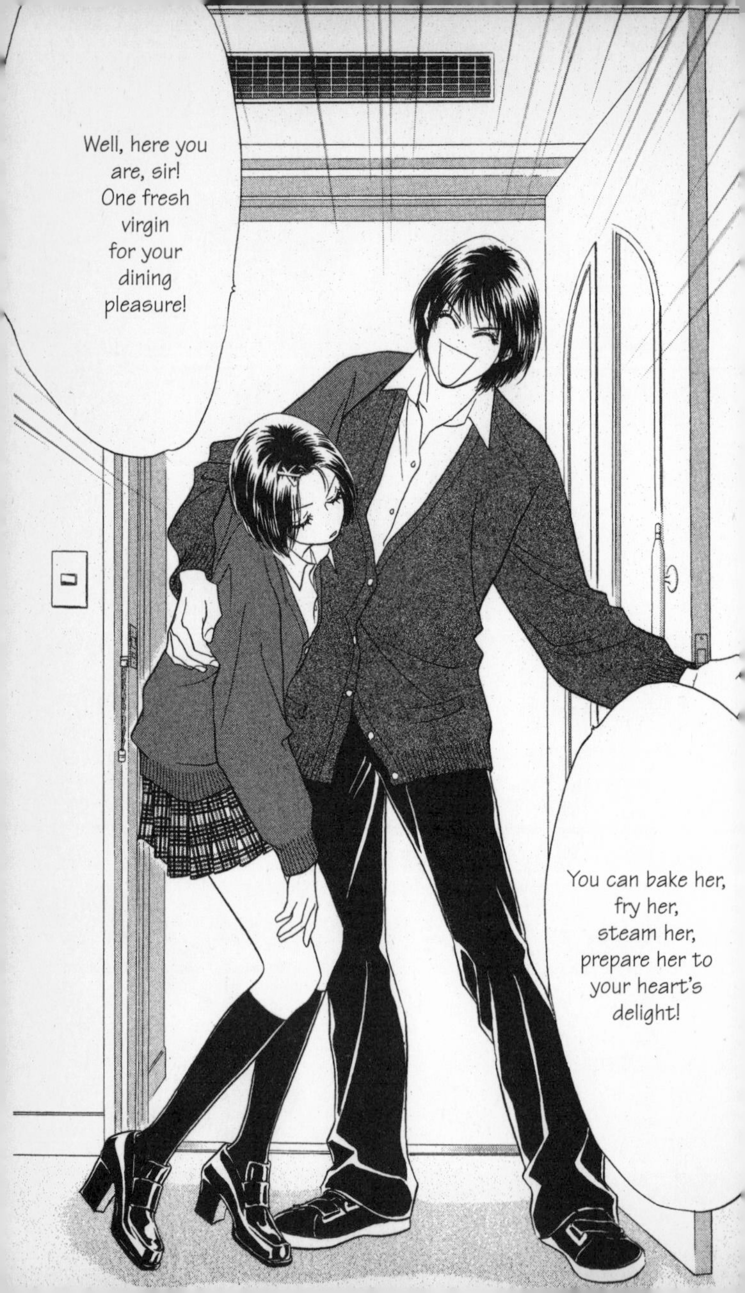
Well, here you are, sir! One fresh virgin for your dining pleasure!
You can bake her, fry her, steam her, prepare her to your heart's delight!

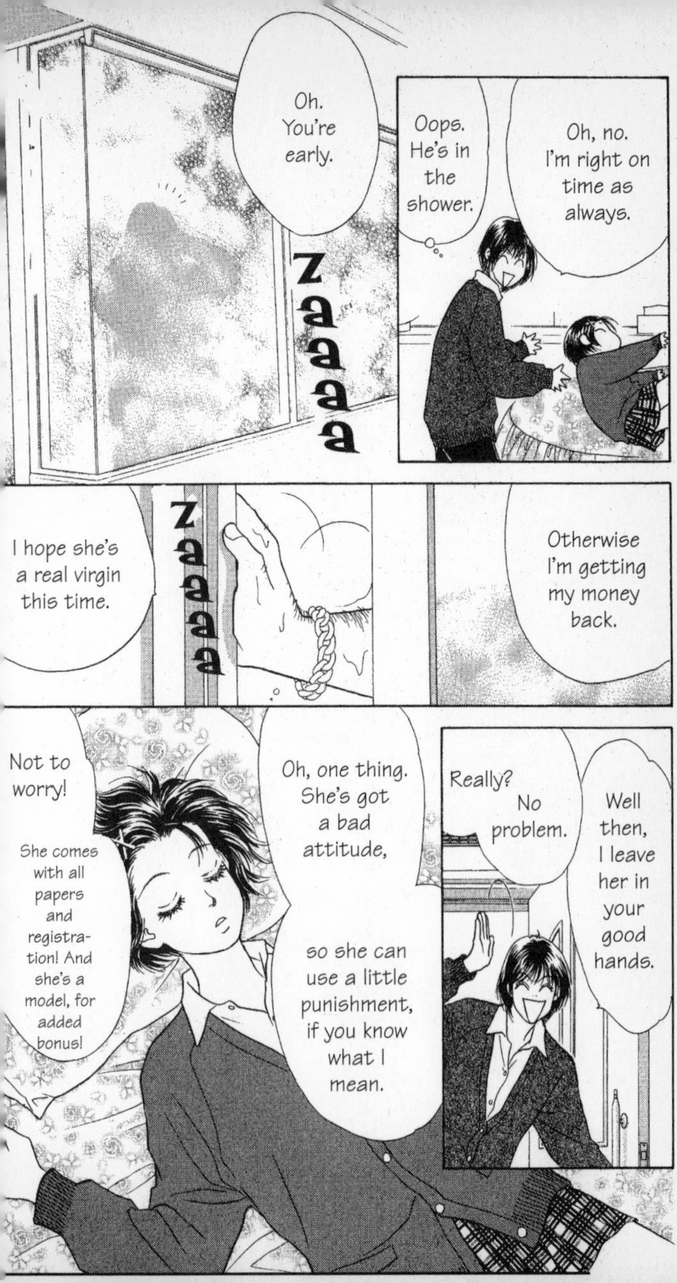
Oh. You're early.
Zaaaa
Oops. He's in the shower.
Oh, no. I'm right on time as always.
I hope she's a real virgin this time.
Zaaaa
Otherwise I'm getting my money back.
Not to worry!
She comes with all papers and registration! And she's a model, for added bonus!
Oh, one thing. She's got a bad attitude,
so she can use a little punishment, if you know what I mean.
Really? No problem.
Well then, I leave her in your good hands.

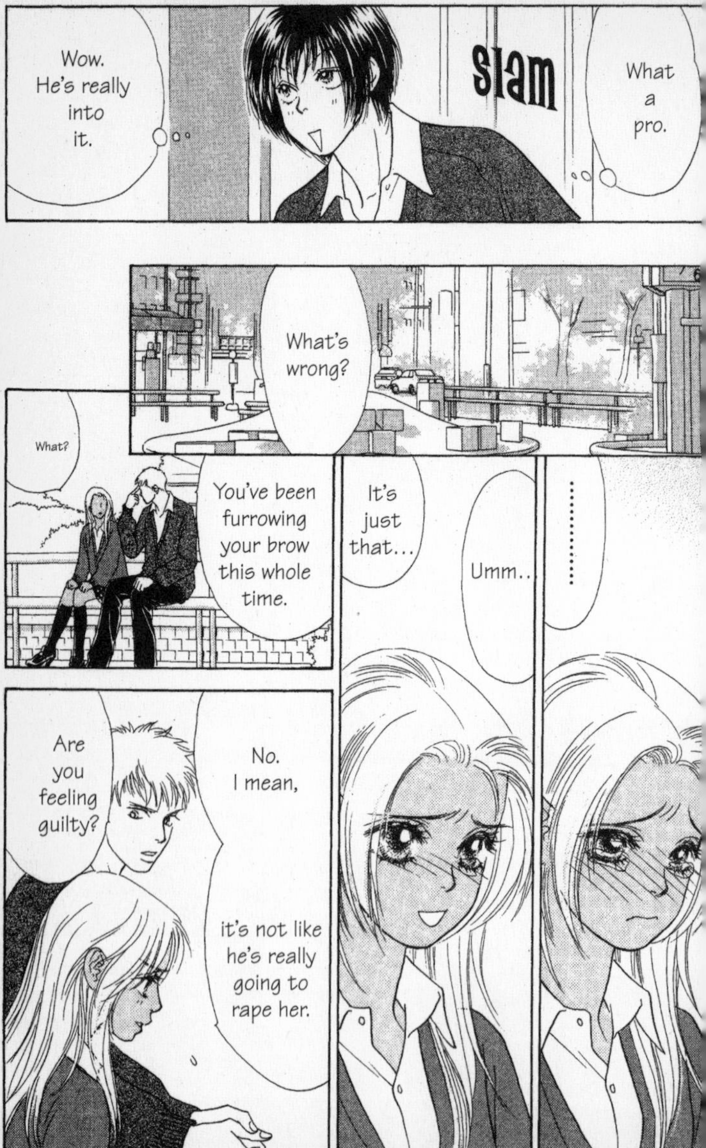
Wow. He's really into it.
SLAM
What a pro.
What's wrong?
What?
You've been furrowing your brow this whole time.
Are you feeling guilty?
No. I mean,
it's not like he's really going to rape her.
It's just that...
Umm..
....

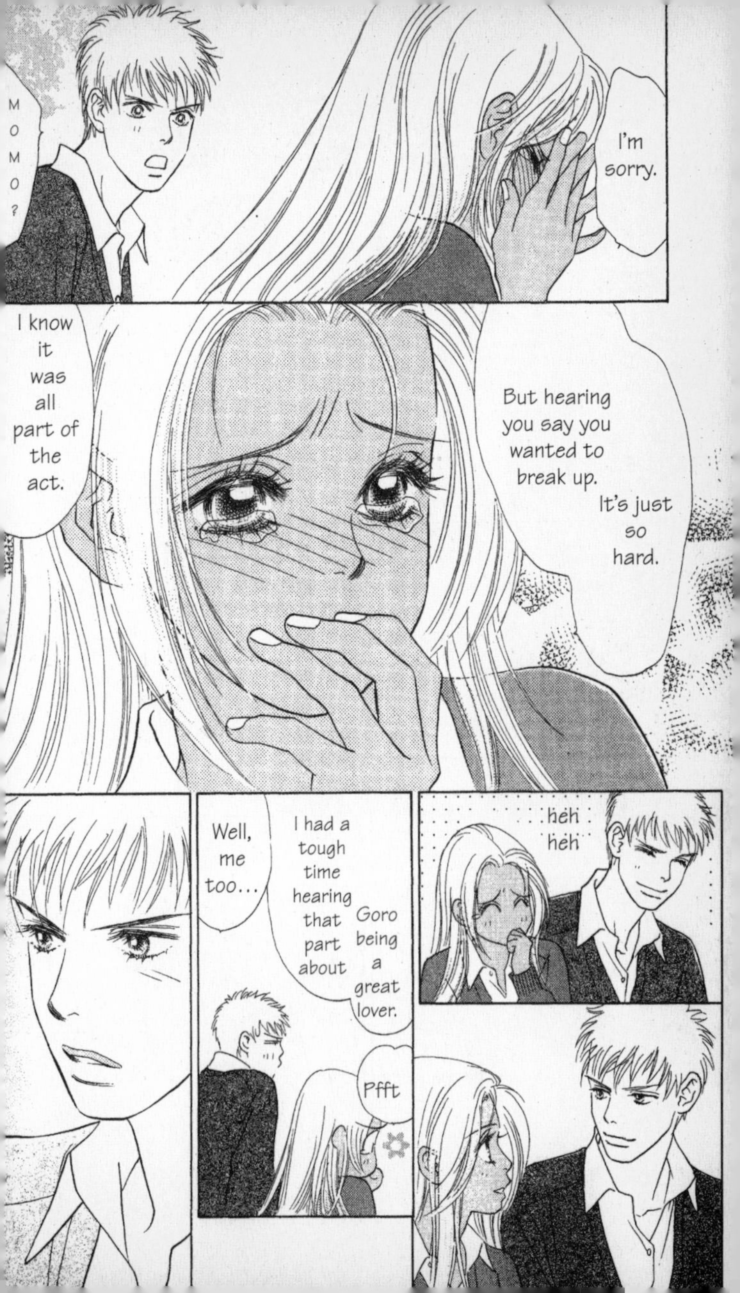
MOMO?
I'm sorry.
I know it was all part of the act.
But hearing you say you wanted to break up.
It's just so hard.
Well, me too...
I had a tough time hearing that part about
Goro being a great lover.
Pfft
heh heh

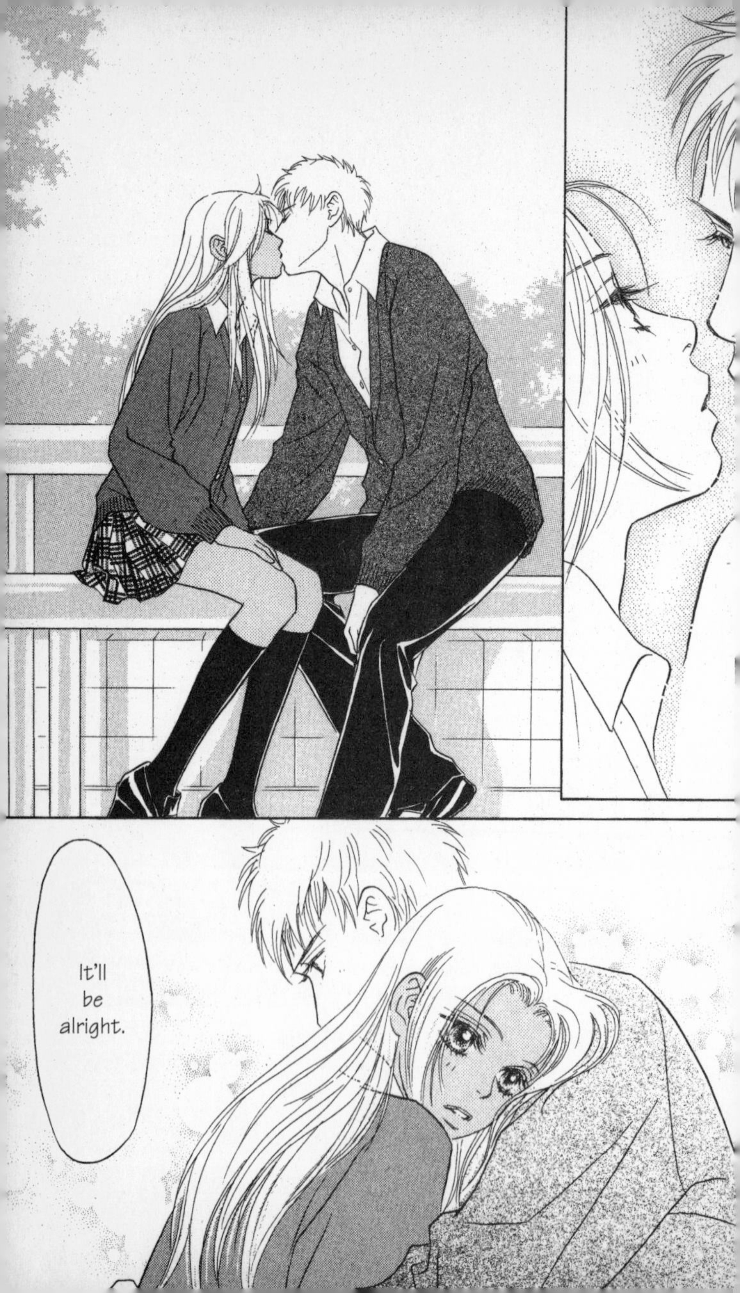
It'll be alright.

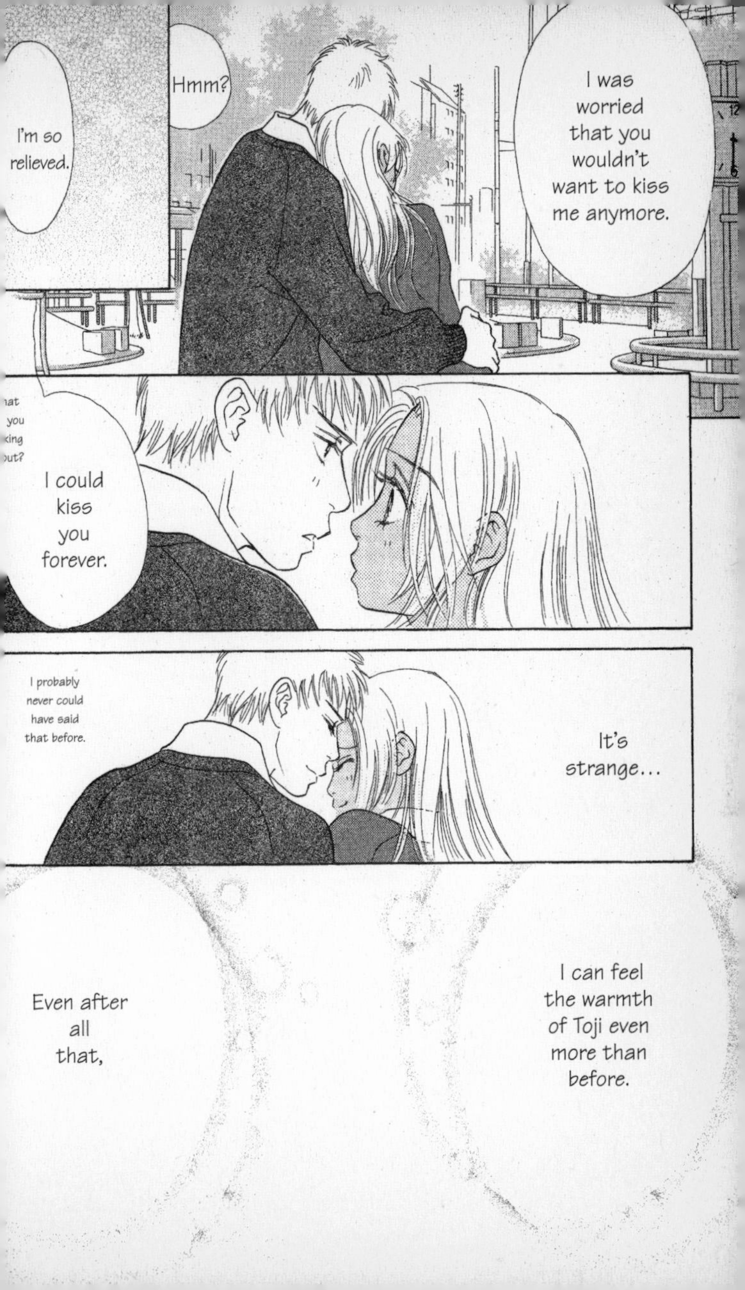
I'm so relieved.
Hmm?
I was worried that you wouldn't want to kiss me anymore.
I could kiss you forever.
I probably never could have said that before.
It's strange...
Even after all that,
I can feel the warmth of Toji even more than before.

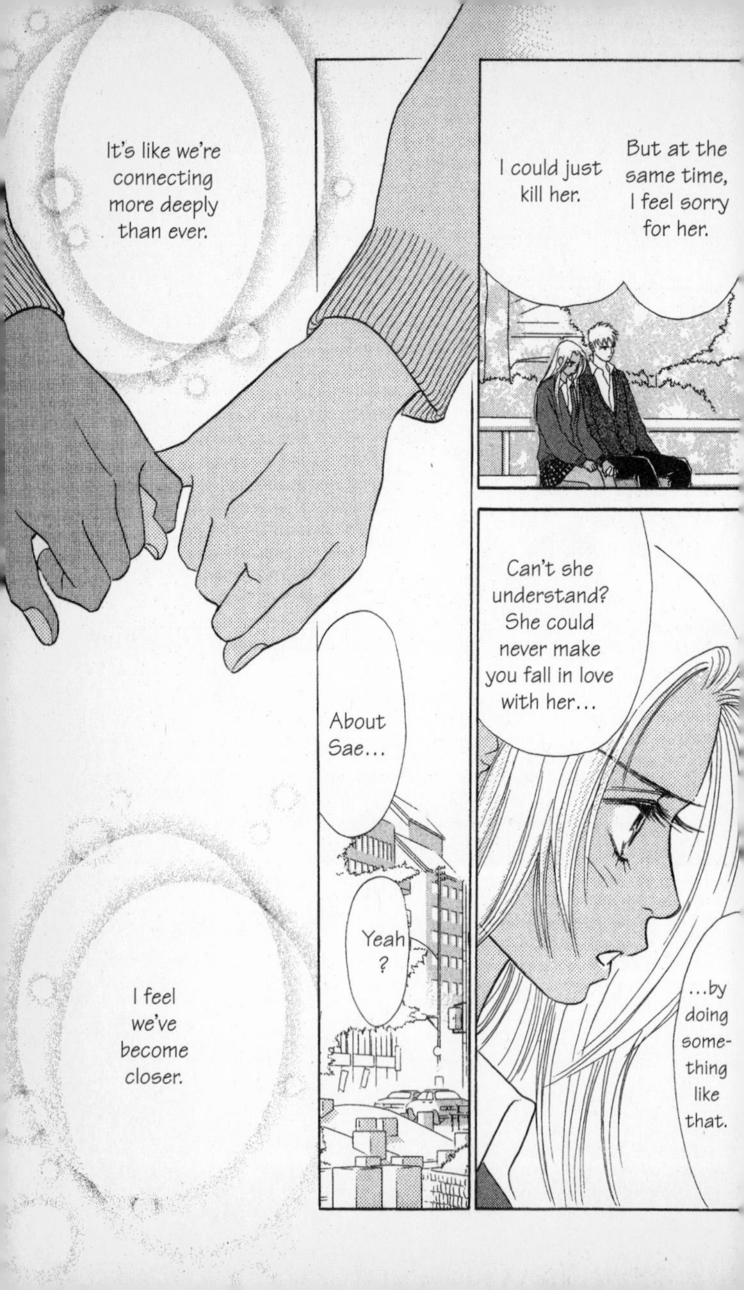
It's like we're connecting more deeply than ever.
I feel we've become closer.
I could just kill her.
But at the same time, I feel sorry for her.
About Sae…
Yeah?
Can't she understand? She could never make you fall in love with her…
…by doing something like that.

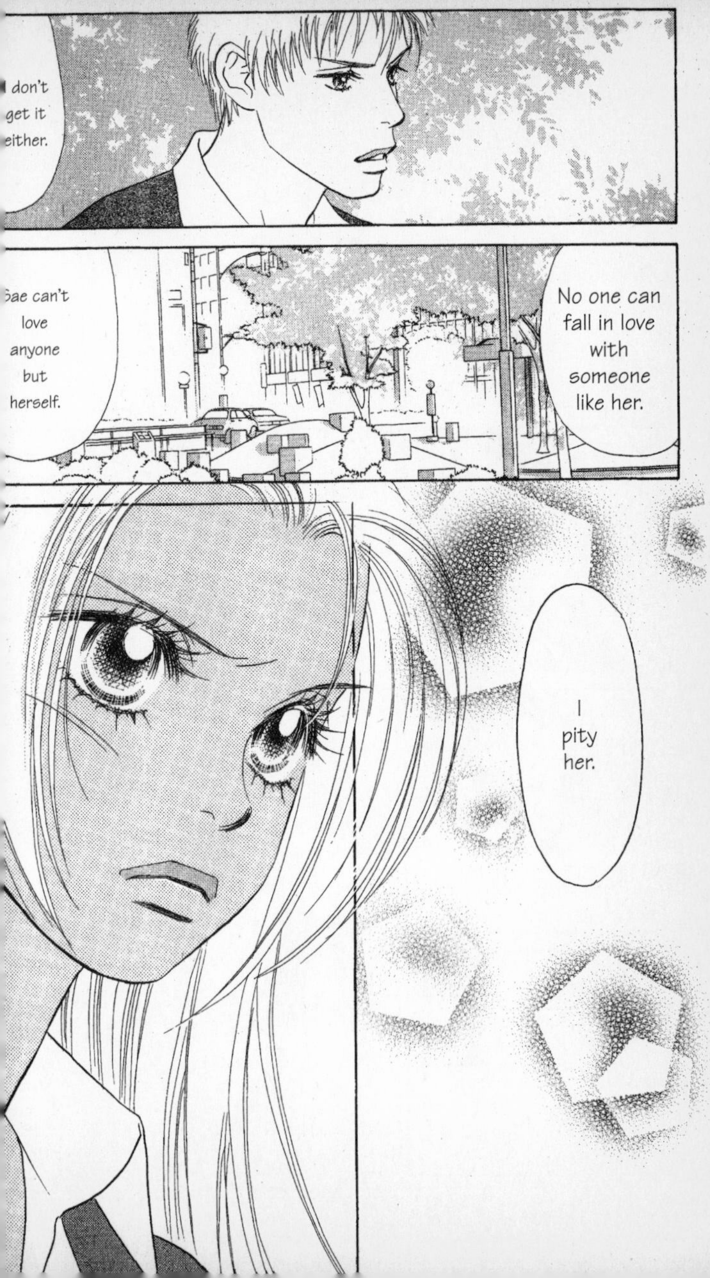

don't get it either.
ae can't love anyone but herself.
No one can fall in love with someone like her.
I pity her.

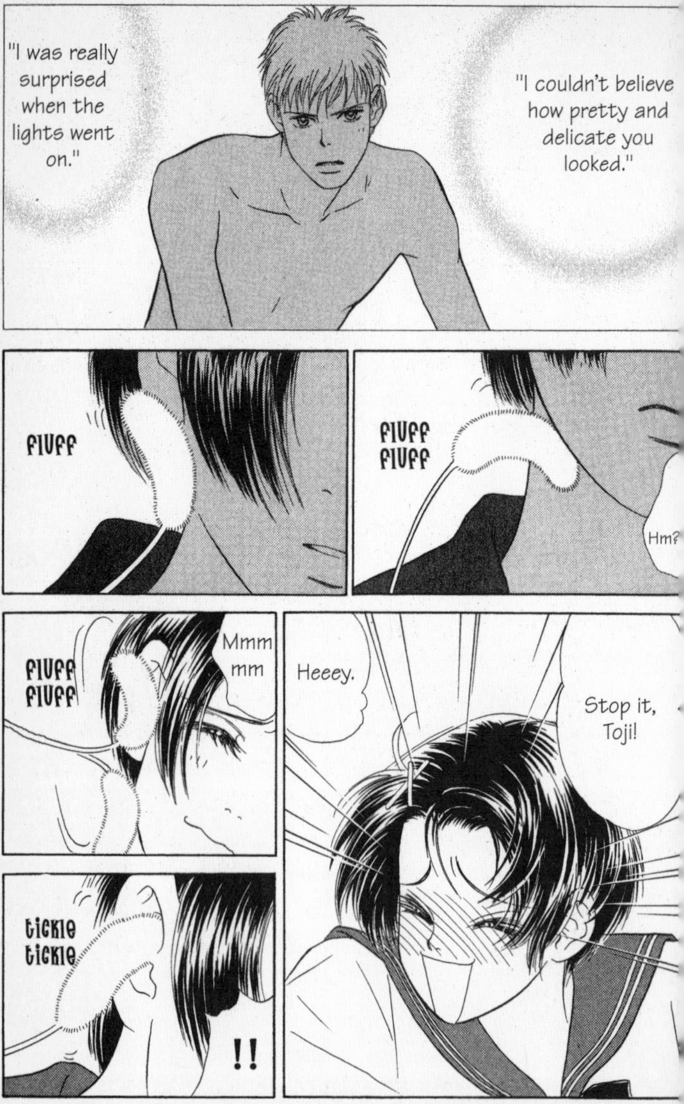
"I was really surprised when the lights went on."
"I couldn't believe how pretty and delicate you looked."
FLUFF
FLUFF FLUFF
Hm?
FLUFF FLUFF
Mmm mm
tickle tickle
!!
Heeey.
Stop it, Toji!

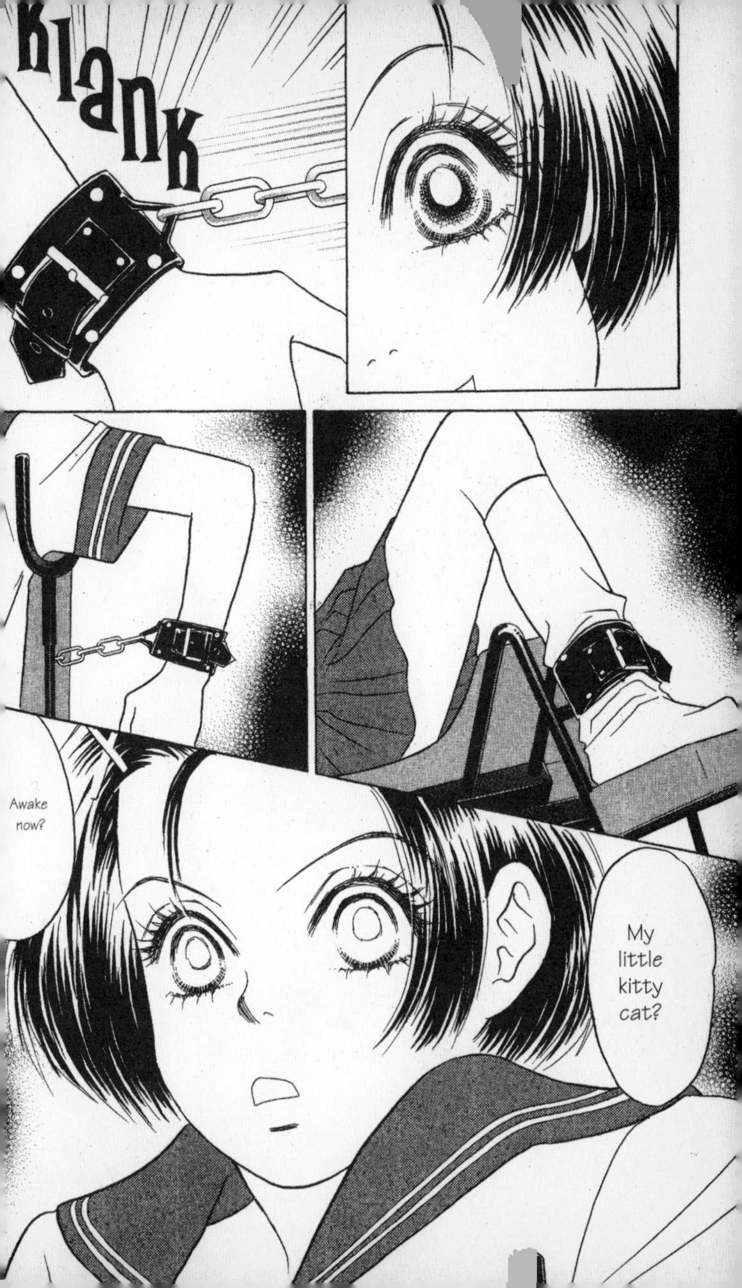
KLANK
Awake now?
My little kitty cat?

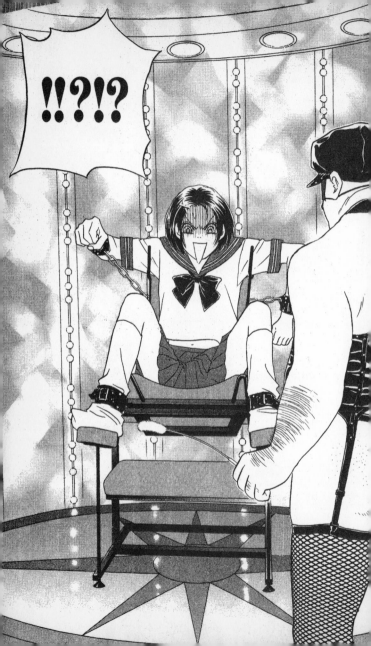

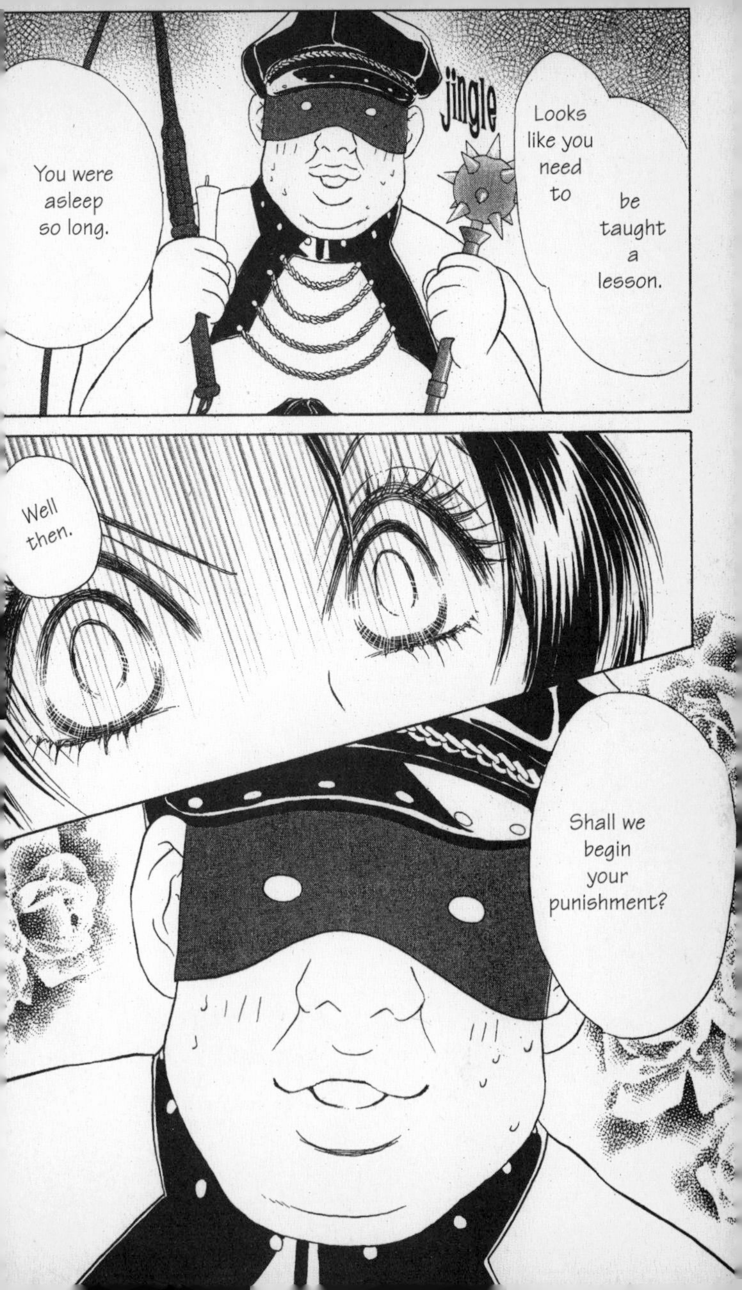
You were asleep so long.
jingle
Looks like you need to be taught a lesson.
Well then.
Shall we begin your punishment?

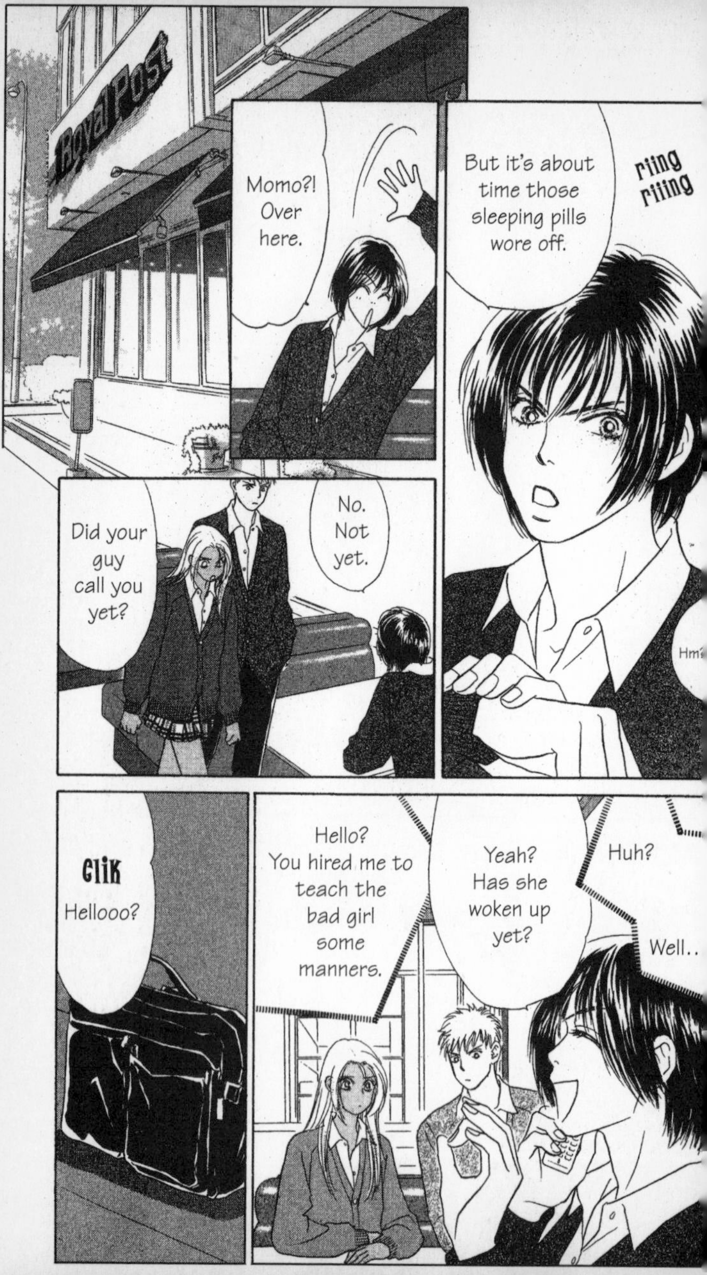
Royal Post
Momo?! Over here.
But it's about time those sleeping pills wore off.
riing riiing
Did your guy call you yet?
No. Not yet.
Hm?
Clik
Hellooo?
Hello? You hired me to teach the bad girl some manners.
Yeah? Has she woken up yet?
Huh?
Well...

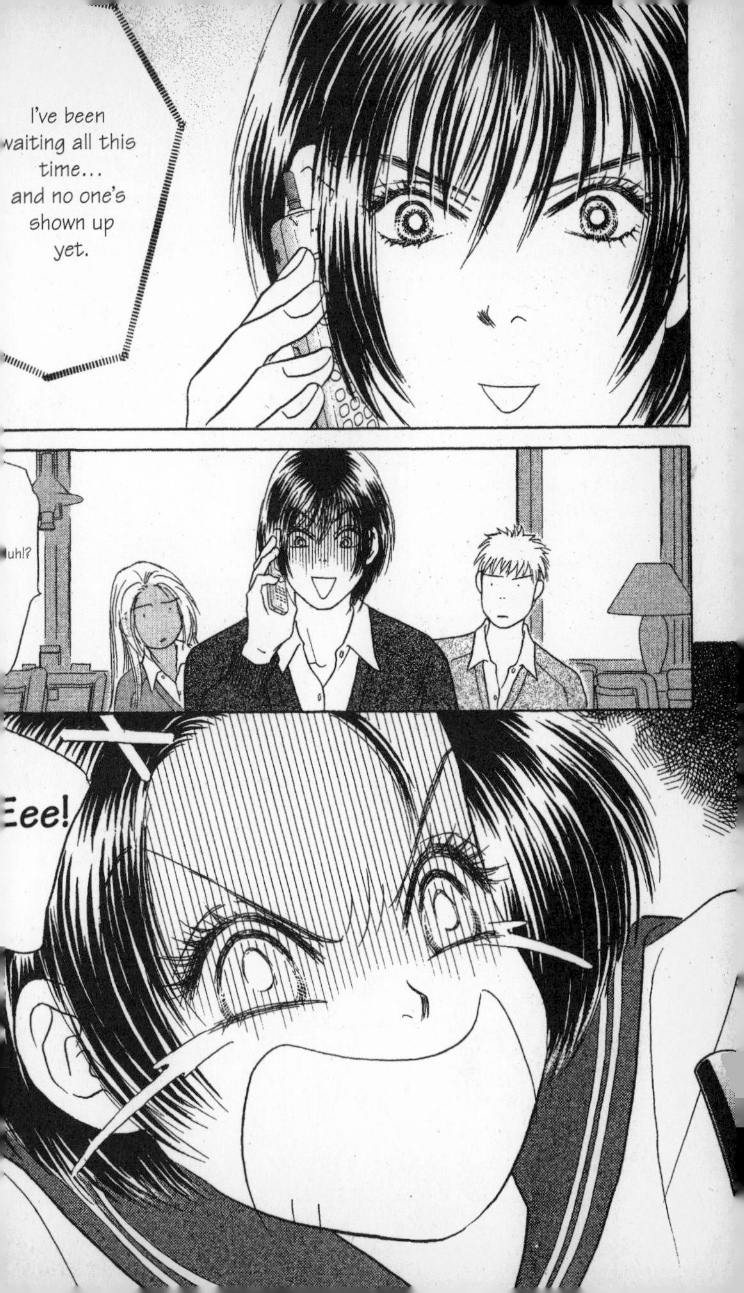
I've been waiting all this time... and no one's shown up yet.
uh!?
Eee!

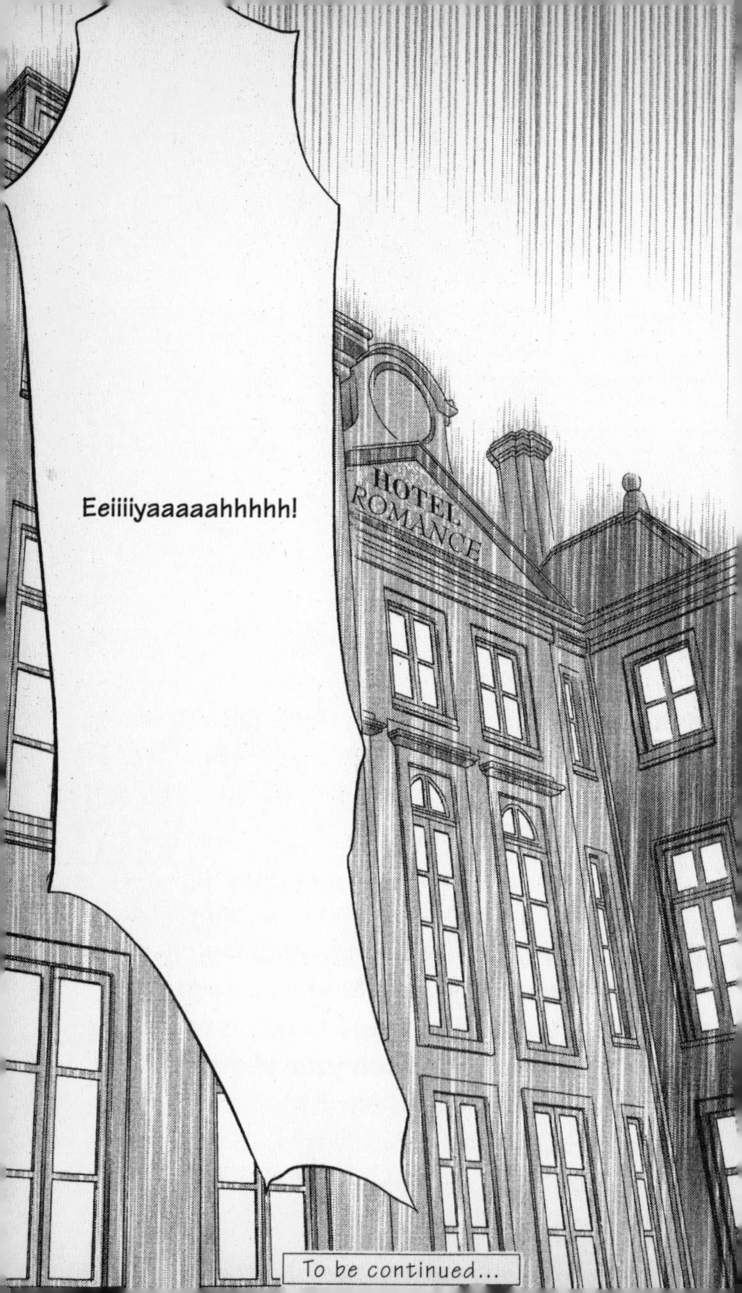
Eeiiiiyaaaaahhhhh!
HOTEL ROMANCE
To be continued...

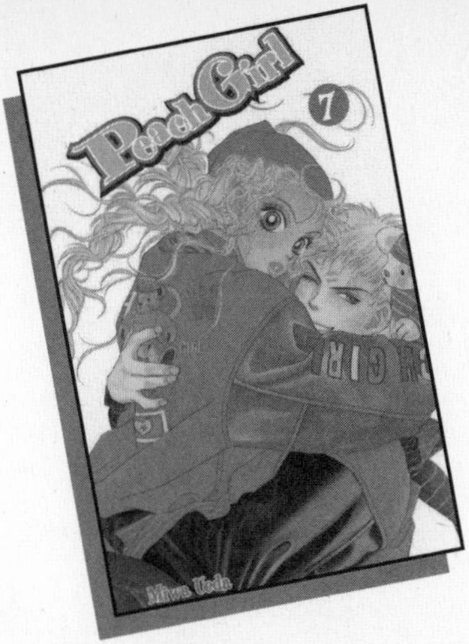
Peach Girl
7
Miwa Ueda

COMING SOON IN PEACH GIRL 7

Sae's gone too far for too long...and now it's time for her to pay! Kiley and Momo decide to set Sae up with her "dream date"—only this is the date from hell. Kiley hires an actor to put the moves on Sae and turn into a major pervert before her very eyes. Serves her right! But when they carry out their conniving plan, something goes drastically wrong...and Sae is put in real danger. It's up to Momo to save the day...but can she find it in her heart to rescue her worst enemy? Fasten your seatbelts and get ready for a wild ride of blackmail, cat-fights, and deceit in this dramatic volume of Peach Girl available in November.

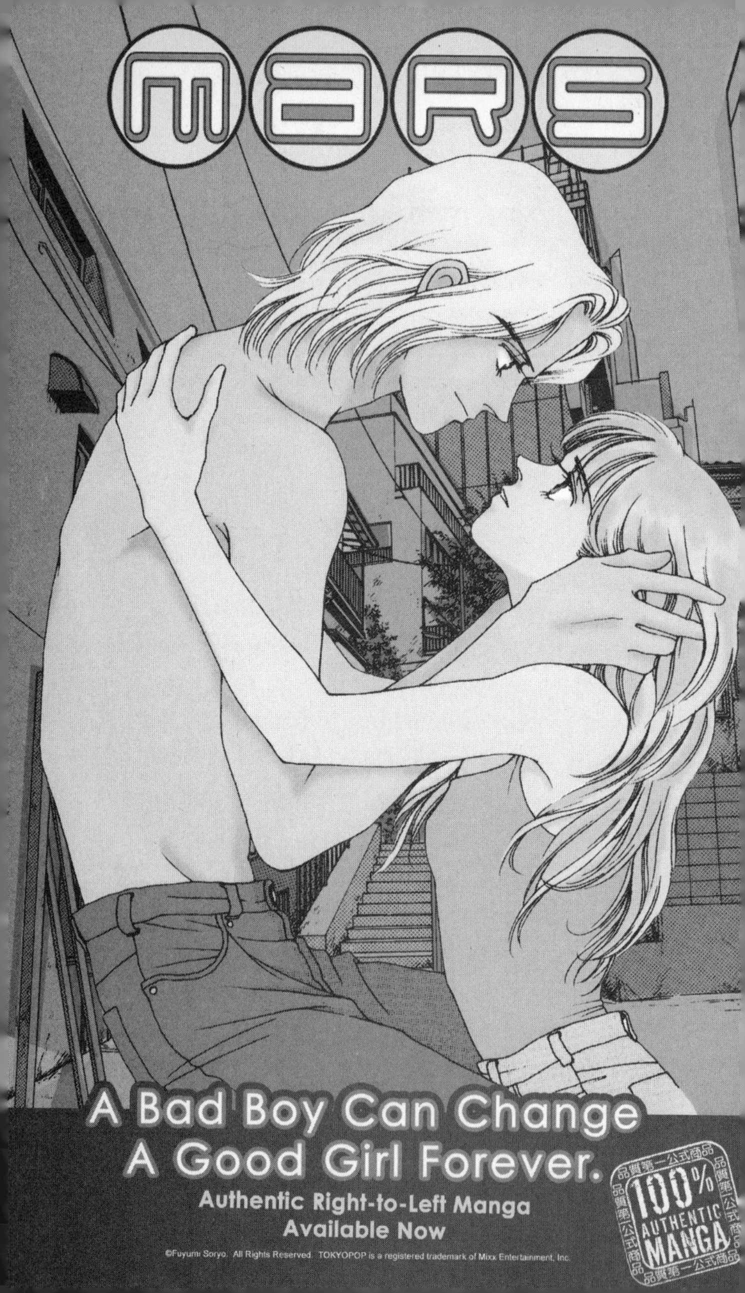
MARS
A Bad Boy Can Change
A Good Girl Forever.
Authentic Right-to-Left Manga
Available Now
©Fuyumi Soryo. All Rights Reserved. TOKYOPOP is a registered trademark of Mixx Entertainment, Inc.
100%
AUTHENTIC
MANGA

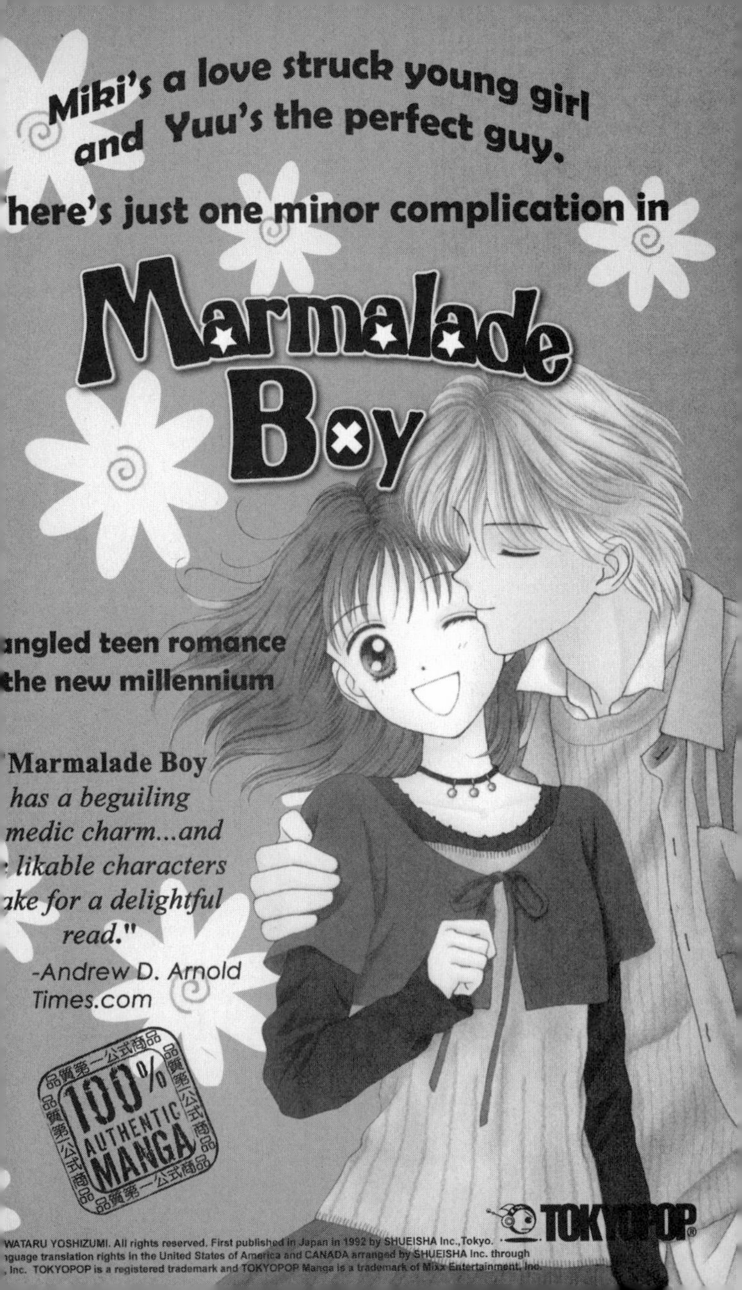

Miki's a love struck young girl
and Yuu's the perfect guy.
here's just one minor complication in
Marmalade Boy
angled teen romance
the new millennium
"Marmalade Boy
has a beguiling
medic charm...and
likable characters
ake for a delightful
read."
-Andrew D. Arnold
Times.com
100% AUTHENTIC MANGA
品質第一公式商品
TOKYOPOP®
WATARU YOSHIZUMI. All rights reserved. First published in Japan in 1992 by SHUEISHA Inc.,Tokyo.
guage translation rights in the United States of America and CANADA arranged by SHUEISHA Inc. through
, Inc. TOKYOPOP is a registered trademark and TOKYOPOP Manga is a trademark of Mixx Entertainment, Inc.

KODOCHA
SANA'S STAGE
Sana Kurata:
part student, part TV star
and always on center-stage
Take one popular, young actress used to getting her way. Add a handful of ruthless bullies, some humorous twists, and a plastic toy hammer, and you've got the recipe for one crazy story.
Graphic Novels
On Sale June 2002
©1994 Miho Obana. All Rights Reserved.
TOKYOPOP is a registered trademark of Mixx Entertainment, Inc.
100% AUTHENTIC MANGA

CORRECTOR YUI

2020:
mputers rule.

l viruses infect.

s superhero daydreams
e suddenly come true.

Wait!
Don't I get a cute sidekick?

A techno-fantasy series
filled with fun,
light-hearted action
from TOKYOPOP®.

Corrector Yui
(Books 1 - 3)
available now.

TOKYOPOP®

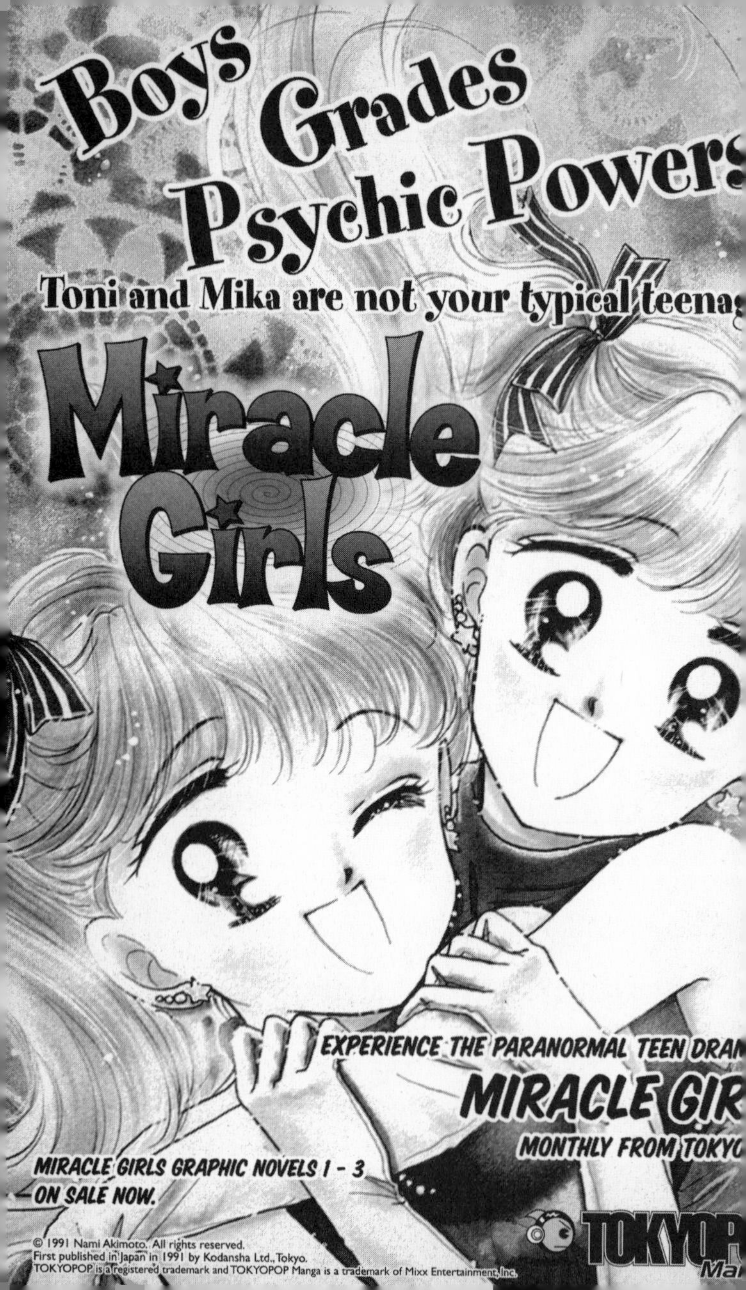
Boys
Grades
Psychic Powers
Toni and Mika are not your typical teenag
Miracle Girls
EXPERIENCE THE PARANORMAL TEEN DRAM
MIRACLE GIR
MONTHLY FROM TOKYO
MIRACLE GIRLS GRAPHIC NOVELS 1 - 3
ON SALE NOW.
TOKYOP
Ma
© 1991 Nami Akimoto. All rights reserved.
First published in Japan in 1991 by Kodansha Ltd., Tokyo.
TOKYOPOP is a registered trademark and TOKYOPOP Manga is a trademark of Mixx Entertainment, Inc.

Meet Misaki, the Prodigy.

...nting-fast fighting doll.
...sane mentor.
...ky promise to be the best.

ANGELIC LAYER

The new manga from CLAMP, creators of Cardcaptor Sakura.

Volume 1 available now!
Volume 2 coming August 2002